LEARNING TO PROGRAM IN C

SECOND EDITION

Thomas Plum

Plum Hall Inc

Library of Congress Cataloging-in-Publication Data

Plum, Thomas, 1943-
    Learning to program in C / Thomas Plum. -- 2nd ed.
      p. cm.
    Bibliography: p.
    Includes index.
    ISBN 0-911537-08-2 : $30.00
    1. C (Computer program language) I. Title.
QA76.73.C15P58 1989
005.13'3--dc20   89-15993
                                    CIP

We wish to thank the following for their kind permission to reproduce excerpts from copyrighted material:

> Rules of Blackjack, from *Gaming Guide*. Copyright © 1980 by Bally Park Place Hotel and Casino. Reprinted by permission.

Acknowledgement of trademarks: UNIX is a trademark of AT&T Bell Laboratories; PDP-11 and VAX are trademarks of Digital Equipment Corporation; Venix is a trademark of VenturCom; Idris is a trademark of Intermetrics; Safe-C is a trademark of Catalytix; Saber-C is a trademark of Saber Software; MC68000 is a trademark of Motorola. C is not a trademark, nor are the names of the software development commands such as cc.

ISBN 0-911537-08-2

10 9 8 7 6 5 4

For Joan

PREFACE

This book is an introduction to computer programming, using the C programming language. It presupposes no previous programming experience. However, readers familiar with other programming languages will find many explanations herein that have proven useful to other experienced programmers in C language training sessions.

The book treats the C language as a general purpose computer language for programmers concerned with portability and efficiency. No special application area is favored; examples are chosen primarily to illustrate the specific features of C. The focus is tutorial rather than reference; no attempt is made to supersede the compiler manuals for syntactic details. The topic sequence has evolved over ten years of teaching C language. I have tried to strike a balance between imparting the fundamentals of programming (which are independent of language and environment) and passing on useful details of the library, compilation procedures, and software maintenance. The goal is to give you the information you need to be a competent programmer in a real software engineering environment.

I hope the book will communicate, beyond the technical details, the delights of working in C language. C is a wonderfully designed tool for programming a variety of modern computers, elegant in its simplicity and yet powerful for many uses. Using it, you can create small, efficient applications that will not be limited to a single computer hardware. As you use it in your computing projects, you may come to appreciate the enthusiastic reception that it has found among professional programmers.

Since the publication of the First Edition in 1983, C has been standardized by ANSI Technical Committee X3J11, of which I had the privilege to serve as Vice-Chair. All the topics and program examples have been revised to reflect the features of the new Standard C.

Appendix A presents a concise guide to the C language and the Standard Library. This guide is not meant to replace the detailed syntactic reference provided by your compiler vendor. It is rather a summary of the rules for writing *readable* C programs.

Frequent checkpoint questions, prefaced by **Question**, are answered in Appendix B of the book.

Programming exercises, marked as **Exercise**, are left to the reader's ingenuity.

Appendix A presents a concise guide to the Standard C language and the Standard Library. This guide is not meant to replace the detailed syntactic reference provided by your compiler vendor. It is rather a summary of the rules for writing *readable* C programs.

Frequent checkpoint questions, prefaced by **Question**, are answered in Appendix B of the book.

Programming exercises, marked as **Exercise**, are left to the reader's ingenuity.

It is a pleasure to acknowledge the encouragement and assistance of many people who have helped in this project. First of all, to P. J. Plauger go my special thanks, for his assistance with the First Edition, for his encyclopedic, witty contributions to X3J11, and for his role in bringing C language to many diverse environments.

I am grateful to my numerous friends who have worked and played as instructors for Plum Hall Inc: David Graham, Steve Schustack, Marc Rochkind, Roland Racko, and Christopher Skelly. Their concern for clear presentation of the language has sharpened many of the examples. Others who commented on various drafts of the material include Jim Brodie, Scott Ehrlichman, C. Gelber, John Justice, Brian Kernighan, Ian MacLeod, Ed Rathje, Greg Rose, Larry Rosler, Teri Whynman, and my mother, Ruby Schunior. Of course, my thanks to them do not mean that they necessarily agree with all points in the presentation — the author who writes, programs, tests, and sets type himself has no one to blame for any misteaks that remain.

For steadfast support and encouragement, my heartfelt thanks go to my family — Halls, Pritchetts, Richters, Schuniors, Schanzes, and Whynmans — and my deepest gratitude to my late father, George E. Schunior, for starting me on my path.

The original author of C language, Dennis Ritchie of Bell Laboratories, deserves the appreciation of all of us in the C language community.

I am delighted to acknowledge Plum Hall's magnificent staff through the years: Sonya Whynman, Linda Deutsch, Cathy Bertino, Suzanne Battista, Dan D'Angio, Terri Chandonnet, and Tina McEvoy, for everything they did in bringing this book into being.

And most of all, thanks to Joan Hall, my wife and Plum Hall's President.

Thomas Plum

CONTENTS

CHAPTER 0: INTRODUCTION

The Computer: TIME Magazine's "Man of the Year" for 1982
("Machine of the Year", actually).

0.1 Introduction

Of special significance for C language fans is that "the computer"
is a tangible piece of hardware for many people. Quite recently, as late
as 1976, one might have predicted that computing would become
increasingly centralized, with widespread terminal access to giant computing centers. The decreasing costs of microcomputers and minicom-
puters have caused a quite different result. Computer users are commonly aware of the memory size and processor speed of the machines
that they use, and the computer as *machine* (as opposed to a *remote
abstraction*) is a fact of life in most offices, and in many homes too.
The situation is favorable for a language such as C, which embodies in
an elegant way many of the common features of modern computing
machines.

Indeed, many of the people whom we have trained in C language
are by occupation not programmers, but rather engineers, who come to
the study of C with considerable knowledge of circuitry and processors.
For them, C programming becomes another important tool in their
engineering toolkit.

Another group interested in C are the systems programmers, who
write the programs that other programmers use — notably compilers and
operating systems, which we will examine in the next section. In such

work, efficiency — making programs fast and small — is a major consideration. Often, there is also a payoff for portable programs that can run on a variety of different machines.

Also, there are the programmers who write applications packages which adapt the computer to the specialized needs of its users. Here again, the combination of efficiency and portability provided by C makes it ideal for the serious software producer.

All these users of C reap the benefits of its role as a small language close to the features of computing machines. C has had these benefits from the start. It evolved from the language B, an adaptation in 1970 by Ken Thompson of Martin Richards's BCPL. The UNIX operating system, originally written in PDP-11 assembler, was rewritten in C shortly after C was created in 1972. The results of the rewrite were overwhelmingly positive, and very shortly C displaced assembler programming in the UNIX environment. (For a fuller account of the history of C, see Ritchie *et al* [1978].)

During most of its history, C has been closely associated with the UNIX operating system, its original home and first major application. Much of the current interest in C is fed by the independent popularity of UNIX. However, the association is largely historical rather than intrinsic, and certain recent trends have promoted the independent status of C language. A series of C compilers for non-UNIX environments have been produced by numerous independent vendors. Indeed, the 80's have seen a proliferation of C implementations on microcomputers, mainframes, RISC (reduced instruction set complexity) machines, massively parallel machines, and supercomputers.

To suggest a deliberate oxymoron, we could call C a "portable high-level assembler" for modern computers. "Portable", in the sense that the same program can be run on a variety of different computers; "high-level", for providing structures for data and control; "assembler", in the sense that the programs are small and fast, with complete control over the data in the machine. Thus, one simple criterion for the suitability for C to a given application is a positive answer to these two questions: "Is assembler language being considered?" and "Might it be useful for the program to run on different hardware?". [We now prefer to punctuate quotation-marks with mechanistic precision.]

Given the variety of uses for C, we will not attempt to give a "cookbook" approach to programming. Our major goal is to give you a clear understanding of the language and its underlying behavior in the computer. The program examples and exercises are chosen not primarily as useful software — although some of them will be useful — but rather as illustrations of the features of C language. Our sequence of topics and explanations has evolved over several years of teaching C language to working professionals. For many of our trainees, their first serious programming project was to be done in C language, so our book covers programming fundamentals as well as the details of C language. Knowing that any sentence in the book may later be quoted in isolation, we will avoid simplifying things with "half-truths" to be undone later in the presentation, but certain topics (such as separate compilation of functions) will be postponed entirely until all the pieces can be put into place.

Thus, the organization of the book is as follows: Chapter 1 (Computers and C) describes the characteristics of modern computers in relation to the theoretically-important "abstract C machine". Using a deliberately introductory approach, we presuppose only that you have some acquaintance with a computer. The experienced computer user can safely skim this chapter.

Chapter 2 (Data) provides an introduction (or refresher) on bits, binary, octal, hexadecimal, and character codes. Declaration of scalar variables is covered in detail. (The enum type is not covered in this book. See *Reliable Data Structures in C*, abbreviated *RDS*.) The "atoms" of a program are defined. Then, a presentation of assignment, flow of control, output, program size, #define and #include provide a foundation for real program examples.

Chapter 3 (Operators), the longest chapter, covers most of the operators of C language. Character input/output is explained early, to permit interactive programs. Precedence and associativity are described throughout the chapter, and summarized at the end. The address-of operator, in its uses for the scanf function, lays groundwork for later discussions of arrays and pointers. A scheme for portable defined-types is presented. The chapter concludes with environmental information about input and output. (Opening and closing named files, and the numerous library functions that process them, are postponed to *RDS*.)

Chapter 4 (Statements and Control Flow) covers all C control structures in full detail. Both syntax and readability are described for each topic. The chapter introduces the *design* of control structures, to facilitate the careful planning required for reliable programs.

Chapter 5 (Functions) covers all syntactic aspects of C functions. Separate compilation and linkage are described, as well as the extended syntax checker, lint. Two-dimensional arrays are postponed to this chapter so that their initialization can be described.

Chapter 6 (Software Development) discusses analysis, design, implementation, and maintenance. A real case study problem (Blackjack) is covered in full detail.

Chapter 7 (Pointers) covers the basics of pointers in C. The advanced applications — dynamic storage allocation, linked lists, and pointers to functions — are not covered in this introductory book.

Chapter 8 (Structures) covers the C language struct. Not included are union, self-referencing structures, and bit-fields.

Appendix A constitutes a "pocket guide" to Standard C, summarizing readable syntax rules and the Standard C Library. Also included are formats for printf and scanf, common C bugs, C "idioms", and ASCII codes.

Appendix B contains answers to all checkpoint questions in the text.

First, the basics.

CHAPTER 1: COMPUTERS AND C

Before we begin the study of programming, we will describe the general characteristics of the computers that we will be using. The machines that are programmed in C have many features in common. To avoid slanting the presentation to a particular machine, we start with a story about a computer-like hotel clerk named Igor who works at the Transylvanian Hilton. Our story is relevant to experienced programmers as well as neophytes; it describes the basic model (or "abstract C machine") for C implementations.

1.1 Igor and the Numbers Game

Igor and his storage mechanism constitute our *computing system*.

1. The system has a *main memory* (or *storage*) consisting of equal-sized, numbered receptacles.

At the Transylvanian Hilton, the storage is embodied in a wall of pigeonholes, each of which can contain one slip of paper. Each pigeonhole is labeled with a number. The hotel happens to have 1024 slots, or *1K* in computer lingo; the slot numbers run from 0 to 1023. The slots look like this:

0	1	2	3	4	5	6	7
8	9	10	11	12	13	14	15
16	17	20	21	22	23	24	25

...

1016	1017	1018	1019	1020	1021	1022	1023

2.   *Input:* Information from the outside world can be entered into the slots, either by giving it to Igor, or by someone else directly placing it into a slot. *Output:* Information can be passed to the outside world by copying the information from a slip and giving it to someone. Again, Igor can do this, or someone else can do it directly.

It makes for a simpler system if Igor does all the input and output himself, but if he is very busy, he may have an assistant to do the copying.

3.   Igor has a repertory of *wired-in (i.e., built-in) capabilities.*

We have already mentioned that he can put information into a slot and copy out what is in a slot. He can copy information from one slot to another, and perform simple calculations like addition, subtraction, multiplication, and division. He can, for example, copy down a number from each of two slots, add them together, and store the result in a slot. The wired-in capabilities are referred to as Igor's *hardware* — "hard" because it cannot be changed.

4.   Igor can only do these few simple operations, but he is *fast and reliable.*

It is essential that Igor work flawlessly for days or even months. This reliability is essential for the proper functioning of the system.

5.   Some of the storage is devoted to *instructions for the processor.*

The manager has discovered that it is useful to store Igor's instructions in a section of slots otherwise unused for information storage. After carrying out the instruction contained in one slot, Igor then proceeds to the *next sequential slot* for further instructions. Also, one slot may contain an instruction directing him to some other slot. Upon arriving for work in the morning, Igor looks in a designated slot for instructions, and starts to work. A complete set of instructions constitutes a *program.* A collection of programs for Igor constitutes his *software* — "soft" because it can be changed relatively easily.

Given this set of capabilities, we can describe a simple program for Igor: totaling a customer's bill.

Slot	Contents
0	Copy slot 9 into slot 13
1	Copy slot 10 to Accounting Department
2	Copy slot 11 to Accounting Department
3	Copy an input from Accounting Department to slot 12
4	If no more inputs, go to slot 7 for further instructions
5	Add slot 12 to slot 13
6	Go to slot 3 for further instructions
7	Copy slot 13 to customer
8	Go to slot 14 for further instructions
9	"0.00"
10	"Please send the charges for room number: "
11	"123"
12	
13	
14	

Now we begin the "numbers game". Written out as above, the instructions are long-winded and cumbersome. But it is possible to streamline matters by assigning a number code to each of Igor's instructions and write them in a more compact form.

6.   The processor's wired-in capabilities are identified by numeric *instruction codes*.

Here are some instruction codes for Igor:

Code	Meaning
1	Go to slot __ for further instructions.
2	If no more inputs, go to slot __ for further instructions.
3	Add slot __ to slot __.
4	Copy slot __ to Accounting Department.
5	Copy an input from Accounting Department to slot __.
6	Copy slot __ into slot __.
7	Copy slot __ to customer.

Using these codes, Igor's program looks like this:

Slot	Contents
0	6, 9, 13
1	4, 10
2	4, 11
3	5, 12
4	2, 7
5	3, 12, 13
6	1, 3
7	7, 13
8	1, 14
9	"0.00"
10	"Please send the charges for room number: "
11	"123"
12	
13	
14	

To summarize: Our system (Igor plus slots) has these properties:

1.   The storage consists of equal-sized, numbered slots.

2.   Data is moved from the outside world to slots (input), and from slots to the outside' world (output).

3.   The clerk has a fixed set of wired-in capabilities.

4.   The clerk is fast and reliable.

5.   Instructions to the clerk are placed in the storage.

6.   The wired-in capabilities are identified by numeric instruction codes.

1.2 Basics of a Real Computer

Now we will convert our story about Igor and the slots into a description of a real computer. The role played by Igor is assigned to a piece of hardware known as the *central processing unit (CPU)*. The role of the slots is played by another piece of hardware, the *main memory*. The transmission of information to and from the system will be done by a *terminal*. These units have all six of the characteristics described above, plus some new ones.

7.   Each character is entered in the storage as a *character code number*.

When a key is pressed at a terminal, it sends the numeric code for that character to the system. Similarly, when a code is sent to a terminal, the corresponding character appears on the screen or printout.

In the early years of C, there were two common schemes of character codes: the ASCII code (American Standard Code for Information Interchange) and the EBCDIC code (Extended Binary Coded Decimal Information Code). The EBCDIC ("EBB-see-dick") code is used almost exclusively by IBM mainframe equipment; other processors usually use ASCII ("ASK-ee"). As C has become more popular internationally, other ISO codes (International Standards Organization) are being supported; they all bear family resemblances to ASCII. Here and throughout the book, our examples will assume that our processor uses the ASCII code, but the principles of C are the same for both codes.

In each scheme, the code for the digit 1 is one greater than the code for 0, the code for 2 is one greater than the code for 1, etc. through the digit 9. In other words, the digits occupy ten adjacent position in the code table, one after the next, in the same sequence as the digits themselves — their natural "collating sequence", to use the technical term. In both schemes, the collating sequence places A after B, B after C, etc., but the letter codes are not all adjacent in the EBCDIC scheme.

Here is a partial table for ASCII character codes:

space	32	@	64	`	96
!	33	A	65	a	97
"	34	B	66	b	98
#	35	C	67	c	99
$	36	D	68	d	100
%	37	E	69	e	101
&	38	F	70	f	102
'	39	G	71	g	103
(	40	H	72	h	104
)	41	I	73	i	105
*	42	J	74	j	106
+	43	K	75	k	107
,	44	L	76	l	108
-	45	M	77	m	109
.	46	N	78	n	110
/	47	O	79	o	111
0	48	P	80	p	112
1	49	Q	81	q	113
2	50	R	82	r	114
3	51	S	83	s	115
4	52	T	84	t	116
5	53	U	85	u	117
6	54	V	86	v	118
7	55	W	87	w	119
8	56	X	88	x	120
9	57	Y	89	y	121
:	58	Z	90	z	122
;	59	[	91	{	123
<	60	\	92			124
=	61	]	93	}	125
>	62	^	94	~	126
?	63	_	95		

(The codes below 32 and those after 126 are special control characters, and not shown here; see Appendix A for a full table.) Using these codes, each of the messages can be entered into the storage as a number. A common convention is to terminate each message with a zero. Thus, "Please" becomes 80, 108, 101, 97, 115, 101, 0.

If ever you should need to know the ASCII codes for a character, you can find it here or in Appendix A. However, memorizing any of this information is a waste of brainpower. Once you know that these numeric codes are used in the storage and that they produce readable characters when printed, you have learned all that is needed.

So far, all that has changed from Igor's program is the numerical storage of the characters. The program has now been encoded entirely into numbers: numbers for the slots, numbers for the instruction codes, and numbers for the characters. The next step, however, alters the way that these numbers are arranged in the storage.

8.   Each slot in the storage can hold only one small number, and is called a *byte*. Each byte has an *address*, a number which identifies its location in the memory.

Each character code is held in a separate byte, and each of the instructions will probably take several bytes for its storage. The CPU must be capable of determining how many bytes each instruction occupies.

With the introduction of this eighth property, we say good-bye to Igor; converting his program into one-byte numbers would be unrewarding. We are now strictly into the world of real computers.

1.3 Basic Architecture

Each of these byte-sized slots is capable of holding one small number. The byte may be (1) an actual number, or (2) part of a machine instruction, or (3) the code for a printing character.

Let us look for a moment at a specific byte whose address is, say, 1660. (Our real machines will usually have many thousand or million bytes of memory, in contrast to Igor's more limited slot storage.) Assume that the code for a printing character is stored there, say the character A whose code is 65 in ASCII. Somewhere else in the memory are machine instructions that will send that character to a terminal. When those instructions are executed, the number 65 is sent to a terminal. The end result is that an A appears on the terminal screen.

To understand the machinery that makes this possible, we will draw a "block diagram" picture of a typical C machine. In the figure below we see four "blocks" (i.e., functional pieces) of hardware that are interconnected   by   an   "omnibus   connection"   (omnibus: "for everything"), or *bus*. The four blocks are

CPU: the Central Processing Unit;

Memory: all the bytes of machine storage;

Disk Controller: which sends data to and from a disk drive;

Terminal Controller: which sends data to and from a terminal.

In our short scenario above, the CPU reads an instruction from the memory and does what that instruction directs it to do. In this case, the instruction tells the CPU to fetch the byte from location 1660 and to send that byte to the terminal controller. The terminal controller then accepts that byte (value 65), and sends it to the terminal.

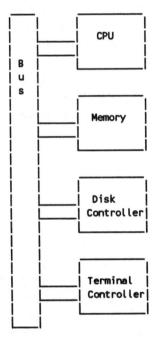

Each of these hardware blocks is typically a *printed circuit board*, and the bus is typically a piece of hardware that the boards plug into, with typically 50 to 100 separate connections between the boards. The time required for the byte-copying is limited mainly by the speed of execution of the boards and the time required for signals to move between them over the bus. The ultimate limit on the speed is the speed of light — the electrical signals travel about 1 billion feet per second, or one foot in one billionth of a second (one nanosecond). (Note: the American "billion" equals the British "thousand million" — but the American and British "nano" are equal.) On a typical C machine, this scenario takes a few millionths of a second. The terminal at the end of the process is usually the limiting bottleneck; terminals range in speed from 10 characters per second to several thousand per second.

The disk typically transfers data much faster than the terminal. Let us modify the scenario above to include the disk. Suppose the user has some data on the disk which is to be printed on the terminal. To be very concrete about it, the user has the disk (or diskette) in hand, inserts it into the disk drive, and executes a program to print some information. After a lot of instructions have been executed that find the appropriate information on the disk, an instruction will be executed that transfers some characters from the disk to the memory. Once the information is in the memory, instructions like our scenario above can transfer it one character at a time to the terminal.

This account will generally be true of any machine that you can use to *execute* your C programs. If you also use your machine to *prepare* C programs, it will also have a collection of software known as an *operating system*. In the operating system are various instructions which make the hardware easier for the programmer to use to produce useful programs.

To summarize: both data and instructions reside in the memory. Certain machine instructions cause the transfer of data to or from the disk or the terminal, producing a result that the user can see. The basic hardware is usually augmented with an operating system to make the hardware easier to use.

1.4 A Typical Environment

One of the great advantages of a language such as C is that it makes it possible to develop software for a great variety of machines and operating systems. The word *environment* is often used to denote the combination of a machine, an operating system, and a compiler. In this sense, C works in a variety of environments. Once you have mastered C in your environment, it is a relatively easy step to write for other environments.

However, this variety poses problems for us in writing a book that attempts to tell you how to do things step-by-step. One solution often taken is to describe the use of the language at a level sufficiently vague to apply to all environments. We prefer to take a more concrete approach: We will give specific pictures and recipes for a Typical Environment and also tell you what needs to be changed in other environments.

Thus, throughout this book there will be a *Typical Environment:* a machine with ASCII codes, in which addresses are 2-byte numbers, running some version of the UNIX operating system and a Standard C compiler. Whenever addresses are shown in our diagrams, they will be shown as 2-byte numbers, ranging from 0 toward 64K.

We strongly recommend that your study of C should make use of a real computer on which you can do the exercises. In each environment that you use, your compiler manuals should provide you with simple instructions for the basic compile-and-execute process. In our Typical Environment, it is described in the next section.

1.5 A Sample Program

The first program to run in any environment is one which simply announces that it is working. In the C language community, the traditional first program says

```
hello, world
```

and then quits. The following C program does nothing but print this message. (The heading `hello.c:` designates the *name* of the file. The next line begins the contents of the file.)

```
hello.c:
    #include <stdio.h>
    main()
       {
       printf("hello, world\n");
       }
```

The program is found in a file named `hello.c` and contains five lines. A file like this, which contains a C program that you can print and read, is known as a *source file* and its readable contents are known as *source code*, or, colloquially, just *code*. The line `#include <stdio.h>` is required for performing input/output (I/O). The word `main` says that this is a *main program*, one that can be executed by itself. The *opening brace* (`{`) marks the beginning of the program, and then the *closing brace* (`}`) marks its end. The line between the braces

```
printf("hello, world\n");
```

writes the 13 characters between the quotes to your terminal. The code \n stands for *newline*, which causes the display to end the current line and start a new one, much like the RETURN key on a typewriter. It consists of two characters (a backslash and an n) in the source file, but during compilation it is translated into one newline character.

If you have access now to a computer, we suggest that you try out each of the steps in the following recipe. Since all the steps of this recipe involve environment-dependent details, refer to your compiler manuals for details.

(1) To get our C program into the computer, we need to use a *text editor*, a program that creates or modifies files of text such as programs. The end result of this editing is a source file named hello.c.

(2) If we have made any mistakes in entering the program, or wish to make changes to an existing program, we again use the text editor to make the changes.

(3) We use the *compiler* to produce an executable program. In our Typical Environment, the compiler is invoked with the command

```
cc hello.c
```

The compiler then goes to work. During its work, it produces a file of *assembler code*, a human-readable version of the machine instructions needed for the program. If you do not tell the compiler to stop with the assembler code, it goes on to produce a file known as an *object-code file*, or *object file*. The object file is simply a series of numbers, the actual hardware instructions to execute your program. The compiler then turns the job over to the *linker*, which combines the instructions for the hello.c program with instructions from a *linkage library*, which contains object files for library functions. The instructions for printf, for example, are found in this library. The end result is an executable program (named a.out in UNIX systems).

(4) We execute or "run" the executable program, and should obtain the printout

```
hello, world
```

The whole sequence is summarized in the figure below. This type of diagram is known as a *data flow diagram;* each box represents a program receiving input from the arrows flowing into it and producing output on the arrows flowing out of it.

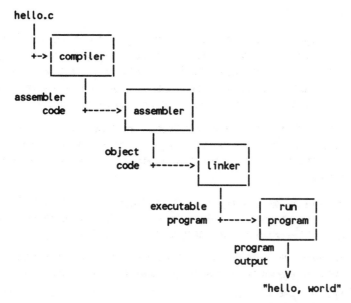

The last step in the process — running the executable program — deserves further explanation. After the compilation process, the program exists as a *file* on a disk, containing machine instructions. When the user asks to *run*, or execute, the program, the process of "asking" is mediated by the *operating system*, which reads the user's commands from a terminal and then performs them. The operating system is itself a program which occupies space in the memory; that part of the operating system which continually "resides" in the memory is known as the *resident*. After the operating system locates the executable file on the disk and reads it into the memory, the memory then looks something like this:

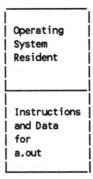

Thus, the loading process has read the instructions and data for a.out into the machine memory. In the diagram, the memory also contains an operating system. Between the two of them, they contain all that is necessary for a.out to do its work.

Such is the picture when the program compiles successfully. Quite often, while learning the language you will have errors in your program which the compiler will complain about. We would like to prepare you now for handling the situation intelligently.

One common type of error is a *syntax error*. This occurs when the format of your program is not what the compiler expects. Unfortunately for the learner, some C compilers are not great at telling you a human-oriented description of the underlying problem. For example, edit your hello.c file and remove the semicolon, to produce

```
helbad.c:
    #include <stdio.h>
    main()
        {
        printf("hello, world\n")
        }
```

On compiling the result, you may encounter messages such as this:

```
helbad.c:5: Statement syntax
```

Each such message tells you what file was being compiled, what line number the compiler was reading, and a description of the problem. In this case, the compiler complains about the syntax of line 5, but line 5 actually is all right — the problem is that the program is missing the semicolon on line 4. Often, the real problem will be *one line before* the compiler tells you.

Continue this exercise by removing other components of the program and observe the results. If you are lucky, you can get the compiler to give you quite a long list of error messages. In this case, fix the first error and see how many messages go away as a result.

A *linkage error* is a different type of error. If, for example, we misspell the name `printf` as `orintf`, we will receive a message like this:

```
undefined: _orintf
```

which means, simply, that the name `orintf` cannot be found in our link library. The correction is usually obvious, as it is in this case.

CHAPTER 2: DATA

Every C machine stores data in the binary number system, so we first present an introduction to the binary system. Then we show how data is stored in variables and constants. And after some discussion of the octal and hexadecimal number systems, we are ready to show programs that print results.

2.1 Bits and Numbers

In this section, we will look at some interesting things that can be done in a world with only two numbers, zero (0) and one (1). The operations on these numbers were invented by George Boole in the 1840's; hence, the system is known as Boolean algebra.

The three basic operations of Boolean algebra are AND (&), OR (|), and NOT (~). Their rules — "0 & 0 is 0", "0 & 1 is 0", etc. — can be written in tables:

```
AND                 OR                NOT
 &   0   1           |   0   1         ~
   --------            --------          ----
0 |  0   0         0 |  0   1       0 |  1
  |                   |                |
1 |  0   1         1 |  1   1       1 |  0
```

Or to put the rules into words, one number AND another number produces 1 only if both numbers are 1; one number OR another number produces 0 only if both numbers are 0; and the negation (NOT) of a number changes 0 into 1 and 1 into 0.

This is certainly a tiny system of arithmetic, with only two numbers. It is interesting because it models some facts of *logic*, when we interpret zero (0) as *false* and one (1) as *true*. "Sentences that can be *true* or *false*" are sometimes known as *assertions*, or to give more credit to Professor Boole, as *Boolean expressions*. Here is an example of a Boolean expression, in words:

"1 is less than n AND n is less than 100".

If n is 50, this expression is *true*. Why? First of all, because it is "obvious", but also, "1 is less than n" is *true*, "n is less than 100" is *true*, and therefore, since "*true* AND *true*" is *true*, the result is *true*. (Or expressed in Boolean algebra, 1 & 1 is 1.)

As we will see in Section 3.5, these operations (& | ~) appear in C language, where we will give them the names *bit-and*, *bit-or*, and *bit-not*. For the moment, we turn instead to *arithmetic*, with the operations *plus*, *minus*, *multiply*, and *divide*. In order to get more interesting arithmetic using *bits* (the digits 0 and 1), we need to use more of them together. The simplest combination we can make is to put two bits together into one number, which would give us these four numbers: 00, 01, 10, 11. Give the leftmost bit the value 2, and the rightmost bit the value 1, and we have an "unsigned two-bit" *binary* arithmetic:

```
0    00
1    01
2    10
3    11
```

Familiar facts of arithmetic have new faces:

```
  0    00        0    00        1    01        1    01
+ 0    00      + 1    01      + 2    10      + 1    01
---------      ---------      ---------      ---------
  0    00        1    01        3    11        2    10
```

But how about 2 + 2? The usual arithmetic result would not fit into two bits; but if we allow our numbers to go to three bits, we can express the result.

```
  2    010
+ 2    010
----------
  4    100
```

But how about 4 + 4? Hmmm. We could keep expanding the size of our numbers to hold bigger and bigger values, but this is not how real computers work. The C machine has data types that are big enough for a fixed number of bits, and no more. Many C compilers provide variables that can hold eight bits for numbers from 0 to 255:

```
0    00000000
1    00000001
2    00000010
3    00000011
4    00000100
...      ...
253  11111101
254  11111110
255  11111111
```

How to convert from binary to decimal? Here is one method that will be of some use later. We are working here with 8-bit numbers, but the same method will work for any size binary number.

Write down the binary number, and next to it label two columns for "ones" and "zeros". For example,

```
01110101    ones | zeros
                 |
                 |
                 |
```

Starting at the rightmost digit, write a 1 below "ones" if that digit is a 1, or below "zeros" if that digit is a 0. In this case:

```
01110101    ones | zeros
                 |
             1   |
                 |
```

As we work from right to left, each digit is worth 2 times the value of the one to its right. So the next digit, the second one from the right, has value 2. In this case, the digit is a zero, so put a 2 under the zeros column.

```
01110101    ones | zeros
                 |
             1   |
                 |  2
                 |
```

Continue the process from right to left until all digits have been recorded either under ones or zeros. The numeric value of the binary number is the sum of the entries in the "ones" column. We can double-check by summing both columns and adding them together; they should total 255, because

255 = 1 + 2 + 4 + 8 + 16 + 32 + 64 + 128.

```
01110101    ones | zeros
                 |
              1  |
                 |   2
              4  |
                 |   8
             16  |
             32  |
             64  |
                 | 128
            ____ |____
                 |
            117  | 138         117 + 138 = 255
```

Question [2-1] What is the decimal value of the following binary numbers?

```
00001111        01010101        10000001
```

_____   _____   _____

How do we add two binary numbers? The process works just like the usual process of decimal addition, except that the sum of 1 and 1 is not 2, but "0 with carry 1". For example, adding the numbers 7 and 2:

```
  00000111      Starting from the right, 1 + 0 is 1.
+ 00000010      Going leftwards, 1 + 1 is 0 carry 1.
-----------     Third digit, carry 1 + 1 + 0 is 0 carry 1.
  00001001      Fourth digit, carry 1 + 0 + 0 is 1.
                The other four digits are all 0.
```

Just for practice, convert the result into decimal by the two-column procedure given above. Your result should look like this:

```
00001001    ones | zeros
                 |
              1  |
                 |   2
                 |   4
              8  |
                 |  16
                 |  32
                 |  64
                 | 128
            ____ |____
                 |
              9  | 246         9 + 246 = 255
```

Noticing how much easier it was here to just add the "ones" column, we suggest leaving off the "zeros" column, since it served mainly for cross-checking.

All these rules can be reduced to the more mathematical interpretation of a *"base two"* (or *base-2*) number system. Recalling that "two to the power N" (or 2^N) means "two times two times two..." repeated N times, and that 2^0 equals 1, then the binary number 10110001 equals

$$1 \times 2^7 + 0 \times 2^6 + 1 \times 2^5 + 1 \times 2^4 + 0 \times 2^3 + 0 \times 2^2 + 0 \times 2^1 + 1 \times 2^0$$

which is

$$1 \times 128 + 0 \times 64 + 1 \times 32 + 1 \times 16 + 0 \times 8 + 0 \times 4 + 0 \times 2 + 1 \times 1,$$

or 177 decimal.

So far we have dealt only with non-negative numbers in our binary system (and nothing bigger than 8 bits, at that). Let us look at some different interpretations of the bits that will allow both positive and negative numbers. The leftmost (or *high-order*) bit will be known as the *sign bit*. If it is a zero, the signed number will have the same value as before; but if the sign bit is a 1, the number value is taken as negative.

The most common scheme for signed numbers is known as the *twos complement system*. In this system, when we add two numbers we get the same binary result whether either of the numbers was interpreted as signed or unsigned. In other words, if we add 11111111 and 00000001, we get 00000000, when the result is truncated to eight bits:

```
  11111111
+ 00000001
----------
  00000000
```

As an unsigned 8-bit number, the bits 11111111 equal 255, and if we add them to 1, we get zero, with a "carry" from the leftmost bit. But in our new signed interpretation, 11111111 equals -1 (negative one), 11111110 equals -2, etc:

Binary value	Unsigned 8-bit value	Signed 8-bit value (twos complement)
00000000	0	0
00000001	1	1
00000010	2	2
00000011	3	3
...	...	...
11111101	253	-3
11111110	254	-2
11111111	255	-1

The rightmost column shows the *twos complement* interpretation of the number.

We arranged the numbers in the table running from 00000000 to
11111111, to show that the set of numbers which we originally interpreted as 0 to 255 can also be interpreted as positive and negative
numbers. Arranging the table according to the (twos complement)
signed value would look like this:

Binary value	Unsigned 8-bit value	Signed 8-bit value (twos complement)
10000000	128	-128
10000001	129	-127
10000010	130	-126
10000011	131	-125
...	...	...
11111100	252	-4
11111101	253	-3
11111110	254	-2
11111111	255	-1
00000000	0	0
00000001	1	1
00000010	2	2
...	...	...
01111111	127	127

How, then, to convert an 8-bit binary number to its signed (twos
complement) decimal representation? For now, the simplest rule is to
first convert to unsigned decimal, which we covered earlier. Then if
the sign bit of the binary number was a 1 bit, subtract 256 from the
unsigned value. A more general rule will be presented in Section 3.6.

The name "twos complement" comes from the fact that when we
add a number with its twos complement value, the sum at each position
is two — zero with "carry", in binary. There is an alternative scheme
called *ones complement* where the sum at each position is a one. In
other words, to find the ones complement of a binary number, change
each 0 bit to a 1, and each 1 bit to a 0. The previous table looks like
this in ones complement:

Binary value	Unsigned 8-bit value	Signed 8-bit value (ones complement)
10000000	128	-127
10000001	129	-126
10000010	130	-125
10000011	131	-124
...	...	...
11111100	252	-3
11111101	253	-2
11111110	254	-1
11111111	255	-0
00000000	0	0
00000001	1	1
00000010	2	2
...	...	...
01111111	127	127

Notice that in ones complement arithmetic there are two binary values for zero: 00000000 and 11111111. Another peculiarity of the ones complement system is the "end-around carry" — if the binary sum produces a high-order carry, a 1-bit is added to the low-order end. For example, when adding "negative zero" (11111111) to itself, ordinary binary addition would give the 8-bit sum 11111110, with a high-order carry. After end-around carry, the result becomes "negative zero" itself, 11111111.

Most C machines work with twos complement arithmetic, and we will show twos complement values whenever they occur in diagrams. The existence of C compilers on ones complement machines does raise some portability questions, which will be addressed in Section 3.21.

Question [2-2] What is the 8-bit sum? What does each number equal in decimal? Do each problem both in unsigned and twos complement signed interpretation.

binary	unsigned decimal	signed decimal (twos complement)
00101011 =	_____	_____
+ 10000011 =	_____	_____

_____	_____	_____
11110000 =	_____	_____
+ 00001111 =	_____	_____

_____	_____	_____
10000000 =	_____	_____
+ 00001010 =	_____	_____

_____	_____	_____

Now compute these 8-bit sums, using ones complement interpretation:

binary	signed decimal (ones complement)
00101011 =	_____
+ 10000011 =	_____

_____	_____
11110000 =	_____
+ 00001111 =	_____

_____	_____
11111101 =	_____
+ 11111110 =	_____

_____	_____

2.2 Integer Variables

Recall from Section 1.2 that the memory of a computer is subdi-vided into bytes, each of which holds one small number. One of the important things that a C compiler does is to associate a *name*, chosen by the programmer, with one or more of the machine memory locations. In a program, each such name is known as a *variable* — so named because its *value* (or "contents") can vary as the program is run. Each variable has a *type*, which specifies its *representation* and its *size*. The two basic representations for variables are

integers (whole numbers with no fractional part) — the *signed* integers and the *unsigned* integers; and

floating-point numbers (numbers with a "floating" decimal point).

We will describe floating-point variables in the next section. Here let's look at the three basic sizes of integer variables found in C: char variables (always 1 byte); short variables (typically 2 bytes); and long variables (typically 4 bytes).

A programmer-chosen name is *declared* to be a certain type of variable by a *declaration*. Here are some declarations:

```
char c;
short i;
long lnum;
```

In our Typical Environment's memory, the storage for these variables would look like this (where each box represents one byte of the memory):

c

i

lnum

C has two "adjectives" that modify integer types: signed and unsigned. Thus, we can use

```
unsigned char,   signed char,   "plain" char,
unsigned short,  signed short,  "plain" short,
unsigned long,   signed long,   "plain" long.
```

For each of the unsigned types, the size is the same as the "plain" type, but the value is interpreted as always being zero or greater. The numeric values of all these variables are stored using the binary number representation. On most machines each byte contains 8 bits, so an unsigned char can hold numbers from 0 to 255; an unsigned short can hold from 0 to 65535; and an unsigned long can hold from 0 to 4294967295.

A signed long can hold values from -2147483648 to 2147483647; signed long and "plain" long are identical. A signed short can hold values from -32768 to 32767; signed short and "plain" short are identical.

However, signed char and "plain" char may have different ranges. In our Typical Environment, signed char can hold values from -128 to 127; "plain" char is *either* signed (-128 to 127) *or* unsigned (0 to 255); the compiler manual tells which. Notice that all three varieties of char variables are just little integers; there are no special "character" properties in C.

There is also an integer type known simply as int. The size of an int depends upon the machine hardware. On some machines, an int is a 2-byte variable, the same as a short. On other machines, an int is a 4-byte variable, the same as a long. Because of this variability in the size of an int, we usually prefer to use either short or long variables.

As with the other types, C also has signed int and unsigned int. The type unsigned int can be abbreviated to unsigned, just as short is really an abbreviation for short int and long is an abbreviation for long int.

As we saw above, each variable is given a *type* by means of a declaration. At run-time (i.e., when the program is run), each variable will have an address in the machine memory. The hardware eventually uses this address as its means of locating the variable when the program runs. For example, if the program contains these declarations

```
short i;
...
short j;
```

the variables might look like this in the memory (where each oblong box represents the 2-byte storage for one short):

NAME	ADDRESS	STORAGE
i	2000	
j	3000	

For purposes of illustration we have shown the variables at particular locations. The actual locations they occupy are up to the compiler, and of no concern to the programmer. All that matters is that each one has an address in the memory.

As a notational convenience, variables with the same type can be declared in the same declaration, by listing them with commas between them:

    short i, j;

When a value is *assigned* to a variable, its storage holds that value until another value is assigned. Thus when the C *assignment statement*

    i = 7;

is executed, the value 7 is put into the storage of i; in this example, the two bytes at machine address 2000 are set to the value 0000000000000111, i.e., 7. When the assignment statement

    j = i;

is executed, the 2-byte value at location 2000 is copied into the 2-byte storage at location 3000. The resulting memory locations look like this:

NAME   ADDRESS   STORAGE

  i   2000 | 7 |

  j   3000 | 7 |

To summarize, a variable has a name and a type, which are specified in a declaration. When the program is run, the variable has a value and location (address). The type of the variable determines the size (number of bytes) and representation (integer or floating-point) of the variable.

2.3 Floating-point Variables

So far, all numbers we have seen are whole-number integers, with no fractional part. *Floating-point* variables are the C .mechanism for handling fractional numbers. The fundamental concept is that of *scientific notation:* any number can be expressed as a decimal fraction multiplied by a power of ten. The value 3.14159, for example, can be written

$$.314159 \times 10^1$$

Similarly, -10000 can be written as

$$-.1 \times 10^5$$

The machine storage for a floating-point number has three parts:

sign (either positive or negative);

fraction (a number somewhat less than 1); and

exponent.

The fraction and exponent are binary rather than decimal on most C machines, but the distinction is important only at a more advanced level of programming. The exact form of the storage of floating-point numbers varies with the machine, but all Standard C compilers offer three flavors of floating-point numbers:

float   which holds at least 6 decimal digits;

double   which holds at least 10 decimal digits; and

long double   which holds at least 10 decimal digits.

The exponent in the floating-point storage allows for numbers to be as small as 10^{-38} or as large as 10^{38}.

Floating-point numbers are thus accurate only to the number of digits in their storage; they can never *exactly* represent fractions such as one-third. However, accuracy to 10 places (or even 6) is often quite sufficient.

2.4 Constants

We have seen that variables have a name, type, and (when the program is run) a location and value. C programs also contain *constants*, which specify an unchanging value. Each constant has a type, but does not have a location, except for the "string constants" which we will see soon.

Decimal constants consist of one or more decimal digits, such as 1, or 2, or 12345. The *type* of decimal constants is int; however, on a machine where int is smaller than long, an integer constant too big to fit an int will have the type long. Also, a constant can be forced to have type long by appending the letter L to the number.

A numeric constant containing a decimal point is a *floating-point constant*, such as 3.14159 or 9.99. A floating-point constant can also be written in E-format, such as 1E-37 (which means 1×10^{-37}) or 1E5 (which means 1×10^5). The *type* of floating-point constants is double.

Decimal and floating-point constants are positive numbers, but negative numbers may be represented using the unary-minus operator, as in -12345 or -1E5 or -.01.

Integer constants can be forced to have an unsigned type by appending the letter U to the number: 255U is an unsigned int with the value 255; 40000UL is an unsigned long with the value 40,000.

Character constants are a means of specifying the numeric value of a particular character. For example, the character constant 'a' is the value which, when sent to a terminal, will print an a. Similarly, the character constant '0' is the value which, when sent to a terminal, will print the digit 0. In ASCII, 48 is the code value for '0' ("single-quote, zero, single-quote"). Note that there is a character constant for an actual zero numeric value; it is written '\0' ("single-quote, backslash, zero, single-quote"). This *null character* is very different from the character constant '0'; when the null character is sent to a terminal, the terminal does absolutely nothing in response, so the null character is sometimes sent as a "delay" to allow time for clearing the screen, etc. (Its uses in C language will be described momentarily.) There are some other special character constants:

```
'\a'    alert ("bell")
'\b'    backspace
'\f'    form feed
'\n'    newline
'\r'    carriage return
'\t'    tab
'\v'    vertical tab
'\''    single-quote (apostrophe)
'\"'    double-quote
'\\'    backslash
'\377'  octal bit pattern
'\xFF'  hexadecimal bit pattern
```

The *type* of character constants is int. (Octal and hexadecimal numbers are discussed in Section 2.5, coming next.)

A *string constant* consists of characters surrounded by double-quotes, such as the famous

```
"hello, world\n"
```

String constants, unlike the others, actually have a *location* in the machine memory. The characters in the string are stored in memory, and the numeric value of the constant is the *address* of this memory. In addition, the compiler stores the null character '\0' at the end of the string to mark the end of it. Assuming the ASCII character set, the string constant "0" looks something like this in the memory:

```
3000      | 48 | 0 |
          | '0'| '\0'|
```

and the value of the constant is its address (in this hypothetical case, 3000) — whereas the value of '0' is simply the number 48 (the ASCII code for '0'). Our representation of the string storage shows both the numeric ASCII code for each byte and the corresponding character constant.

The shortest string constant is the *null string*, which is written "" ("double-quote, double-quote") and is stored in memory as a single null character, '\0'.

Two adjacent string constants are catenated by the compiler into a single string. Thus

```
printf("hello, world\n");
```
and
```
printf("hello,"   " world\n");
```

produce identical results.

Question [2-3] What is the *type* of each constant:

123	_____	1.2	_____
'x'	_____	1.5E4	_____
5L	_____	'2'	_____

What does this string constant look like in memory:

```
"000"
```

```
| | | | |
|_|_|_|_|
```

2.5 Octal and Hexadecimal Numbers

So far, we have written binary numbers using only the bits 0 and 1. You can easily see a couple of problems with this system. It tends to get verbose even for the small 8-bit numbers we have used so far. Also, it increases the likelihood of making mistakes with the larger numbers. For a more compact notation of binary numbers, we can use *octal* and *hexadecimal* numbers.

To convert a number from binary to octal, group the bits into groups of three, starting at the right. Next, write down one digit for the binary value of each group of three (or fewer) bits. Here is an example:

    11001010 --> 11 001 010 --> 3 1 2

The translation between octal and binary can be given by a table:

    binary octal

     000   0
     001   1
     010   2
     011   3
     100   4
     101   5
     110   6
     111   7

In C programs, any numeric constant that starts with a leading zero is interpreted as an octal number. Therefore, if we wanted to write the binary number 11001010 in a C program, we could write it as 0312. C also employs octal numbers (without the leading zero) in the *arbitrary bit pattern* style of character constants. The character constant '\23' has the decimal value of 19, for example.

Converting from octal to binary is very easy: Translate each octal digit into the corresponding group of three bits.

Question [2-4] Write down the octal equivalent for each binary number:

10110010   11111111

0__ __ __   0__ __ __

1101100100110110   1111111111111111

0__ __ __ __ __   0__ __ __ __ __

Question [2-5] Write down the binary equivalent (8 or 16 bits) for each octal number:

014   0177

_____   _____

0200   014662   052525

_____   _____   _____

Octal numbers constitute a *"base-8"* arithmetic system: The octal constant 0123 corresponds to

$$1 \times 8^2 + 2 \times 8^1 + 3 \times 8^0$$

which is

$$1 \times 64 + 2 \times 8 + 3 \times 1$$

or 83, in decimal.

As you see, the octal number system serves as a shorthand for writing binary numbers, using groups of three bits each. An alternative system, which uses groups of four bits each, is the *hexadecimal* (or "hex") number system. (The roots of the name "hexadecimal" are "hexa" for "six" and "deci" for "ten", hence "based on sixteen".)

To convert a number from binary to hexadecimal, start with the rightmost four bits and convert them to a hexadecimal digit. Then working leftwards, keep grouping into four-bit digits. The table for hexadecimal digits includes the usual 10 decimal digits and the letters "A" through "F" to stand for digits with values 10 through 15:

binary	hexadecimal	binary	hexadecimal
0000	0	1000	8
0001	1	1001	9
0010	2	1010	A
0011	3	1011	B
0100	4	1100	C
0101	5	1101	D
0110	6	1110	E
0111	7	1111	F

In C programs, hexadecimal constants appear with 0x prefixed to them; e.g., 0x1F is the number 31. For various historical reasons, most of the early work in C language favored the octal number system (e.g., plain '\23' is octal; hex '\x23' takes an extra letter). However, most modern C machines have data sizes of 8, 16, and 32 bits, which divide more conveniently into 4-bit digits, so hex is now more common. In our book, we will show both octal and hexadecimal where appropriate, but generally favor decimal numbers in our programs and diagrams.

To convert from hexadecimal to binary, just convert each digit to its corresponding binary value.

Question [2-6] Write down the hexadecimal equivalent for each binary number:

10110010   11111111

0x__ __   0x__ __

1101100100110110   1111111111111111

0x__ __ __ __   0x__ __ __ __

Question [2-7] Convert from the hexadecimal to the corresponding binary:

0xFE   0x40

_____   _____

0x7FFF   0x9A6E

_____   _____

2.6 Atoms of a C Program

One of the first things that the compiler does when reading a program is to split it into "words and punctuation". These basic pieces of a program are known as its *atoms*. Each variable name constitutes one atom; so does each constant. Here is a complete list of the categories of atoms:

1. *Names* or *identifiers,* chosen by the programmer. Identifiers may be as long as you like, but some compilers will only look at the first 31 characters of the name. Identifiers are composed of letters and numbers, and must start with a letter. The underscore character (_) counts as a letter, but names that *start* with an underscore are reserved for the system software, and should not be used in regular application code. The compiler sees the difference between lower-case characters and upper-case characters; the names MAIN, Main, and main are three different names in C. The most common C style is to use only lower-case characters for your variable names. Examples that illustrate these rules:

   Valid identifiers: i j x1 total user_id

   Invalid identifiers: %_of_change 57flavors

   Bad style, but valid: TOTAL _x

   There are some "conventional" meanings for simple names: c is a character; i, j, and n are integers; x, y, and z are floating-point. Over 90% of the hundreds of C programmers we surveyed share these conventions.

2. *Constants:* As we saw in the previous section, C has the following types of constants:

   Decimal integer constants (both int and long): 63 9999 40 40L 255U

   Octal integer constants: 077 040 0 0L 07U

   Hexadecimal integer constants: 0x37 0xFFFF 0x9000 0x9000L 0xFFU

   Character constants: 'a' '0' '\0' '\n' '\xFF'

String constants: `"help"` `"hello, world\n"` `""`

Floating-point constants: `1.5` `.001` `1E-5` `1000.`

3. *Punctuators* separate the other atoms. Examples:

    `,` `;` `{` `}` `:` `#`

4. *Operators* (such as "plus", "minus", "times", or "divided-by") are described in Chapter 3. Examples:

    `+` `-` `*` `/`

5. *Keywords* are "built-in" words of the language. These are *reserved* words, meaning that you are not allowed to use them as identifiers. A complete list of C keywords:

auto	double	int	struct
break	else	long	switch
case	enum	register	typedef
char	extern	return	union
const	float	short	unsigned
continue	for	signed	void
default	goto	sizeof	volatile
do	if	static	while

6. *Header-names*, such as `<stdio.h>` and `"local.h"`, appear on `#include` lines.

    Regarding *whitespace:* Any number of blanks, tabs, formfeeds, and newlines may be used to separate the atoms in a program; the seldom-used "vertical-tab" character also counts as whitespace. The whitespace characters are not atoms; they serve to *separate* atoms. Good style dictates that you use tabs and spaces to arrange your program in a readable layout.

    Comments also constitute whitespace. The compilation process behaves as if each comment were simply replaced by one blank. A comment starts with the two characters `/*` and continues (possibly over several lines) to the two characters `*/`.

    Notice that the comment format in C allows multi-line comments; all comments extend until the closing `*/`. It is always good style to place a comment before each program to describe what is done in that program. A useful style for such *prolog comments* is to align the asterisks in the second position of each line, as in the programs that follow.

Another useful style is to attach a comment to each declaration, explaining the properties of each variable. We suggest that the comment contain a description (if needed), a colon, and an abbreviation of the variable's properties, such as its range. Let the notation ⟨0,2,4⟩ mean "the set containing 0, 2, and 4", and let ⟨-99,0:100⟩ mean "the set containing -99 and the range 0 through 100". Then a typical declaration might look like this:

```
short nmonths;  /* number of months : {0:12} */
```

which says that this variable will range from 0 through 12.

These two programs would compile the same:

```
hello2.c:
    /* hello2 - print greeting
     */
    #include <stdio.h>
    main()
        {
        printf("hello, world\n");
        }


hello3.c:
    #               include              <stdio.h>
    main
    (
    )
    {
    printf
    (
    "hello, world\n"
    )
    ;
    }
```

The second program, hello3.c, has more space around the atoms. (The #include <stdio.h> must be all on one line; see Section 2.10.)

Question [2-8] Write the category of atom next to each atom of hello3.c.

2.7 Flow of Control

An *assignment statement* such as

```
c = 'A';
```

assigns the value on the right-hand side of the equal-sign to the variable on the left of the equal-sign. After the assignment, the new value is remembered in the storage of the variable until yet another new value replaces it. The best verbalization of the assignment operator is "gets", as in "c *gets* 'A'". It should definitely *not* be read as "equals".

We now combine some declarations, constants, and assignment statements to make a simple C program. Each line of this program is identified by a *line number* at the left-hand margin. (The line numbers are added for illustration only and are not part of the source file.)

```
asst.c:
 1  /* asst - examples of assignment
 2   * (No output is produced)
 3   */
 4  main()
 5      {
 6      char c;     /* 1-byte integer : ('A','X') */
 7      short i;    /* short integer  : (65, -4) */
 8
 9      c = 'A';
10      i = 65;
11      c = 'X';
12      i = -4;
13      }
```

For this program, or any other one, its life history can be divided into four stages or "times":

Edit-time: The source file is created using a text editor.

Compile-time: The compiler reads the source file and creates an executable program.

Load-time: The executable program is loaded into the memory of the computer.

Run-time: Control of the computer is given to the executable program that is loaded in memory.

Thus, "run-time" is the time when the program actually performs what it was programmed to do. In order to understand what happens at run-time, you need to know that the computer has a mechanism for keeping track of where it is in the execution of a program. On most C machines, this mechanism is known as the *program counter (PC)*. At each instant of time as the machine is running, the PC contains the location of the next instruction that it is about to execute.

After the executable program is loaded into the memory by the operating system, the operating system turns control of the machine over to the executable program by loading the PC with the address of the first instruction of the program. After that, the PC keeps track of where it is in the program, until the program is finished. Then the PC reverts to an address in the operating system again.

Each C statement may create more than one machine instruction in the executable program, and each machine instruction may consist of several bytes. However, for the time being, we will treat the PC as though it kept track of the execution by the *line number* of the program, rather than by actual machine addresses. Thus, when our program is started, the PC starts at line 9, the first executable statement of the program. (The declarations on lines 6 and 7 do not generate any instructions; they just give information to the compiler.) After the code for line 9 is executed, the PC points to line 10. This statement is then executed by the machine, and the PC points to line 11, and so forth. The time that these events take is measured in *microseconds* (millionths of a second), but they still follow each other in strict sequence. This strict sequence is known as the *flow of control*. If you are looking at a printed program in front of you, you can simulate the flow of control by moving your finger from top to bottom of the program printout. The PC is the machine's equivalent of your pointing finger.

The run-time flow of control looks like this:

PC=9   The storage of the variable c receives the value 65 (the ASCII code for 'A'). Its eight bits in memory now look like this: 01000001. (Before this statement is executed, the variable has what is known as a "garbage" value — whatever bits happened to be lying in the memory.)

PC=10   The storage of the variable i receives the value 65; its 16 bits in memory look like this: 0000000001000001. The variable c continues to hold the value it received before.

PC=11   The storage of the variable c is changed to 98 (the ASCII code for 'x'); i is still 65.

PC=12   The storage of the variable i is changed to -4; its bits now look like this: 1111111111111100. c is still 98.

PC=13   The end of the program is reached, and control returns to the operating system.

This program has not produced any observable result; all it has done is to store some values into certain locations inside the machine, then abandon them.

In order to see what is going on during the execution of the program, we must perform some *output*, the subject of our next section. Our sample program has simply illustrated the sequential flow of control through an executable program: execution starts with the first executable statement and proceeds statement-by-statement until the end of the program. Each assignment statement stores a certain value into the storage of some variable, and that value abides in that location until something else is stored in that variable.

2.8 Output and Printf

To see what our program is doing, we need to add *output* to our program. The most common way of producing output is the function printf. Its simplest use is to print messages — the string constants that we saw in section 2.4:

```
printf("hello, world\n");
```

A more significant use of printf is to print variables using an output format string:

```
printf("%d\n", c);
```

Here we are printing the char variable c, using the *format string* "%d\n". The format says to print as a decimal number and then to return the cursor or carriage to start a new line. Other output conversions are available: %o specifies octal format, %x specifies hexadecimal format (with lowercase letters), %X specifies hexadecimal format (with uppercase letters), %u specifies unsigned decimal format, and %c prints as one character, unconverted. More than one format is allowed by a single call to printf, and ordinary printing text may be interspersed in the format string, as in

```
printf("c: dec=%d oct=%o hex=%X char=%c\n",
    c, c, c, c);
printf("i: dec=%d oct=%o hex=%X unsigned=%u\n",
    i, i, i, i);
```

Naturally, the c format should not be used if the variable being printed does not contain a printable character. Because we are adding output to the program, we need the "Standard I/O" (i.e., "Standard Input/Output") header. We will add #include <stdio.h>; more details will come in Section 2.10. Adding these calls to printf gives the following revised program:

asst2.c:

```
/* asst2 - print assigned values
 */
#include <stdio.h>
main()
    {
    char c;       /* : {'A', 'X'} */
    short i;      /* : {65, -4} */

    c = 'A';
    i = 65;
    printf("c: dec=%d oct=%o hex=%X char=%c\n",
        c, c, c, c);
    printf("i: dec=%d oct=%o hex=%X unsigned=%u\n",
        i, i, i, i);
    c = 'X';
    i = -4;
    printf("c: dec=%d oct=%o hex=%X char=%c\n",
        c, c, c, c);
    printf("i: dec=%d oct=%o hex=%X unsigned=%u\n",
        i, i, i, i);
    }
```

Note that the same variable can be printed using several different formats; the choice of output representation is given entirely by the format string, not by the type of the variable being printed.

Some practical suggestions on entering and compiling this program: The procedure of editing the source file is just as we saw in Section 1.5. But if you use this simple recipe for compilation

    cc asst2.c

you will create a file named a.out (on UNIX systems), which will effectively destroy the executable version of your hello.c program. For simple learning examples such as these, it matters little — less space on your disk or diskette will be taken up by seldom-used executable programs. But as you advance, you will obviously not want to re-compile a program every time you want to use it. The more sophisticated formula for compilation is

    cc -o asst2 asst2.c

The option -o asst2 says to place the executable program in a file named asst2. Then to execute it, you run asst2 instead of a.out. Try this option on the compilation of asst2.c.

Question [2-9] What does the output of asst2 look like (in our Typical Environment with ASCII codes and 16-bit int's)?

There are also floating-point formats available from `printf`. Suppose the variable `x` is either `float` or `double`, and contains the value 123.5. We could print it in *fixed-point* format with one decimal place using the format `"%.1f"` (which would print `123.5`), or in E-notation using the format `"%.3E"` (which would print `1.235E+02`), or with the format `"%.3e"` (which would print `1.235e+02`). In each case, after the decimal-point in the format, we find a *precision* specifier, which tells how many decimal fraction places to print.

All these formats shown so far will accept an additional specification of *printing width*, by giving the desired width immediately after the percent-sign of the format. For example, the statement

```
printf("%6c %6d %6o %6X\n", c, c, c, c);
```

specifies six print positions for each output. This allows printouts with lined-up columns of numbers. Without the width specification, C takes only as many positions as are needed to print the data.

We can obtain leading zeroes on the output by putting a "precision" onto the integer format. Thus,

```
printf("%3d 0x%2.2X 0%3.3o\n", 10, 10, 10);
```

will produce

```
10 0x0A 0012
```

Question [2-10] If each format in `asst2.c` is changed to a 6-position width (without leading zeroes), what does its output look like?

In the floating-point formats, the width and precision may be combined. If `dollars` is a `float` or `double` variable, we could print numbers up to 999,999.99 with the format `"%10.2f"`, as in

```
printf("%10.2f\n", dollars);
```

The comma after the thousands place cannot be produced by `printf`, but we have left one space for a possible leading minus-sign. Thus, if `dollars` equals -999,999.99, the output will be `-999999.99`.

To summarize the formats with a few examples:

character:	%c	%6c	
decimal integer:	%d	%6d	%3.3d
unsigned integer:	%u	%6u	%3.3u
octal integer:	%o	%6o	%3.3o
hexadecimal integer:	%X	%6X	%2.2X
fixed-point:	%.1f	%10.2f	
E-notation:	%.3e	%10.6E	

Note that the number of formats must match the number of items separated by commas appearing after the formats. If there are too many items, some items will be left unprinted. If there are too few items, extra garbage may be printed.

Exercise 2-1. Write and test a program which will print (decimal, octal, hex) the numeric value of the special character constants:

```
'\a'     alert ("bell")
'\b'     backspace
'\f'     form feed
'\n'     newline
'\r'     carriage return
'\t'     tab
'\v'     vertical tab
'\''     single-quote (apostrophe)
'\"'     double-quote
'\\'     backslash
'\377'   octal bit pattern
'\xFF'   hexadecimal bit pattern
```

2.9 Program Size

Your compiler or operating system probably has a command to tell you how much memory your program will require when run. On UNIX systems, the size command will give the answer. The execution looks something like this:

```
cc -o asst asst.c
size asst
 142+2+2  = 146b = 0222b
cc -o asst2 asst2.c
size asst2
 2326+402+1040 = 3768b = 07270b
```

Forget for the moment about the first numbers with plus-marks between them; they concern "text" and "data" segments of the program, which we will cover in Section 5.8. Notice the difference in the total program size: 146 bytes (0222 octal) versus 3768 bytes (07270 octal). The difference comes from using printf, which generally takes several thousand bytes of object-code space. Those of you who work on large, time-shared computers will not care much, but if you are programming for a small, dedicated engineering application, the size of the resulting program is important.

Exercise 2-2. Determine the size required by hello, asst, and asst2 on your system.

2.10 Define and Include

C language has a mechanism called #define, which can make program constants easier to read. Consider the following revision of hello.c:

```
hello4.c:
    /* hello4 - print greeting
     */
    #include <stdio.h>
    #define VERSION 4
    main()
        {
        printf("hello, world [Version %d]\n", VERSION);
        }
```

The first step in compilation is the *preprocessor* which processes lines starting with a # such as

```
#define VERSION 4
```

The result of the preprocessing is to replace any occurrence of VERSION with 4.

We are just specifying the constants in a way that will be easier for someone to change later. As a general rule, any constant that could conceivably be modified (during a revision of the program) should be given a readable upper-case name via #define, making it a *defined constant*.

A collection of commonly-used #define constants can be entered once into a file, and can be brought into a C source program using #include. Such a file is known as an *include-file* or *header*. At this point, you should refer to Section 2.10 in Appendix B, and create the file local.h that you will find listed there. Be sure to type the upper and lower case characters just as you see them there. We will explain the items from that file as we come to them. For now, just notice that it causes <stdio.h> to be included automatically. After creating local.h, you should be able to compile the following hello5.c program.

```
hello5.c:
    /* hello5 - print greeting
     */
    #include "local.h"
    #define VERSION 5
    main()
        {
        printf("hello, world [Version %d]\n", VERSION);
        }
```

We are introducing headers quite early, because they are commonly used on large projects to collect conventional values used throughout the project. The name local.h is chosen merely to suggest the "local" name that your organization may adopt for its standard headers.

One source of very important #define's is the Standard header <limits.h>. Here are found definitions such as

```
#define INT_MAX 32767
```

which describe a particular machine. These are the most important definitions:

SCHAR_MIN	the minimum value of a signed char
SCHAR_MAX	the maximum value of a signed char
CHAR_MIN	the minimum value of a char
CHAR_MAX	the maximum value of a char
UCHAR_MAX	the maximum value of an unsigned char
SHRT_MIN	the minimum value of a short
SHRT_MAX	the maximum value of a short
USHRT_MAX	the maximum value of an unsigned short
INT_MIN	the minimum value of a int
INT_MAX	the maximum value of a int
UINT_MAX	the maximum value of an unsigned int
LONG_MIN	the minimum value of a long
LONG_MAX	the maximum value of a long
ULONG_MAX	the maximum value of an unsigned long

Besides their uses in making your programs portable across different machine types, these defined constants are also useful in documenting ranges of variables, such as

```
short ncategories;      /* number of categories : {0:SHRT_MAX} */
```

CHAPTER 3: OPERATORS

The operators of C are a faithful reflection of the built-in machine operations of modern computers. They provide the programmer with nearly all the capabilities that are available in assembler languages, without limiting the program to one specific computer hardware.

3.1 Arithmetic Operators

Arithmetic is the school subject dealing with addition, subtraction, multiplication, and division, and is pronounced "a-RITH-me-tick". In C, we have the *arithmetic operators*, in which the adjective "arithmetic" is pronounced "a-rith-MET-ick". There are five arithmetic operators:

+   plus (addition)

-    minus (subtraction)

*   times (multiplication)

/   divided by (division)

%   remainder

All these operators are *dyadic* ("dye-ADD-ick") operators, meaning that they require two *operands* (the things being operated upon). (Another term for "dyadic operator" is *binary operator*, but we are avoiding this term to avoid confusion with "binary numbers".) Examples are a + b ("a plus b") and c / d ("c divided by d"). Furthermore, the "minus" operator can be used as a *monadic* ("moan-ADD-ick"), or *unary*

("YOU-nary"), operator, meaning that it is applied to only one operand. *Unary minus* is the operation that takes the negative value of a number, as in -x ("minus x"), or -99 ("minus 99").

In programming languages, an *expression* is the name for the construction formed by an operator and its operands. (An operand by itself also constitutes an expression.) Examples of expressions are

```
a + b     c / d     -x     x
```

When this statement is executed

```
x = y + z;
```

the (run-time) value of y and the value of z are added together, and the result is assigned to x. More interestingly, when

```
x = y + z * w;
```

is executed, a *temporary result* is created for the product of z and w. The value of this temporary result and the value of y are added together, and the result is assigned to x. This last statement illustrates a *precedence rule* of C; multiplication has *higher precedence* than addition, and hence it *binds tighter* to its operands. If we wanted to add y and z before the multiplication, we would need to use *parentheses* like this:

```
x = (y + z) * w;
```

Note that one expression may form a part of a bigger expression. Thus in the above statement there are eight expressions:

```
x
y
z
w
y + z
(y + z)
(y + z) * w
x = (y + z) * w
```

When one expression forms a part of a bigger expression, it is known as a *subexpression*. Of the eight expressions above, seven are subexpressions; the largest one is not a subexpression — it is the *full expression*. (The concept of the full expression will be important when we discuss "side effects" later.)

These examples illustrate a portion of the *precedence hierarchy* of C. Using only the operators shown so far, the hierarchy would look like this:

( )	parentheses	TIGHTEST
-	unary minus	
* / %	multiplicative	
+ -	additive	
=	assignment	LOOSEST

Unary minus groups the tightest of the arithmetic operators:

```
x = y * -z;
```

multiplies y by negative z.

There is a conventional method of depicting the grouping of expressions: the *expression tree*. Such a tree is formed by placing the operands of each operator slightly below the operator, joined by a connecting line. Thus, each subexpression forms a tree, and the whole expression forms a tree. These trees grow downward, in contrast to biological trees, which grow upward. The reason for this convention probably comes from "organization charts" in which the president or "big cheese" is usually at the top. In C, the "big cheese" operator at the top of the tree is the one which is not part of any subexpression. The expression tree for

```
i = (j + k) * -m
```

looks like this:

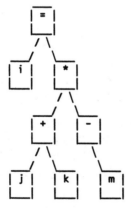

Notice that no parentheses are needed in the tree, because the information that they convey in the expression is conveyed by the tree notation. Another way to fully depict the grouping of an expression is the *fully parenthesized form*, in which every subexpression (except a simple variable or constant) has parentheses around it. For the expression

```
i = (j + k) * -m
```

the fully parenthesized form looks like

```
i = ((j + k) * (-m))
```

which, if used in an actual program, would be considered verbose, unreadable C. This tree (like the expression that generates it) does not specify the *order of evaluation* of its subexpressions. The only rule for arithmetic operators is that before an operator can be evaluated, its operands must first be evaluated. Thus the compiler is free to evaluate (j + k) first and then evaluate -m, or it could do them in the other order.

Question [3-1] Draw expression trees for the following expressions:

```
a + b % c          -a / b          a * -b
```

Question [3-2] How many subexpressions are there in this expression? _____ List them.

```
(a + b) * (c + d) + e
```

Let us look at the *semantics* (i.e. "meaning") of these arithmetic operators in more detail. Addition and subtraction accomplish their usual result. Division, when applied to integers, produces a whole-number result with no fraction; thus, 6 / 4 is equal to 1 exactly. If it is the remainder that we are interested in, the % operator will tell it; 6 % 4 yields 2, an integer result. When applied to floating-point numbers, division yields a fractional answer (to as much precision as can be held in the floating-point type). Thus, 6. / 4. will yield 1.5 exactly. The remainder operator (%) is therefore not defined for floating-point data. Otherwise, the arithmetic operators can be applied to all the variable types that we have seen so far — both integers and floating-point.

Of course, with either integer or floating-point data, division by zero is not a good idea, and the results are unpredictable.

Question [3-3] What does this program print?

```
arith.c:
    /* arith - arithmetic practice
     */
    #include "local.h"
    main()
        {
        printf("%d %d %d %d\n",
            1 + 2,    5 / 2,    -2 * 4,   11 % 3);
        printf("%.5f %.5f %.5f\n",
            1. + 2.,  5. / 2.,  -2. * 4.);
        }
```

Notice that we are able to put these arithmetic expressions right into the output list of the printf statements. This is one of the excellent features of C: an expression may be used anywhere a value is allowed. Furthermore, if the operands are constants (rather than variables), then the expression is a *constant expression*, computed by the compiler at compile time, saving execution time later.

Negated constants, such as -99, are the simplest form of constant expressions: the operator is unary minus, and the operand is the decimal constant 99.

Question [3-4] If a equals 8, b equals 2, and c equals 4, what is the resulting value of each expression:

a + b % c   -a / b   a * -b

─────   ─────   ─────

3.2 Relational Operators

So far, the program examples we have shown are all "straight-through" programs: the machine executes the first instruction, then goes on to the next, then the next, and so forth until the program is finished.

Now we will introduce *loops* and *conditionals*, both of which alter the straight-through flow of control through the program. The following program, blast.c, illustrates a *loop*, known in C as the for statement:

```
blast.c:
    /* blast - print countdown
     */
    #include "local.h"
    main()
        {
        short n;      /* countdown timer : {-1:10} */

        for (n = 10; n >= 0; n = n - 1)
            printf("%d\n", n);
        printf("Blast off!\n");
        }
```

English translation of program:

> Start the variable n at 10.
> Count it down to zero, printing each value.
> Print "Blast off!" when done.

A flow chart for this program looks like this:

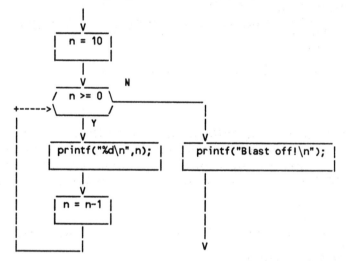

We will generally prefer to show program logic with a *program outline* (or *pseudo-code*), which is formatted like a program but contains a readable mixture of English and programming abbreviations:

> *for n = 10 down to 0*
>   *print n*
> *print "Blast off!"*

An equivalent loop can be written with the while statement:

```
n = 10;
while (n >= 0)
    {
    printf("%d\n", n);
    n = n - 1;
    }
```

The flow-chart is the same as above. The expressions to initialize and to step the variable n must be written in separate statements, because the while statement contains only a single test within the parentheses. The *body* of the loop (the statements that are to be repeated) becomes two statements, and braces are required around the body any time it contains more than one statement.

The simplest form of *conditional* statement in C is the if statement, such as this example:

```
if (n == 3)
    printf("We have ignition!\n");
```

The statement under the if is executed only if the condition in the parentheses is *true*. If we add this if statement to blast.c, we obtain

```
blast2.c:
    /* blast2 - print countdown
     */
    #include "local.h"
    main()
        {
        short n;     /* countdown timer : (-1:10) */

        for (n = 10; n >= 0; n = n - 1)
            {
            printf("%d\n", n);
            if (n == 3)
                printf("We have ignition!\n");
            }
        printf("Blast off!\n");
        }
```

Notice the braces around the body of the for statement; they became necessary when the body grew to more than one line.

C has a full set of *relational operators*, such as the == ("is equal to") that we just used. Here is the full set of relational operators:

```
<=    less than or equal to
<     less than
>=    greater than or equal to
>     greater than
==    equal to
!=    not equal to
```

Each of these operators takes two operands and produces a numerical result which is either 0 or 1 according to whether the relation is *false* or *true*. The while statement tests the *result* of the comparison: a *zero* stands for *false*, and any *non-zero* value stands for *true*. We will call this behavior of the while statement a *semi-Boolean* logic, because "zero equals *false*" is the proper Boolean interpretation, but "non-zero equals *true*" is the semi-Boolean interpretation.

The precedence of the relational operators is just below that of the arithmetic operators. This allows us to write expressions such as

```
a + b < c + d
```

with the meaning "a plus b is less than c plus d". Incidentally, when code makes sense in English when read aloud, we say that it "passes the telephone test" — i.e., would make sense when read aloud over the telephone. This is a rough test for program readability; when code fails the telephone test, try rewriting it. (For this and other useful style rules, see Kernighan and Plauger [1978].)

3.3 Logical Operators

The results of relational operators can be combined using the *logical operators:*

```
&&    and
||    or
!     not
```

For example,

```
a < b && b < c
```

is *true* (equals 1) if a is less than b *and* b is less than c; otherwise the expression is *false* (equals 0). The precedence of the logical operators is below that of the relational operators, so expressions such as this example can be written without parentheses.

The operators && and || are dyadic operators; they take two operands. The negation operator ! is unary; it takes only one operand. It produces a 1 when the operand is *false* (zero), and a 0 when the operand is *true* (non-zero). (This is the same semi-Boolean logic that we saw previously in the if, for, and while statements.) Thus,

```
!a
```

means the same as

```
a == 0
```

The *and* and *or* operators are "short-circuit" operators; evaluation proceeds left to right and stops when the result is determined. Thus in

```
d != 0 && n / d < 10
```

if the first comparison gives a *false* result, the second operation is not performed. In this example, this prevents a divide-by-zero problem. This property of logical operators is commonly used in C programs for situations in which the second operand should not be evaluated if the first comparison determines a case that should not be tested further.

Combining logical and relational operators allows us to test whether a character is a digit:

```
if ('0' <= c && c <= '9')
    printf("c is the digit %c\n", c);
```

Or to test for an uppercase letter:

```
if ('A' <= c && c <= 'Z')    /* ASCII only */
    printf("c is the uppercase letter %c\n", c);
```

Or to test for a printable character (refer to the code table in Section 1.2):

```
if (' ' <= c && c <= '~')    /* ASCII only */
    printf("c is the printable character '%c'\n", c);
```

(These latter tests assume ASCII, which is not universal for C. We will shortly describe a technique that is better because it is *portable* — that is, it is not tied to a particular machine or compiler, but can be run in a variety of environments.)

Using several of these tests, we can create a program to generate a simple "code table":

codes1.c:

```
/* codes1 - print ASCII codes
 */
#include "local.h"
main()
    {
    short c;     /* an ASCII code value : {0:128} */

    for (c = 0; c <= 127; c = c + 1)
        {
        printf("%3d 0x%2.2X 0%3.3o", c, c, c);
        if (' ' <= c && c <= '~')
            printf(" '%c'", c);
        if ('0' <= c && c <= '9')
            printf(" digit");
        if ('A' <= c && c <= 'Z')
            printf(" uppercase");
        if ('a' <= c && c <= 'z')
            printf(" lowercase");
        printf("\n");
        }
    }
```

Question [3-5] When the variable c reaches the value 0x20 (ASCII blank, or ' ') how many of the relational expressions in codes1.c evaluate to a *true* (1) result? _____

How many evaluate to *true* for the value 126 (tilde, '~')? _____

Write the value of each expression (0 or 1):

```
1 < 4 && 4 < 7            _____
1 < 4 && 8 < 4            _____
!(2 <= 5)                 _____
!(1 < 3) || (2 < 4)       _____
!(4 <= 6 && 3 <= 7)       _____
```

3.4   Character Input/Output

All our programs so far have generated their own output, without any input at run time. Thus, none of them were interactive, that is, responsive to the keyboard. Input is required if a program is to be interactive, and as our first example of getting input to a program, we present getchar. Each time a program invokes getchar like this

```
c = getchar()
```

getchar will wait for terminal input from the user, and return one character back to the program. At some point during the execution, the user may indicate "no more input", and the special value EOF (i.e., "end-of-file") will be returned from getchar. On UNIX systems, "no more input" is indicated by hitting the <ctrl-d> key (the letter d with CONTROL shift); MS-DOS systems use <ctrl-z> (followed by RETURN); other environments have other equivalents.

Both names, EOF and getchar, are defined in the Standard header named <stdio.h>, which is automatically included by our local.h "local header".

The integer value that is returned by getchar will be either the negative integer value EOF (typically -1), or a non-negative character code value, ranging from 0 to UCHAR_MAX (the largest unsigned char value).

An interactive version of our "codes" program looks like this:

```
codes2.c:
    /* codes2 - print ASCII codes
    */
    #include "local.h"
    main()
        {
        short c;     /* character or EOF : {EOF, 0:UCHAR_MAX} */

        while ((c = getchar()) != EOF)
            {
            printf("%3d 0x%2.2X 0%3.3o", c, c, c);
            if (' ' <= c && c <= '~')
                printf(" '%c'", c);
            if ('0' <= c && c <= '9')
                printf(" digit");
            if ('A' <= c && c <= 'Z')
                printf(" uppercase");
            if ('a' <= c && c <= 'z')
                printf(" lowercase");
            printf("\n");
            }
        }
```

In codes2.c, we have introduced a notational convenience of C, the *embedded assignment*, in the expression

```
(c = getchar()) != EOF
```

which combines two steps: First, getchar returns a value which is assigned to the variable c. Next, this value is compared against EOF.

If this expression — (c = getchar()) != EOF — evaluates *true* (non-zero), the loop continues. If the expression is *false* (zero), the loop terminates. There are no statements after the loop, so the program terminates. The parentheses around

```
(c = getchar())
```

are necessary, because assignment has lower precedence than all the other operators that we have seen so far.

Question [3-6] If you type one line of input to the codes2 program, consisting of the characters 1aA! followed by a newline, what would the output be? Compile the program and try it.

If you try the codes2 program at the keyboard, you will notice the typical *line-by-line buffering* provided by most environments: even though getchar returns one character at a time, you will see no output until you type an entire line and hit the RETURN (or ENTER, or the corresponding newline key on your terminal). This is because the codes2 program does not see the input characters until you hit the newline key. This line-by-line buffering allows you to correct typing mistakes at the terminal and is generally a useful behavior. Most environments will also provide you with a "raw keyboard" entry mode in which the buffering is turned off, but this is entirely different in each environment. For the rest of this book, we will continue to assume that input is buffered line-by-line.

You may be wondering why the variable c was declared to be a short integer. It must be bigger than any of the characters returned by getchar, because the EOF returned value must be distinguishable from any possible character value. In most environments, EOF is actually equal to the integer -1 and if assigned to a char variable, this could be confused with a possible char value.

To emphasize this last distinction, we introduce a name for the range of returned values from getchar — the name metachar will be an abbreviation for the range ⟨EOF, 0:UCHAR_MAX⟩. (In words, this range means "either the negative EOF value, or a number between 0 and UCHAR_MAX, inclusive".) With the inclusion of this metachar comment, our program becomes

codes3.c:
```
/* codes3 - print ASCII codes
 */
#include "local.h"
main()
    {
    short c;     /* return from getchar: metachar */

    while ((c = getchar()) != EOF)
        {
        printf("%3d 0x%2.2X 0%3.3o", c, c, c);
        if (' ' <= c && c <= '~')
            printf(" '%c'", c);
        if ('0' <= c && c <= '9')
            printf(" digit");
        if ('A' <= c && c <= 'Z')
            printf(" uppercase");
        if ('a' <= c && c <= 'z')
            printf(" lowercase");
        printf("\n");
        }
    }
```

So far, we have used printf to print strings, even if they contain only one character, as in

```
printf("\n");
```

The same result is achieved by

```
putchar('\n');
```

with a smaller and faster program. The argument to putchar should be one individual character, either variable or constant. We can combine getchar and putchar to create a program that simply copies its input to its output:

copy1.c:
```
/* copy1 - copy input to output
 */
#include "local.h"
main()
    {
    short c;     /* input character : metachar */

    while ((c = getchar()) != EOF)
        putchar(c);
    }
```

Exercise 3-1. Write a program hex.c that will read characters from the terminal (until EOF), printing the code for each character in hexadecimal representation. (Use octal, if you prefer.) Each code should be printed with two numeric digits (with possible leading zero), one code per line of output.

Exercise 3-2. Write a program `chksum.c` that will compute the sum of all its input bytes.

Exercise 3-3. Write a program `strip.c` that will remove all characters from its input except for whitespace, letters, and digits.

Exercise 3-4. Write a program `plot.c` that will read characters from its input until EOF, printing a line of asterisks proportional in length to the binary value of the character that was read. In other words, the program functions as a simple plotter, treating the input line as a digital input signal. Apply a scaling factor, so that the largest ASCII character will fit onto an 80-character line.

3.5 Character-type Tests

Character-type tests occur frequently enough in programming that they have been incorporated into the Standard Library. We can accomplish the same thing as

```
if ('0' <= c && c <= '9')
```

by saying

```
if (isdigit(c))
```

And we can replace

```
if ('A' <= c && c <= 'Z')   /* ASCII-only */
```

with

```
if (isupper(c))
```

Besides brevity, the advantage is portability; these library tests will work for either ASCII or EBCDIC.

In order to use these library tests, we need to be sure that the header `<ctype.h>` has been `#include`'d. This header is among those that are automatically included by our `local.h` header.

These are the tests available from `<ctype.h>`:

isalpha(c)	c is a letter
isupper(c)	c is an uppercase letter
islower(c)	c is a lowercase letter
isdigit(c)	c is a digit
isxdigit(c)	c is a hexadecimal digit
isalnum(c)	c is an alphanumeric character
isspace(c)	c is a "whitespace" (space, tab, newline, carriage return, vertical tab, or formfeed)
ispunct(c)	c is a punctuation character
isprint(c)	c is a printing character (including space)
isgraph(c)	c is a printing character (excluding space)
iscntrl(c)	c is a non-printing character (less than ' ', in ASCII)

Also available in <ctype.h> are two translation functions:

tolower(c)	if c is upper-case, return its lower-case value
toupper(c)	if c is lower-case, return its upper-case value

Returning to the version of codes that printed a complete table, we can add all these tests to obtain a fully portable version of the code table, codes4.c:

codes4.c:

```
/* codes4 - print character types for all 8-bit codes
 */
#include "local.h"
main()
    {
    short c;     /* arbitrary code value : {0:256} */

    for (c = 0; c <= 255; c = c + 1)
        {
        printf("%3d 0x%2.2X 0%3.3o", c, c, c);
        if (isprint(c))
            printf(" '%c'", c);
        if (isgraph(c))
            printf(" G");
        if (isdigit(c))
            printf(" D");
        if (isxdigit(c))
            printf(" X");
        if (isupper(c))
            printf(" UC");
        if (islower(c))
            printf(" LC");
        if (isalpha(c))
            printf(" L");
        if (isalnum(c))
            printf(" AN");
        if (isspace(c))
            printf(" S");
        if (ispunct(c))
            printf(" P");
        if (iscntrl(c))
            printf(" C");
        if (islower(c))
            printf(" toupper(c)='%c'", toupper(c));
        if (isupper(c))
            printf(" tolower(c)='%c'", tolower(c));
        printf("\n");
        }
    }
```

See Appendix B for its output. Compile and run codes4.c in your environment and compare the results.

3.6 Bitwise Logical Operators

We return now to the three Boolean operators AND &, OR |, and NOT ~, and introduce a fourth operator, EXCLUSIVE-OR ^. The operators are defined by these tables:

```
AND              OR              NOT         EXCLUSIVE-OR
 &   0   1       |   0   1        ~           ^    0   1
 --------        --------        ----         --------
0 |  0   0      0 |  0   1       0 |  1       0 |  0   1
  |              |               |             |
1 |  0   1      1 |  1   1       1 |  0       1 |  1   0
```

In C, these operators are applied in parallel to the individual bit positions. Hence they are called *bitwise logical operators* (or just *bitwise operators*). They must be carefully distinguished from the *logical operators*, && || !, which we saw in Section 3.3. The logical operators have similar names, but treat the entire operand as one single *true-or-false* value. We will avoid confusion over names by terming the bitwise operators *bit-and*, *bit-or*, *bit-not*, and *exclusive-or*.

Taking *bit-not* ~ as the simplest example, consider the binary number

0000000000000111 (i.e., 0x0007 or 0000007 or just 7).

The *bitwise negation (bit-not)* of this number would be written

~0x7   or   ~07   or just   ~7

and its value would be

1111111111111000 (written in C as 0xFFF8 or 0177770)

on a 16-bit-word computer, and

0xFFFFFFF8 or 037777777770

on a 32-bit-word computer. Bit-not is its own inverse;

~0x0007 equals 0xFFF8, and

~0xFFF8 equals 0x0007.

assuming a 16-bit word.

Question [3-7] Convert each number to 16-bit binary, and then negate it:

0x40 = _____   01 = _____

~0x40 = _____   ~01 = _____

The dyadic ("two-operand") bitwise operators are shown in the following table:

```
    m     0001001101111111 (i.e., 0x137F or 011577), and
    n     1111011100110001 (i.e., 0xF731 or 0173461).
  m & n   0001001100110001 (i.e., 0x1331 or 011461).
  m | n   1111011101111111 (i.e., 0xF77F or 0173577).
  m ^ n   1110010001001110 (i.e., 0xE44E or 0162116).
```

In other words, the *bit-and* & of two numbers has a 1 bit in each position where both numbers have a 1 bit; all other positions are 0 bits. The *bit-or* | has a 0 bit in each position where both numbers have a 0 bit; all other positions are 1 bits. The *exclusive-or* ^ has a 1 bit in each position where the numbers have opposite bits; all other positions have 0 bits.

Question [3-8] Write the binary result of these operations:

```
  0000000001111111        0000000011000000        1111111111111100
& 0111010110011010      | 1000000000000100        1000000001111111
```

_____   _____   _____

Portability suggests using unsigned integers for bitwise operations. Thus, ~7 is a negative signed integer (with different properties in ones- and twos-complement), but ~7U is an unsigned int.

Notice that the result of bit-and and bit-or does not depend on the word size of the computer, but the result of bit-not and exclusive-or does. If we want to write a unsigned binary value which consists of all 1-bits except for three low-order 0-bits, we should write this value as ~7U, not as 0xFFF8U (its 16-bit value), nor as 0xFFFFFFF8U (its 32-bit value). When examining code for portability to other machines, give the bit-negation operators special attention.

The precedence of the bitwise operators is intrinsically confusing, and we recommend *always* fully parenthesizing any expression that involves the operators left-shift, right-shift, bit-and, bit-or, and exclusive-or. In other words, write

```
    n = ((a & b) | c);
```

not

```
    n = a & b | c;
```

The bitwise operators are not allowed upon floating-point numbers, but they may be used upon integer data of any size.

One last note about bitwise operators. The bitwise negation operator ~ is also known as the *ones complement* operator. One way to accomplish the twos complement negation is to take the bit-negation and add 1 to the unsigned result. For example, the bit-negation of 0u is a word filled with 1-bits:

    1111111111111111 equals ~0U

The twos complement negation of 0u is simply 0u, or

    0000000000000000

and we could have gotten this result by adding 1 to ~0u (which would be done in unsigned int arithmetic).

Question [3-9] Write the ones complement and twos complement of these numbers:

    9U = 0000000000001001   0xFF00U = 1111111100000000

    _____   _____
    (ones complement)   (ones complement)

    _____   _____
    (twos complement)   (twos complement)

3.7 Shift Operators

The *left shift* operator << takes two integer operands and produces an integer result. Let us look in detail at the operation

    0x10 << 3

The operation starts by placing the left operand (0x10 here) into an int sized temporary:

    | 0000000000010000 |
    |_____|

Next the bits within this temporary are all moved ("shifted") to the left by the number of places given by the right operand (3 here). The result looks like this:

```
--------------------
|  0000000010000000  |
|_____|
```

Thus, 0x10 << 3 equals 0x80, or 128 in decimal.

An interesting arithmetic fact about shifting is that the left-shift operator is equivalent to a multiplication by a power of two. In this example, 3 places were shifted. Two to the third power is 8, 0x10 is 16, and 16 times 8 is 128.

The bits shifted into the number at the right-hand edge (the *low-order bits*) are always zero bits.

This example has shown the shifting of int sized numbers. If the number being shifted is a long integer, the expression result is similarly a long.

The *right-shift* operator >> works in similar fashion by shifting to the right. Thus, 0x10 >> 3 produces 2 as a result:

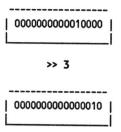

```
--------------------
|  0000000000010000  |
|_____|

        >> 3

--------------------
|  0000000000000010  |
|_____|
```

Notice that the bits shifted from the left-hand edge are filled with zeroes. If the number being shifted is a non-negative number, the fill bits are always zeroes. (And, of course, if the left operand is an unsigned variable, it is guaranteed to be non-negative.) Right-shift when applied to *negative* numbers can give different results in different environments, and we suggest never doing it, in the interests of portability.

Restricting ourselves, then, to right-shifting only non-negative numbers, the right-shift operation is equivalent to a division by a power of two. In this example, 0x10 >> 3 equals 0x10 / 8, or 2.

Here is a program which builds a binary number within an unsigned int variable:

```
getbn.c:
    /* getbn - get a 16-bit binary number and print it
     */
    #include "local.h"
    main()
        {
        short c;                    /* the input character : metachar */
        unsigned int n;             /* the binary number : {0:UINT_MAX} */

        n = 0;
        c = getchar();
        while (c != EOF && isspace(c))  /* skip any leading whitespace */
            c = getchar();
        while (c == '0' || c == '1')     /* process each binary digit */
            {
            n = ((n << 1) | (c - '0'));
            c = getchar();
            }
        n = n & 0xFFFF;                      /* mask n to 16 bits, as per spec */
        printf("%5u 0x%4.4X 0%6.6o\n", n, n, n);
        }
```

This program skips over any whitespace input characters. Then, as each
'0' or '1' character is read, the previous value of n is doubled (shifted
left by one bit) and a 0 or 1 is bit-or'ed into the low-order bit. Thus, if
the input is

    1011

the program produces the value 11 (0x000B hex, 000013 octal).

Question [3-10] What output will the program produce for input 100001?

What output will the program produce for input 1111111111111111?

Exercise 3-5. Write a program wrdcnt.c that will tell how many bits there
are in a "word" (int) on your computer.

3.8 Functions

Consider this C program which uses the previous section's binary conversion code:

```
getbn2.c:
    /* getbn2 - get and print 16-bit binary numbers
     */
    #include "local.h"
    unsigned int getbin(void);   /* get one number : {0:0xFFFF} */
    main()
        {
        unsigned int number;     /* the returned number : {0:0xFFFF} */

        while ((number = getbin()) != 0)
            printf("%5u 0x%4.4X 0%6.6o\n", number, number, number);
        }
    /* getbin - get binary input number
     */
    unsigned int getbin(void)
        {
        short c;                 /* the input character : metachar */
        unsigned int n;          /* the binary number : {0:UINT_MAX} */

        n = 0;
        c = getchar();
        while (c != EOF && isspace(c))  /* skip any leading whitespace */
            c = getchar();
        while (c == '0' || c == '1')    /* process each binary digit */
            {
            n = ((n << 1) | (c - '0'));
            c = getchar();
            }
        n = n & 0xFFFF;                 /* mask n to 16 bits, as per spec */
        return n;
        }
```

We see here our first C program that contains a function other than `main`. From a practical point of view, functions save the programmer much work. Several new concepts must be explained:

1. Call and return

2. Declared type of the function

3. Local variables and scope of names

4. Returned value

5.   Specification and manual page

6.   Arguments

(1) Call and return: The *function-call operator* consists of a left parenthesis appearing after an identifier; the identifier is the name of the function being called. The left parenthesis must be matched by a subsequent right parenthesis; between the parentheses may appear *argument* expressions. The simplest function call has no arguments at all, such as

```
getbin()
```

When our getbin2 program reaches this expression, the main function *calls* the getbin function. (Thus, main is the *calling function* and getbin is the *called function*.) The position of the program counter "PC" in main is memorized for later use. The code of the called function begins executing, starting with the statement

```
n = 0;
```

Statements from getbin keep executing until a return statement is executed. (Reaching the function's closing brace, or "falling off the end", also causes a return.) At this point, control returns to the remembered place in the calling function.

(2) Declared type of the function: The getbin function produces an unsigned int result, and it takes no arguments, so its first line is

```
unsigned int getbin(void)
```

This tells the compiler that the number coming back from getbin will be an unsigned int value, and the void indicates that getbin should be called with *no* argument.

A function declaration such as this one, which contains parameter information between the parentheses, is known in Standard C as a *function prototype*. A matching prototype for getbin appears prior to main, so that the call to getbin will know what type of function getbin is.

(3) Local variables and scope of names: The open-brace (on the next line means "BEGIN" — it marks the beginning of the function. And the close-brace) at the bottom marks the "END" of the function. Between these markers, the function may have its own local variables.

At the top of the getbin function come declarations of variables:

```
short c;           /* the input character : metachar */
unsigned int n;    /* the binary number : {0:UINT_MAX} */
```

These are *local* variables, meaning that any code outside this function has no access to these names. The *scope* of each name extends from the line where it is declared, down to the closing brace. Thus, these names are not *visible* in this main function; only the variables declared in main can be used there. This means that two different programmers could write the two functions without needing to coordinate their choice of names.

After the declarations comes a blank line — not a requirement of C, but added for readability. Then come the *executable statements*, which do the work of the function. The algorithm (or "precise method") is the same as we saw in getbn.c: skip over whitespace and build the number bit by bit.

(4) Returned value: When control reaches this line

```
return n;
```

control passes back to the calling function, and the value of n is delivered to the expression that called getbin. Assembler programmers may be interested in knowing that on most machines this *returned value* is placed in a machine register, and the calling program knows to look in this register for the returned value.

In this example, the calling program stores the returned value into the variable number and then compares this value to zero. As long as it is non-zero, the program prints the number in three formats: unsigned decimal, hexadecimal, and octal.

Question [3-11] If the input to getbn2 consists of these three lines

```
101
1111
00000
```

what does the output look like?

(5) Specification and manual page: We provide a concise description of the information needed to use the getbin function in the format introduced by UNIX manuals. The NAME entry gives a brief description of the function. The SYNOPSIS entry shows how the function is defined. The DESCRIPTION entry discusses how to use the function. The NOTES entry describes any quirks, "features", or actual errors in

the existing implementation. It is poor practice to distribute software with actual errors in it, but even poorer practice to distribute it with no warnings.

---

getbin   USER MANUAL   getbin

NAME
    getbin - get a 16-bit binary-coded number from input

SYNOPSIS
    unsigned int getbin(void)

DESCRIPTION
    Getbin first reads and ignores any whitespace input characters, then reads any number of '0' and '1' characters. This latter string is converted to a binary integer and returned as an unsigned int. If end-of-file is reached, 0 is returned.

NOTES
    The end-of-file return is indistinguishable from actual 0 input.

Now is a good time to become familiar with the reference manual provided with the compiler that you are using. In the section where C functions are described, find the page describing printf. You will notice that it has more capabilities than we have described so far.

Question [3-12] Referring to the printf manual page, how can the output be printed *left-adjusted* in its field width?

(6) Arguments: Data may be passed from the calling function to the called function via arguments. The values to be passed are listed, separated by commas, between the parentheses that follow the function name. In the called function, *parameter* names are declared to access these argument values, and the names are used thereafter as ordinary variables are. We need a new function to see the mechanism, since getbin had no arguments.

It is good programming practice to write the manual page first before you write the function; accordingly, here is the manual page for our new function.

---

putbin   USER MANUAL   putbin

NAME
putbin - print 16-bit integer in binary format

SYNOPSIS
void putbin(unsigned int n)

DESCRIPTION
The parameter n is printed as a 16-bit binary number.

And now the function:

```
/* putbin - print low-order 16 bits of number in binary format
 */
#include "local.h"
void putbin(
    unsigned int n)       /* any number : {0:UINT_MAX} */
    {
    short i;              /* loop index : {-1:15} */

    for (i = 15; i >= 0; i = i - 1) /* for each of the 16 low bits ... */
        {
        if ((n & (1 << i)) == 0)        /* print either 0 or 1 */
            putchar('0');
        else
            putchar('1');
        }
    }
```

This new function begins with

```
void putbin(unsigned int n)
```

The declared type of the function putbin is void, meaning that this is a function that does not return a value. In the calling program, putbin should be called without an assignment of result, as in

```
putbin(0xFF);
```

The parameter declaration

```
unsigned int n
```

declares an unsigned int named n as the parameter — the value to be processed by the function. The putbin function looks at the bits of n, printing a 0 or 1 for each one. Notice the else in the if statement; it means "if the previous condition is *false*".

Here is a program that uses both the getbin and the putbin functions:

```
bdrill.c:
    /* bdrill - binary arithmetic practice
     */
    #include "local.h"
    unsigned int getbin(void);      /* get 16-bit number : {0:0xFFFF} */
    void putbin(unsigned int);      /* put 16-bit number */
    main()
        {
        unsigned int a, b;          /* numbers from input : {0:0xFFFF} */

        while ((a = getbin()) != 0 && (b = getbin()) != 0)
            {
            printf("\n    a = ");
            putbin(a);
            printf("\n    b = ");
            putbin(b);
            printf("\na + b = ");
            putbin(a + b);
            printf("\na & b = ");
            putbin(a & b);
            printf("\na | b = ");
            putbin(a | b);
            printf("\na ^ b = ");
            putbin(a ^ b);
            printf("\n");
            }
        }
    /* getbin function goes here */
    /* putbin function goes here */
```

Question [3-13] What output will bdrill produce from this input? Compile it and try it.

```
10101
11001
```

3.9 Lvalue, Rvalue, Increment, Decrement

The assignment statement

```
x = y;
```

typically produces assembler code that looks like this:

```
LOAD y
STORE x
```

On some machines, the value of y (the "right-hand side" of the assignment) is loaded into a temporary register and then placed into the storage of the variable x (the "left-hand side" of the assignment). On other machines, the assignment produces assembler code like

```
MOVE y TO x
```

with the same end result. Thus in C (as in most high-level languages), the left-hand side of the assignment must be an *lvalue* — an expression that references storage in the machine.

In contrast, the right-hand size of an assignment may be an lvalue, or it may be an *rvalue*, which is any expression that is not an lvalue. A constant provides a simple example of an rvalue, such as the 0 in the statement

```
x = 0;
```

No machine memory is required to hold the zero. For example, the compiler might generate a "CLEAR x" instruction as the assembler code for this assignment statement.

Another way to describe the language's restriction is that rvalues are not allowed on the left-hand side of an assignment:

```
0 = x;
```

is invalid, as well as nonsensical.

We consider now some more operators that require lvalue operands: the *increment* ++ and *decrement* -- operators. In the statement

```
x = ++y;
```

the value of ++y is one greater than the original value of y. In addition, there is a *side effect*: the incrementation of y. The operator ++, when applied *to the left of* its operand, is known as a *prefix* operator.

Conversely, when ++ is written *to the right* of its operand, it is known as a *postfix* operator. The postfix form is different in that the value of y++ is the value of y *prior* to the incrementation.

To use some concrete values, if y initially contains the value 99, the statement

```
x = ++y;
```

will produce 100 in both x and y. If y now contains 100, the statement

```
x = y++;
```

will produce 100 in x and 101 in y.

Everything said about ++ applies to --, except that it *decrements* instead of incrementing. Thus if y is initially 99, the statement

```
x = --y;
```

will produce 98 in both x and y. If y now contains 98, the statement

```
x = y--;
```

will produce 98 in x and 97 in y.

Increment and decrement cannot be applied to rvalues. It is invalid to write --0 or 0++. In such cases, the compiler will produce some diagnostic such as "lvalue required", because the operator must have an lvalue operand.

These operators may be used for their side effect alone, without forming part of a larger expression; for example, the statement

```
++x;
```

will increment x. When used solely for side effects, the prefix and postfix forms are equivalent; the statement above is equivalent to this one:

```
x++;
```

For consistency, we suggest using the prefix form when using the operators for side effects only. This makes the operator more visible.

The precedence of these operators is higher than any others we have seen, except for parentheses, which have the highest precedence. Thus we can write

```
x = y + z++;
```

without parentheses, although it would be more straightforward to write simply

```
x = y + z;
++z;
```

As we will see in Section 3.15, C is not precise about the exact moment that the side effect takes place; tricky expressions such as

```
n++ + n++
```

will give different results in different environments. Such expressions, which do not produce a well-determined result, are known as "grey expressions". (Good compilers can diagnose them for you.)

These operators are often written as the *step* expression of a `for` statement. For example, in `putbin.c` (Section 3.8), we wrote

```
for (i = 15; i >= 0; i = i - 1)
```

whereas more fluent C would read

```
for (i = 15; i >= 0; --i)
```

Or in `codes4.c` (Section 3.5), where we wrote

```
for (c = 0; c <= 255; c = c + 1)
```

we would now write

```
for (c = 0; c <= 255; ++c)
```

There may be a small improvement in speed of execution from these changes.

3.10 Assignment Operators

"Add 2 to x" can be written as

```
x = x + 2;
```

using the (simple) assignment operator, or as

```
x += 2;
```

The *compound assignment operator* `+=` is a combination of the `+` (add) and `=` (assignment) operators. All the arithmetic and bitwise operators are available in compound forms like this:

```
x += n    Add n to x
x -= n    Subtract n from x
x *= n    Multiply x by n
x /= n    Divide x by n
x %= n    x gets the remainder of dividing x by n
x <<= n   Shift x left by n
x >>= n   Shift x right by n
```

```
x &= n   x gets x bit-and'ed with n
x |= n   x gets x bit-or'ed with n
x ^= n   x gets the exclusive-or of x and n
```

With some compilers, the assembler code produced by

```
x += n
```

is shorter and faster than the assembler code produced by

```
x = x + n;
```

Besides, once you are familiar with it, the brevity actually aids readability.

Each of these operators produces a result equal to the new value of the left-hand side; it is valid to say

```
x = (y += z);
```

However, for readability we prefer

```
y += z;
x = y;
```

The precedence of these operators is the same as that of simple assignment — the lowest of all the operators we have seen so far. Thus, in order to say "divide x by y minus 3", we need no parentheses:

```
x /= y - 3;
```


3.11 Nesting of Operators

Each of the C operators produces a result that can be *nested* inside a larger expression. This is because C language accepts an expression anywhere a value is allowed. For example, we have often seen loops that start like this:

```
while ((c = getchar()) != EOF)
```

The assignment c = getchar() is *nested inside the comparison*. This is the sequence of events in evaluating the expression

```
(c = getchar()) != EOF
```

Call getchar, producing an int result.

Store the result in c.

Compare c with EOF, producing *true* or *false*.

When the assignment is nested like this, be sure to enclose it in parentheses; it is lower in precedence than most of the operators.

Another common form of nesting is the multiple assignment statement:

```
x = y = 0;
```

In this case, parentheses are not needed, because C interprets it properly:

STORE 0 IN y.

MOVE y TO x.

3.12 Address-of Operator and Scanf

C provides an operator which tells the *address* of its operand: &x gives the address of x. The operand of & must be an lvalue, something which has storage in the machine. (Actually, there are also addresses of functions; see *RDS* for details. In this book, we will deal only with addresses of data.)

Our first use of & is to read numerical data with the scanf function. This function uses *formats,* just as printf does, to specify how input data is to be read. For example, the format "%hd" specifies a short (h for "halfword") integer in d ("decimal") format. To read a short integer into the variable n, use

```
scanf("%hd", &n);
```

The argument &n tells scanf where to store the data that it reads. If, for example, n is located at address 8730 and contains the value 99,

then the expression n has the value 99, and the expression &n has the value 8730. So if the program executes scanf("%hd", &n), after the user types "1000" (followed by newline), the storage of n will contain the numeric value 1000:

```
n   8730   |   1000  |
           |_____|
```

The scanf function knows to store the 1000 into location 8730 because that is the number that was passed as the value of &n. If instead we made the common mistake of calling scanf("%hd", n) the value passed to scanf would be 99, the *value* of the variable n. What would happen next is unpredictable. On some machines, the attempt to store the 1000 into location 99 would cause a hardware error; on others, the memory at location 99 would suddenly receive the value 1000, leaving the value 99 unchanged in n.

Using scanf, several numbers can be read by a single call to scanf:

```
scanf("%hd %hd %hd", &n1, &n2, &n3);
```

When the user types

```
123    456    789 (NEWLINE)
```

the variables n1, n2, and n3 will receive the new values 123, 456, and 789. The numbers typed on the input must be separated by whitespace (such as blanks, tabs, or newlines).

The formats used by scanf are similar to those used by printf, but there are some differences. The distinction between short data (h prefix) and int data (no prefix) is vital to scanf; so is a similar distinction between float (no prefix) and double (l prefix). Here are some of the formats:

```
%c     char - reads one input character
%hd    short - reads one decimal number
%ho    short - reads one octal number
%hx    short - reads one hexadecimal number
%ld    long - reads one decimal number
%lo    long - reads one octal number
%lx    long - reads one hexadecimal number
%d     int - reads one decimal number
%o     int - reads one octal number
%x     int - reads one hexadecimal number
%f     float - reads one decimal number
%e     same as %f
%lf    double - reads one decimal number
%le    same as %lf
```

Question [3-14] Write a program, pr2a.c, to read two hexadecimal numbers into long variables, and print the two variables and their sum. Make another such program, pr2b.c, with double variables, using the proper formats.

3.13 Conditional Operator

The *conditional operator* produces a choice between two alternatives:

```
c ? x : y
```

("c *choose* x *or* y") produces the value of x if c is *true* (non-zero) and produces the value of y if c is *false* (zero). Thus,

```
a = n == 0 ? b : c;
```

does the same thing as

```
if (n == 0)
    a = b;
else
    a = c;
```

The conditional operator is sometimes useful in making a program shorter:

```
printf("%d\n", a > b ? a : b);
```

does the same thing as

```
if (a > b)
    printf("%d\n", a);
else
    printf("%d\n", b);
```

and usually generates less code.

The conditional operator is commonly used for such constructs as the *minimum (min)* of two numbers, the *maximum (max)* of two numbers, and the *absolute value* of a number:

```
minxy = x < y ? x : y;

maxxy = x < y ? y : x;

absx  = x < 0 ? -x : x;
```

Question [3-15] Modify your pr2b.c program to create maxmin.c which prints the max and min of the two input numbers.

The conditional operator is *triadic (ternary)*, meaning that it requires three operands: the expression being tested, and the two alternative outcome expressions. It is the only triadic operator in C.

Precedence of conditional is slightly above assignment, which allows all the conditional expressions above to be written without parentheses.

3.14 Arrays and Subscripting

So far, we have looked at variables which are single items of data; these are called *scalars*. Now we will look at variables which contain multiple items of data; in C, such variables are known as *arrays*.

A variable is declared to be an array by putting a *subscript* after the variable name in the declaration. For example, to declare an array s which contains 512 char data items, we would write this declaration in C:

```
char s[512];
```

In the machine memory, s would look like this:

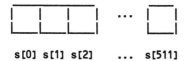

Each little box in the diagram represents the space to hold one char value; on all C machines, this amount of space is one byte. Thus, the variable s occupies 512 bytes of memory. Notice that the subscripts of the individual elements start at 0, and run upwards to 511 — one less than the declared number of elements. This scheme is known as *zero origin subscripting*, and it is the only scheme that C provides. By the way, we *strongly* suggest that you form a verbal habit of saying "*initial* element", not "first element", when referring to array element *sub* zero, such as s[0].

It is worth being precise about the *type* of an array variable. (Many problems that novices have with C can be traced to confusion about the types of the variables.) The data types of the scalar variables we have seen so far are all simple names, such as char or int. A very important rule can be given for determining the precise type of a C variable: the type is whatever is left by scratching out the name of the variable from its declaration. So for example, given the declaration

```
int i;
```

the type consists of whatever remains after scratching out the name i, namely the word int. And similarly, the type of our array variable s is just what is left after scratching out the name s, namely char[512]. To say this type out loud, one might say literally "char bracket five-twelve bracket", but the proper way to say it is "array of 512 char's". In other words, a declaration in C forms a "sandwich" of two things: the *type* is the "bread", and the name being declared is the "meat". (If the type is a simple type like int, the "sandwich" is "open-face".)

Another general rule is that the *memory size* of a variable is completely determined by its type. Thus, the size of s is the memory size for the type char[512], namely 512 bytes. C language even has an operator which will tell the memory size of an expression — the sizeof operator. And sizeof can also tell the size of a *type*, as well. Consider this little program:

```
sizes.c:
    /* sizes - report the size of some types and expressions
     */
    #include "local.h"
    main()
        {
        char c;            /* the type of c is  char        */
        char s[512];       /* the type of s is  char[512]    */
        short n;           /* the type of n is  short        */
        short m[40];       /* the type of m is  short[40]    */

        printf("%3d %3d\n", sizeof(c), sizeof(char));
        printf("%3d %3d\n", sizeof(s), sizeof(char[512]));
        printf("%3d %3d\n", sizeof(n), sizeof(short));
        printf("%3d %3d\n", sizeof(m), sizeof(short[40]));
        }
```

Here we are simply asking the compiler to print out the sizes of our data, specified once by the variable name and once by the type. And the output, as we expect, is

```
  1   1
512 512
  2   2
 80  80
```

The variable s is an array of 512 individual char's; each element can be referenced using a *subscript*, which can be any expression that produces an integer. Thus, s[0], s[1], and s[511] are all elements of s, as is s[i], where i is an integer variable. (Strictly speaking, i must have a value between 0 and 511 if s[i] is to designate an element of this array s. Most compilers do *no checking* to determine if a subscript is indeed

within the bounds of an array; it is entirely the programmer's responsibility to use valid subscripts.) Each of these elements of the array designates a piece of the memory in the machine; the determination of the
address of an element is given by a formula known as the *subscripting
formula*. In C, the subscripting formula is this:

address of i-th element =

address of 0-th element + i * (size of each element)

In this example, the size of each element is 1 byte. Therefore, if the
array s is located at address 2000 in the machine, the address of s[101] is
2000 + 101, or 2101. So s[101] is a single char of storage which is located
at 2101.

Let us look at another example:

```
short m[100];
```

According to our rules above, this declaration says that m has the type
short[100], i.e., an array of 100 short's. If each short occupies 2 bytes,
then the size of m is 200 bytes. Suppose that m is located at address 4000
in the machine; then the address of m[40] is 4080.

By the way, another common name for *subscripting* is *indexing* —
the terms "zero-origin subscripting" and "zero-origin indexing" are
equivalent.

String constants, in C language, are arrays of char's. The array
contains the characters of the string, followed by the null terminator
character '\0' which marks the end of the string in memory. Thus the
string "april" looks like

97	112	114	105	108	0
'a'	'p'	'r'	'i'	'l'	'\0'

in the memory. There is a useful function, strlen, in the Standard
Library which will tell us the length of a string. *Length*, when applied
to arrays of characters, refers to the number of non-null characters
appearing before the null terminator. Thus, the length of the string
constant "april" is 5 —

```
strlen("april")
```

would return the value 5 — whereas the *size* of "april" is 6 (including
the null terminator).

An array of characters can be copied into another array with the strcpy function. For example, if s has the type char[512], we can safely copy "april" into s by writing

```
strcpy(s, "april");
```

One character array can be tacked onto the end of another ("catenated") with strcat(s1, s2):

```
strcpy(s, "april");
strcat(s, " fool");
```

will leave s containing the characters "april fool" plus a null terminator.

Two strings can be compared using strcmp(s1, s2). One by one, the string characters are compared until corresponding characters differ (or a null character is reached). The returned value is negative, zero, or positive according to whether s1 sorts lower than, equal to, or higher than s2. (Note that the sorting order can be different in different character sets.) Thus,

```
strcmp("123", "124")
```

is negative (the 3 sorts lower than the 4),

```
strcmp("3", "12")
```

is positive (the 3 sorts greater than the 1), and

```
strcmp("ab", "ab")
```

is zero (the comparison reaches the null terminators).

We can write our own simple version of the Standard Library "string copy" function. The names of all the Standard Library functions are *reserved names* (not to be used for user-defined functions), so we will name our version strcpy1:

```
/* strcpy1 - copy characters from s2 to s1
 */
#include "local.h"
void strcpy1(
    char s1[],   /* array of char to receive string */
    char s2[])   /* source : string */
    {
    int i;       /* subscript for string : {0:INT_MAX} */

    for (i = 0; s2[i] != '\0'; ++i)
        s1[i] = s2[i];
    s1[i] = '\0';
    }
```

This version of strcpy is simpler than the one in the Standard Library; it has no returned value. To use the Standard Library functions, the header <string.h> needs to be #include'd; our local.h includes it automatically.

It is the programmer's responsibility to be sure that there is enough space in the receiving array for the operation of strcpy and strcat. The functions do no checking for length. (However, some special debugging environments such as *Safe-C* and *Saber-C* do perform this checking.)

The simplest way to print a string is with the "%s" format of printf. If a1 is an array of characters, calling

```
printf("%s", a1);
```

will deliver each character of a1 to the output, up to the first '\0' null character. Any '\n' newline characters in a1 will be printed along with the others, but no extra newlines will be added. If one or more newlines are desired besides whatever is in the array a1, they may be put into the format string, such as "%s\n".

Question [3-16] What does the following program print? (The defined constant BUFSIZ comes from <stdio.h>; it is usually 512 or 1024, large enough for the largest line of input.)

```
string.c:
    /* string - practice with character arrays
     */
    #include "local.h"
    main()
        {
        char a1[BUFSIZ];        /* : string */
        char a2[BUFSIZ];        /* : string */

        strcpy(a1, "every ");
        strcpy(a2, "good boy ");
        strcat(a2, "does ");
        if (strlen(a1) < strlen(a2))
            strcat(a2, "fine ");
        else
            strcat(a1, "very ");
        if (strcmp(a1, a2) < 0)
            {
            strcat(a1, a2);
            printf("%s\n", a1);
            }
        else
            {
            strcat(a2, a1);
            printf("%s\n", a2);
            }
        }
```

The "get line" function from Kernighan and Ritchie [1988] is a good way of reading one input line into a string. However, this function is not part of the Standard Library, so we have provided a definition of the name getln in our local.h header. With this definition, the expression

```
getln(s, n)
```

will read one line (including the newline '\n') into the string s. A null terminator will be put at the end of s. If the input is at end-of-file, the value EOF is returned; otherwise, the new length of s is returned. Thus, this program will copy lines of input onto the output:

```
copy2.c:
    /* copy2 - copy input to output
     */
    #include "local.h"
    main()
        {
        char s[BUFSIZ];       /* : string */

        while (getln(s, BUFSIZ) != EOF)
            printf("%s", s);
        }
```

Exercise 3-6. Write a program `byttab.c` that reads input and tabulates the number of times it sees each one of the UCHAR_MAX character values. At the left margin, print the numeric code for the first tabulation on that line, followed by eight tabulations. But if all eight numbers are zero, do not print the line.

Exercise 3-7. Write a program `words.c` that reads input and prints each word on a separate line. (A word, in this context, is a sequence of non-whitespace characters.) Along with each word, print its hash-sum (the sum of the characters in the word), once as a four-digit hex number and once as a 5-digit decimal number. Print the hex number with leading zeroes, the decimal number with leading blanks.

3.15 Comma Operator

So far, we have seen two uses of the comma symbol in C. It serves to separate a list of variables in a declaration, as in

```
double a, b;
```

And it separates the arguments to a function, as in

```
printf("%d\n", n);
```

In both of these cases, the comma is a *separator* of C; it is part of the punctuation of declarations and function arguments.

But there is another use of comma in which it is an *operator*. Two expressions can be "spliced" together with the *comma operator*. For example, this line counts as one statement in C:

```
t = s[i], s[i] = s[j], s[j] = t;
```

The effect of this line is to "swap" two array elements s[i] and s[j], using a temporary variable t. One reason for using this "comma-spliced" construction is to indicate that the statement forms one "atomic" operation, in this case a "swap" operation. It alerts a maintenance programmer that these lines constitute one operation that should be kept together.

A second use of the comma is to perform more than one expression in the initialization, or the step, of a for loop. Both uses of comma are found in the following revers.c program, which reverses the lines of its input. An early use of the program was to create a "crossword-puzzle" dictionary of words sorted by their endings. Instead of creating a new sort program (which would be a big effort), it was easier to reverse the words, sort them, and then reverse them again. The algorithm uses two indexes, i and j, to point to the left-hand and right-hand sides of the string that is to be reversed. Rather than artificially making one of them the "controlling" variable of the loop, we can give both variables equal status in the loop. Here is the program:

```
revers.c:
    /* revers - print input lines reversed
     */
    #include "local.h"
    void reverse(char []);        /* function to reverse string */
    main()
        {
        char line[BUFSIZ];        /* the line of input text : string */
        short len;                /* length of line : (EOF, 1:BUFSIZ-1) */

        while ((len = getln(line, BUFSIZ)) != EOF)
            {
            if (line[len - 1] == '\n')
                line[--len] = '\0';
            reverse(line);
            printf("%s\n", line);
            }
        }
    /* reverse - reverse string s end-for-end
     */
    void reverse(
        char s[])             /* to be reversed : string */
        {
        char t;               /* temporary for swap */
        short i;              /* L-hand index : (0 : strlen(s)/2) */
        short j;              /* R-hand index : (-1+strlen(s)/2 : strlen(s)-1) */

        for (i = 0, j = strlen(s) - 1; i < j; ++i, --j)
            t = s[i], s[i] = s[j], s[j] = t;
        }
```

In the function reverse we see three different uses of the comma operator. The for loop is initialized with the single expression

```
i = 0, j = strlen(s) - 1
```

The *step* of the loop is the expression

```
++i, --j
```

And the "swap" is spliced together as we saw earlier.

It is considered poor style to string expressions together with commas just to save printout paper; it makes the programs harder to maintain later.

3.16 Order of Evaluation

The actual sequence in which operands are evaluated is unspecified for most of the C operators. Consider these functions:

```
short f1(void)
    {
    printf("reached f1\n");
    return 1;
    }
short f2(void)
    {
    printf("reached f2\n");
    return 2;
    }
```

If we write

```
x = f1() * f2();
```

the result is guaranteed to be 2 (1 times 2), but in which order will the printf messages be printed? C does not say; either order is possible.

Some operators, however, *do* guarantee sequence of evaluation:

```
1.  a, b          comma
2.  a && b        logical and
3.  a || b        logical or
4.  a ? b : c     conditional
```

In each case, the evaluation of a will take place before the evaluation of b (or c). Moreover, in case 4 exactly one of the two expressions b and c will be evaluated.

Furthermore, when a function-call takes place, all the arguments are fully evaluated before control transfers to the function. Thus, in

    5. **a(b)**   function-call

the operand b will be evaluated before the function a is called.

To this list of five guarantees, C adds one more sequence guarantee:

    6. full expression

C guarantees that each "full expression" (the enclosing expression that is not a subexpression) will be evaluated completely before going further.

The five operators above, plus the "full expression", will be called the *sequence points* of C.

One vital reminder: The comma that separates the arguments in a function call is *not* a sequence point; the compiler is free to evaluate the arguments left-to-right or right-to-left, or randomly. Thus the function call

```
printf("%d %d\n", f1(), f2());
```

does not guarantee whether f1 will be called before or after f2.

Besides governing the sequence of evaluation, the sequence points are important for controlling *side effects*. Any operation that affects an operand's storage is said to have a side effect. These are the operators with side effects:

++ --	increment and decrement
=	simple assignment
+= -= *= /= %=	compound assignment operators
<<= >>= &= |= ^=	

In addition, whenever a function-call appears in an expression, some side effects might take place during the execution of the function.

In C, the exact time at which the side effect takes place is indeterminate. All that is guaranteed is that the side effect will be complete by the time the next sequence point is reached. For example, this code cannot be guaranteed to produce a consistent result:

```
a[i] = i++;
```

If the side effect of the increment takes place before the subscript is evaluated we get one result; if the side effect takes place after the subscripting, we get a different result. Moral: do not write code which depends upon the timing of side effects. As mentioned in Section 3.9, such instances are sometimes called "grey expressions", because the behavior is not properly "black-and-white". Here is a simplistic but useful rule:

> A variable which is the operand of increment, decrement, or embedded assignment should not have any more appearances in the same arithmetic expression.

Question [3-17] Mark Y or N whether each of these statements contains a *grey expression*:

____   n = n++;

____   printf("%d %d\n", ++n, ++n);

____   n = ++m;

____   n = y *= 2;

____   a[i++] += 3;

____   a[i++] = a[i++] + 3;

3.17 Floating-point Computation

Most of the operators that we have seen can be applied to floating-point data as well as to integers. (The exceptions are the remainder operator and the bitwise operators: & | ~ ^ << and >>.) Several special considerations apply to floating-point computation.

To begin with, because machines differ in their floating-point mechanisms, answers may be slightly different on different machines. And on any machine, answers are only approximate — accurate only to a limited number of decimal places. Comparing two floating-point results for exact equality is generally risky. Adding a long series of numbers can create a noticeable *roundoff error;* the more numbers in the series, the larger the error. Subtracting two nearly equal numbers can also create a roundoff error. A small roundoff error can also creep in when decimal input is converted to internal binary format or vice versa. Before attempting serious scientific or engineering computations with long sequences of floating-point operations, you should first consult a text on numerical analysis, such as Press *et al* [1988].

If you use floating-point numbers for currency computations, you must pay attention to roundoff behavior. Let us assume that our machine holds 12 digits in a double number; the defined-constant DBL_DIG in the Standard header <float.h> would thus equal 12. (The minimum allowable is 10.) Also assume that we want to hold 8 digits of currency. Then if we read the input 123456.78 into a double variable payment, perhaps using scanf("%lf", &payment), the resulting internal value of payment might be closer to 123456.779999 or 123456.780001 than to 123456.780000. And if we added payment ten thousand times into a double sum, the sum might be off by a penny.

The word *mite* means "a very small coin" — see Mark 12:42 for a Biblical reference — so we could call the "smaller-than-pennies" digits the *mite-digits*. Then our floating-point representation of currency looks like some number of currency digits plus some mite-digits:

```
currency   mite
digits     digits

 123456.78 0001
```

The total number of digits — currency-digits plus mite-digits — equals DBL_DIG (12, in these examples). Assume, in the worst case, that every addition or subtraction adds an error of 1 in the mite-digits, because some decimal fractions do not have an exact binary representation:

```
  currency   mite
  digits     digits

  123456.78 0001
+ 111111.11 0001
  --------------
  234567.89 0002
```

Let us assume that the various library functions perform proper rounding as they should. Then a simple, overly-conservative rule would be that our program could perform adds and subtracts until the mite-digit errors carry into the high-order mite digit. Thus, in this example, where DBL_DIG equals 12, and assuming we desire 8 currency-digits, if we do no more than 1000 adds and subtracts, we are guaranteed that the total will still print correctly. If, however, our environment supports DBL_DIG of 15, and we desire 9 currency-digits, we would have 6 mite-digits and we could safely perform 100,000 (10 to the 5th power) adds and subtracts.

If we need to do more adds and subtracts than our mite-digits allow, we can reset the mite-digits to (almost) zero by *rounding* (to the nearest penny):

```
/* round - returns adjusted dollars amount rounded to even pennies
 */
#include "local.h"
double round(
    double money,               /* value to be rounded : dollars */
    double adjust)              /* rounding adjustment : dollars */
    {
    double pennies;             /* adjusted value : pennies */

    if (money >= 0.)
        pennies = floor((money + adjust) * 100.);
    else
        pennies = ceil((money - adjust) * 100.);
    return pennies/100.;
    }
```

Calling `round(1137.2965, .005)` produces the result 1137.30 (rounding to the higher penny), but `round(1137.2923, .005)` produces 1137.29 (rounding to the lower penny).

In addition to any rounding of mite-digits after sequences of adds and subtracts, you should always round the mite-digits back to even pennies after every multiply, every divide, and every math function that produces a fractional result.

Alternatively, you can eliminate all these add-and-subtract round-off errors by storing all currencies in whole numbers of pennies, since it is the fractional part that causes the roundoff problem. You still have to round fractional results (multiply, divide, and function-calls) to the nearest penny.

A number of useful functions are available in the Standard Library for floating-point computation. Some of the more common functions are

`ceil(x)`	"ceiling" — smallest integer not less than x
`cos(x)`	cosine of x
`exp(x)`	e raised to the x-th power
`floor(x)`	"floor" — largest integer not greater than x
`log(x)`	natural logarithm of x
`log10(x)`	base-10 logarithm of x
`pow(x, y)`	x raised to the y-th power
`sin(x)`	sine of x
`sqrt(x)`	square root of x

All these functions accept `float` or `double` arguments, and return a `double` result. When you use these math functions, you should be sure that the `<math.h>` header has been `#include`'d; our `local.h` includes it automatically.

The following program, `mortg.c`, computes the monthly payment of a mortgage:

```
mortg.c:
    /* mortg - compute table of payments on mortgage
     */
    #include "local.h"
    double round(double, double);   /* rounding function */
    main()
        {
        double intmo;          /* monthly interest : fraction */
        double intyr;          /* annual interest : fraction */
        double bal;            /* balance remaining : dollars */
        double pmt;            /* monthly payment : dollars */
        double prinpmt;        /* payment allocated to principal : dollars */
        double intpmt;         /* payment allocated to interest : dollars */
        double dnpmts;         /* number of payments, in double */
        short i;               /* loop index */
        short npmts;           /* number of payments */
        short nyears;          /* number of years */

        printf("Enter principal (e.g. 82500.00): ");
        scanf("%lf", &bal);
        printf("Enter annual interest rate (e.g. 16.25): ");
        scanf("%lf", &intyr);
        printf("Enter number of years: ");
        scanf("%hd", &nyears);
        printf("\nprincipal=%.2f  interest=%.4f%%  years=%d\n\n",
            bal, intyr, nyears);
        intyr /= 100.;
        intmo = intyr / 12.;
        npmts = nyears * 12;
        dnpmts = npmts;
        pmt = bal * (intmo / (1. - pow(1. + intmo, -dnpmts)));
        pmt = round(pmt, .005);
        printf("%8s %10s  %10s %10s %10s\n",
            "payment", "total", "interest", "principal", "balance");
        printf("%8s %10s  %10s %10s\n",
            "number", "payment", "payment", "payment");
        printf("%8s %10s %10s %10s %10.2f\n",
            "", "", "", "", bal);
        for (i = 1; i <= npmts; ++i)
            {
            intpmt = round(bal * intmo, .005);
            if (i < npmts)
                prinpmt = pmt - intpmt;
            else
                prinpmt = bal;
            bal = round(bal - prinpmt, .005);
            printf("%8d %10.2f %10.2f %10.2f %10.2f\n",
                i, intpmt + prinpmt, intpmt, prinpmt, bal);
            }
        }
    /* include  round  function here */
```

The execution of mortg.c looks like this:

```
Enter principal (e.g. 82500.00): 10000.00
Enter annual interest rate (e.g. 16.25): 18.00
Enter number of years: 1

principal=10000.00  interest=18.0000%  years=1
```

payment number	total payment	interest payment	principal payment	balance
				10000.00
1	916.80	150.00	766.80	9233.20
2	916.80	138.50	778.30	8454.90
3	916.80	126.82	789.98	7664.92
4	916.80	114.97	801.83	6863.09
5	916.80	102.95	813.85	6049.24
6	916.80	90.74	826.06	5223.18
7	916.80	78.35	838.45	4384.73
8	916.80	65.77	851.03	3533.70
9	916.80	53.01	863.79	2669.91
10	916.80	40.05	876.75	1793.16
11	916.80	26.90	889.90	903.26
12	916.81	13.55	903.26	0.00

The computation embodies the following formula:

$$pmt = bal \times \frac{intmo}{1 - (1 + intmo)^{-dnpmts}}$$

The example computation actually produces a pmt of 916.799929 (etc.); the rounding brings it back to even pennies.

One general environmental note: some machines have special hardware for floating-point operations, and your programs will run many times faster if it is used. If you are running on a large time-sharing system, the standard compile command will probably take advantage of any special hardware. If you have your own system, you should consult your compiler manual to determine how it handles floating-point operations.

3.18 Precedence and Associativity

In the individual sections on operators we have seen specific rules of precedence. Now we describe them all together in one table. (For completeness, we are showing the primary operators . and ->, and the unary usage of *; their details will wait until Chapter 7.)

Operator Type	Precedence Level	Operators
Primary	15	() [] -> .
Unary	14	! ~ ++ -- + - (cast) * & sizeof
Arith-metic	13	* / %
	12	+ -
Shift	11	>> <<
Rel-ational	10	< <= > >=
	9	== !=
Bitwise Logical	8	&
	7	^
	6	|
Logical	5	&&
	4	||
Cond.	3	?:
Asst.	2	= += -= *= /= %= |= ^= &= >>= <<=
Comma	1	,

As undigested information, this table is formidable and leads many programmers into cop-out attitudes like "when in doubt, use parentheses". However, the design of C embodies real insight and programming experience, and a few simple rules give full mastery of C precedence.

Bitwise operators have intrinsically confusing precedence and should *always* be used with parentheses. The confusion comes from their dual nature — they are both quasi-arithmetic and quasi-logical. They are quasi-arithmetic in that n & 3, which gives the rightmost two bits of n, is prone to usage in contexts such as n & 3 == 2 which is wrong; it should be written (n & 3) == 2. But they are quasi-logical in that one could write

```
a == b & c == d
```

where the precedence is correct — but the logical operator && is generally preferred. Therefore, always parenthesize the operators

```
<<  >>  &  |  ^
```

With bitwise operators thus excluded, we can group the others into eight intuitive levels:

Level 1: *Primary* operators () [] -> . are naturally the strongest operators. In any scheme, parentheses must be the strongest. The other primary operators serve to describe the access to data and should be stronger than any other operators upon that data.

Level 2: *Unary* (monadic) operators are naturally stronger than other arithmetic operators. Levels 1 and 2 are illustrated in

```
a = -b + c[d]
```

Here the tight binding of -b and c[d] is natural and intuitive.

Level 3: *Arithmetic* operators should be higher than relational because

```
a + b < c + d
```

sounds natural (passes the "telephone test") when read aloud as *a plus b is less than c plus d*. Within the arithmetic level, multiplicative operators * / % are traditionally stronger than additive operators + -.

Level 4: *Relational* operators should be, by the "telephone test" again, stronger than logical:

```
a < b && c < d
```

reads aloud properly as *a is less than b and c is less than d*. In readable code, one never needs to remember that equality operators == != have slightly lower precedence than comparison operators < <= > >= and we therefore simply group them all under the category of *relational* operators.

Level 5: *Logical* operators are thus the next level. Within the logical operators, the Boolean multiplicative "and" && is stronger than the Boolean additive "or" ||.

Level 6: *Conditional* is higher than assignment, because a "choice" can be assigned to a variable:

```
a = b ? c : d;
```

Level 7: *Assignment* is lower than all these operators, because expressions using these operators can be assigned to a variable.

Level 8: *Comma* is lowest of all, because assignments can be strung together with commas:

```
a = b, c = d
```

Thus, by these rules there are really eight levels to remember, with five mnemonic examples:

LEVELS	EXAMPLES
1. primary	
2. unary	a = -b + c[d]
3. arithmetic	
4. relational	a + b < c + d
5. logical	a < b && c < d
6. conditional	a = b ? c : d
7. assignment	
8. comma	a = b, c = d

plus the historical convention placing *multiplicative* above *additive*.

Question [3-18] Parenthesize to show the binding:

```
a  ==  b  &&  c  !=  d

y  =  3.14  *  -  d
```

Precedence rules by themselves do not answer all questions about grouping; there still are cases of adjacent operators all having the same precedence, such as

```
a - b - c - d
```

To most people, this would mean *subtract b from a, then subtract c, then subtract d* (a "left-to-right" reading), rather than *subtract d from c, then subtract this from b, then this from a* (a "right-to-left" reading). C therefore associates operators of equal precedence left-to-right, with these exceptions:

(1) *Assignment* groups right-to-left to allow multiple assignments:

```
x = y = 0;
```

which is indeed the "natural" grouping.

(2) *Unary* operators are generally written to the left of their operand: ~~x means ~(~x) and therefore right-to-left association is more natural. It also hardly matters, except in the case of *p++ which groups as *(p++) and is also beyond the scope of this chapter.

(3) *Conditional* ?: groups right-to-left, but in readable programs conditionals are never nested inside each other, so the rule is irrelevant.

These rules can easily be memorized. They eliminate all uncertainty about precedence and associativity in C.

3.19 Conversion

C has a preference for int data types when it evaluates expressions. On most C machines, there are machine registers that are big enough to hold an int result, and smaller data will be widened to int size when used in an expression. (That is, the storage for the variable does not expand; a temporary is created, usually in a register, and this temporary has int size.) Of course, if long numbers are bigger than int numbers on your machine, it would not work very well to shorten them down to int in calculations. Therefore, long is also a preferred type. Furthermore, all the floating-point types are preferred types, in Standard C.

These rules can be summarized like this: There are certain preferred sizes. Any value not already occupying one of these sizes will be widened to the next-largest preferred size when it appears in an expression. The more general technical name for this widening process is *promotion*.

A second rule concerns the dyadic and triadic operators: After any promotions to preferred size, if the operands are still of different size, the smaller one will be promoted to the size of the larger one. The result will be of this larger size. This part of the process is known as *type balancing*.

A third rule concerns unsigned data. Whenever an unsigned item is promoted to a larger size, there is enough room to express it as a signed number in the wider size. But if after promotions to preferred size, one of the operands is signed and the other is unsigned, the signed operand is converted to an unsigned value, and the result of the operation is unsigned.

The effect of these rules can be summarized in a table (slightly simplified). Each of the preferred types is marked with an asterisk (*). Each operand will be promoted to the nearest larger preferred type, and if two operands are involved, the smaller will be promoted to the type of the larger.

2-byte machine	4-byte machine
* long double	* long double
* double	* double
* float	* float
* unsigned long	* unsigned int, unsigned long
* long	* int, long
* unsigned int, unsigned short	unsigned short
* int, short	short
char (any form)	char (any form)

Another set of conversion rules applies for *simple assignment* and the *compound assignment operators* (+= -= etc.). In such cases, the only conversion required is that the result value is converted to the type of the left-hand side of the assignment.

Some examples will illustrate these rules. In our first example, we will perform some arithmetic with short, long, and float data. Consider this code fragment, in which the intended ranges are documented:

```
short n;        /* : {0:99} */
long lnum;      /* : {0:10} */
float f;        /* : {10:100} */

/* ... */
n = n * lnum / f;
```

The product n * lnum involves a short variable n and a long variable lnum. The variable n will be promoted to long, and the operation takes place in long arithmetic. (The range of the result will be {0:990}.) Then the long result is divided by the float variable, f, so the long result is promoted to float, and the division takes place in float arithmetic. (Result range is {0:99}.) Finally, the float result is assigned back to a short variable, causing a loss of any fraction digits, and a truncation to the size of a short.

By the way, most machines can hold more in a long than in a float, even though long can promote to float. As we have emphasized throughout, the programmer must anticipate the possible numeric ranges of data, and program accordingly.

These promotion rules apply to constant expressions as well as to variables. This causes one strange problem when writing the most-negative twos-complement integer: If (positive) 32768 is too large for an int, its type becomes long, so -32768 ("unary minus" applied to the decimal constant 32768) would also be long, even though its value would fit into an int. However, the constant expression (-32767 - 1) has the proper value and its type is int.

Conversion can be specified explicitly with the *cast* operator, which consists of a type enclosed in parentheses. For example, remembering that the square-root function, sqrt, requires a double argument, one could take the square root of a short variable i like this:

    sqrti = sqrt((double)i)

However, in Standard C this cast is optional, because the prototype for sqrt (found in <math.h>) specifies that the argument is a double, and the conversion is performed automatically.

This covers the rules for conversions between scalars in C. A different kind of conversion is needed to convert between scalars and numbers stored in strings. This kind of conversion has no built-in operator in C; one must call functions to do it. For example, if in the string s we have stored the character representation of a number such as 123, it might look like this in the memory:

s

49	50	51	0
'1'	'2'	'3'	'\0'

To convert the contents of s into a char, short, or int number n, we could write

    n = atoi(s);

The atoi ("ASCII to int") function takes a character array argument, and treats it as the decimal representation of an integer. Similarly, for a long number lnum, we could convert it from s via

    lnum = atol(s);

using the atol ("ASCII to long") function. And for a double number d, there is atof for "ASCII to float". (This is a slight misnomer; the name should mean "ASCII to double". And the "ASCII" in each name is unduly specific; the functions use the execution character set, whichever it is.)

All these functions will skip over any leading whitespace in the string, and stop converting when they reach a character that cannot be part of the number they are converting.

The most general way to convert the other direction — from scalar numbers into printable representations in character arrays — is to use the sprintf ("string printf") function. This handy function formats its arguments just as printf does, but its output goes into a string instead. For example,

```
char s[BUFSIZ];
short n;

n = 246;
sprintf(s, "%d", n);
```

will leave s looking like this:

s

50	52	54	0
'2'	'4'	'6'	'\0'

Of course, sprintf is much more powerful than this simple example suggests. We can format a whole list of scalars and other strings into one string:

```
sprintf(s, "%3s %3s %2d %2d:%2.2d:%2.2d %4d",
    weekday, mo, day, hh, mm, ss, yr);
```

could leave s looking like this:

```
"Fri Nov 11 15:47:04 1982"
```

The receiving array s must be large enough to hold all the generated characters, or they will run over into other storage.

The scanf function also has a "string" counterpart called sscanf. It "reads" from a string instead of from the input; if s looks like the result above, we could read from it a list of strings and short integers like this:

```
sscanf(s, "%3s %3s %2hd %2hd:%2hd:%2hd %4hd",
    weekday, mo, &day, &hh, &mm, &ss, &yr);
```

After the conversion is complete,

weekday	contains	"Fri",
mo	contains	"Nov",
day	contains	12,
hh	contains	15,
mm	contains	47,
ss	contains	4, and
yr	contains	1982.

Just like scanf, sscanf returns the number of successful assignments performed (seven, in this case), and this returned value should be tested to be sure that sscanf succeeded. In Section 3.22, we will see some useful things that we can do if the returned value indicates a conversion failure.

3.20 Overflow

Overflow is what happens when when a value is computed which is too large for the space available to hold the result. You can see the phenomenon of overflow with a hand calculator. If the calculator holds six digits, you can enter the number 999,999:

```
| 999999 |
L_____|
```

If you then add 1 to this value, the calculator may overflow in a computer-like fashion:

```
| 000000 |
L_____|
```

Or, more likely it will complain about the result:

```
| ERROR  |
L_____|
```

Most C machines never complain about overflow. They just keep running with the portion of the overflowed number that fits the storage that is available.

The operators that can overflow are + - * ++ -- and <<. When you use these operators, be sure that the result is not marred by overflow problems. The responsibility for guarding against overflow rests entirely with the programmer. As we have suggested, follow the discipline of using a range ⟨LO:HI⟩ notation in comments to foster continual awareness of data ranges.

Exercise 3-8. The unsigned types wrap-around to zero when the largest value is exceeded; this is completely well-defined. Make use of this behavior to write a function maxuint which returns the largest positive unsigned int value on whatever computer the program is compiled for. Include your maxuint function in a program maxui.c which prints your result.

Exercise 3-9. Write a similar function maxulng which returns the largest positive unsigned long value on whatever computer the program is compiled for. Include your maxulng function in a program maxul.c which prints your result.

3.21 Defined-types, Constants, and Properties

In the preceding sections, we have occasionally used names to describe the properties of variables. Now, here is the entire collection of these property names (from our own style usage, not required by Standard C):

bits(*n*)   Used for bitwise operations on *n* bits.

bool   Tested for either *false* (zero) or *true* (non-zero).

metachar   Used to receive the returned value from functions such as getchar which return either a unsigned char value or the EOF indication.

dollars   Represents currency in dollars; i.e. the value 12.34 means 12 dollars and 34 cents.

pennies   Represents currency in pennies; i.e. the value 12.34 means 12 and 34/100 cents.

string   Designates an array of characters in which a null-terminator appears.

In our header local.h, there are some convenient *defined-types* which can be used as synonyms for basic C types. These synonyms are created using the typedef facility of C:

```
typedef signed char    schar;
typedef unsigned char  uchar;
typedef unsigned short ushort;
typedef unsigned int   uint;
typedef unsigned long  ulong;
```

After these typedef's have been seen by the compiler, the name ulong (for example) is *equivalent in every way* to unsigned long. The briefer names are useful for aligning variable declarations neatly.

The local.h header also provides a defined-type named bool (created using typedef) for an integer type with the bool property. (In this book we define bool to be int, but some people use char instead; your programs should not assume any particular size for the bool type.)

There is also a defined-type named metachar for an integer type with the metachar property. (In this book metachar is short, but some people use int; again, do not assume any particular size.)

The `bits(n)` property deserves special mention. It is intended to alert the maintenance programmer that bitwise operations are being performed upon the data. As we saw in Section 3.6, various machine differences require that one be very careful when mixing bitwise and arithmetic operations upon the same data. In particular, our rule about not right-shifting negative data can be made more specific: when right-shifting, always cast the left-hand operand either to `ulong` (if the operand is larger than `unsigned int`), or else to `uint`. Some examples are shown in the following `bits.c` program.

```
bits.c:
    /* bits - examples of bitwise operations
     */
    #include "local.h"
    main()
        {
        ushort b1, b2;  /* : bits(16) */

        b1 = 0xF0F0 & 0x1234;
        b2 = b1 | 0x60;
        printf("b1=0x%4.4X, b2=0x%4.4X\n", b1, b2);
        b1 = ~1 & 0307;
        b2 = (uint)b1 >> 2;
        printf("b1=0%3.3o, b2=0%3.3o\n", b1, b2);
        b1 = 0xF001 | 0x8801;
        b2 = b1 & 0xB800;
        printf("b1=0x%4.4X, b2=0x%4.4X\n", b1, b2);
        }
```

Question [3-19] What does `bits.c` print?

Will it give the same results on any C machine? _____

The header `local.h` also provides some *defined constants*:

Name	Where defined	Meaning
YES	local.h	"yes" ("true"), 1
NO	local.h	"no" ("false"), 0
EOF	<stdio.h>	"end-of-file" return, often -1
BUFSIZ	<stdio.h>	a useful buffer size, often 512 or 1024

One final note on defined-types: we are using lower-case names for these new type names. Our convention is that type names which are defined by organization-wide headers should be written as ordinary lower-case names, because these names acquire essentially the same immutable status as the reserved words of the language. As a rule, however, one should distinguish any other names created via `#define` or

typedef by some typographical convention such as putting them into
upper case.

3.22 More about Input/Output

So far, all your input and output has gone through the interactive
terminal — input from the keyboard, output to the screen (or printer).
The full treatment within C is much more general.

Each program starts its execution with access to three streams of
data, one for input and two for output:

stdin   The "standard input", the usual source of input characters.

stdout   The "standard output", the usual destination for output char-
         acters.

stderr   The "standard error output", where error messages are sent.

It is often helpful to depict these connections with a simple
diagram:

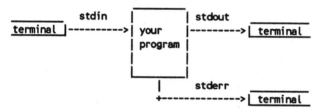

In many environments (such as UNIX and MS-DOS), the same program can be made to put its standard output into a file instead of the
terminal, simply by adding a *redirection* request to the command line
when you execute the program. Thus, using the codes4 program as a
useful example, we could create a file containing the code-table output
by executing

        codes4 >table

Error messages, if any, will continue to come out on the terminal,
instead of being buried inside the output file:

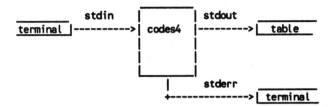

Exercise 3-10. Compile and run codes4.c on your system. Print the resulting file and compare it carefully to the output that was shown in Appendix B.

A similar redirection is possible for the standard input. If we wish to run our mortg program using data that we have stored in a file called house1, we can execute the program like this:

```
mortg <house1
```

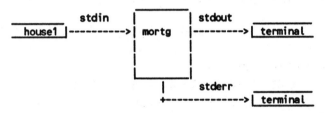

In this case, the output will come out to the terminal. If we wish instead to capture the output in a file, we can run

```
mortg <house1 >house1.out
```

If we execute our copy1 program with both input and output redirection, we achieve a simple file-to-file copy:

```
copy1 <filein >filout
```

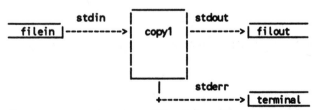

As before, error messages (if any) will come to the terminal, not the output file. We can print error messages with the fprintf function, as in

```
fprintf(stderr, "goodbye, world\n");
```

Here is a useful function for printing two error-message strings:

```
/* remark - print non-fatal error message
 */
#include "local.h"
void remark(
    char s1[],  /* message : string */
    char s2[])  /* message : string */
    {
    fprintf(stderr, "%s ", s1);
    fprintf(stderr, "%s\n", s2);
    }
```

Providing two different string arguments to the remark function allows us to print a message plus a character array variable, often useful in situations like this:

```
n = sscanf(s, "%lf", &x);
if (n != 1)
    remark("I cannot read x from ", s);
```

In this last example, once the error message has been printed, the program continues on its way. Often, we want it to stop in its tracks and give up. The function exit provides us the means to stop instantly, while providing the operating system with a "status code" reporting on the success or failure of our program. The header <stdlib.h>, which is #include'd by our local.h, provides two defined constants, EXIT_SUCCESS and EXIT_FAILURE, for use with the exit function. Thus, a program can report a failure to the operating system by calling

```
exit(EXIT_FAILURE);
```

and similarly for success. However, the C Standard specifies that the value zero will always mean the same as EXIT_SUCCESS, so we favor the brevity of

```
exit(0);
```

Every program should announce its successful completion in this way.

Adding an error exit to our previous example gives

```
n = sscanf(s, "%lf", &x);
if (n != 1)
    {
    remark("I cannot read x from ", s);
    exit(EXIT_FAILURE);
    }
```

This combination of error message followed by exit occurs often enough to deserve its own function, error:

```
/* error - print fatal error message
 */
#include "local.h"
void error(
    char s1[],   /* message : string */
    char s2[])   /* message : string */
{
fprintf(stderr, "%s ", s1);
fprintf(stderr, "%s\n", s2);
exit(EXIT_FAILURE);
}
```

And in the interests of encouraging "defensive programming" — preventing programs from going haywire when given bad input — we suggest attaching error calls at each unrecoverable error point:

```
if (sscanf(s, "%lf", &x) != 1)
    error("I cannot read x from", s);
```

(We have not followed our own prescription in several preceding programs; if you have entered them on your system, take a moment to add the error function to them and protect all calls upon scanf.)

So far, we have been using getln(s, n) to read input. To use the Standard C Library directly we would use fgets(s, n, stdin). The fgets ("file-get-string") function is like getln in that it stops when newline is encountered and that it will store no more than n-1 characters into s (plus the null terminator), but it returns zero at end-of-file. Thus instead of writing

```
if (getln(buf, n) != EOF)
```

we could write

```
if (fgets(buf, n, stdin) != 0)
```

The fgets function will be noticeably more efficient than getln.

3.23 Methodology and Trade-Offs

This book shows you a particular approach to programming, one which we call *project programming*. It urges heavy commenting (especially of declarations), constant attention to ranges and properties of data, strict consistency of layout, use of project-wide headers, and attention to portability. (See *C Programming Guidelines (Second Edition)*, for detailed suggestions.)

Not everyone programs this way. Many programs, often in textbooks or magazine articles, favor brevity of presentation to highlight the essence of the algorithm. Only the Standard headers are used, so that the reader need not invest time in building scaffolding. We might call this *publication programming*.

We believe that both approaches have validity in different circumstances, but project programming more closely resembles what you will produce in real commercial practice. Furthermore, if you know how to use a particular technique (such as declaring properties of variables), you can evaluate the trade-offs for yourself (the extra clarity versus the extra keyboarding time).

There are similar trade-offs regarding portability. If you can write the majority of your functions in strictly portable C, your code will be commercially viable for a longer time, in this rapidly-changing business. But in some situations, the simplest approach is to implement some critical features with environment-dependent methods, making perhaps a few napkin-notes on the porting strategy you would use if your program became so popular that you needed to widen its audience.

These are the trade-off decisions that make programming challenging and interesting.

CHAPTER 4: STATEMENTS AND CONTROL FLOW

The flow of execution through a program is controlled by statements such as if, while, and for. The convenience that they provide to the programmer and the clarity that they give to the program are major advantages of high-level languages like C over low-level assembler languages. There is also an important correspondence between these control structures and the structure of data, which we will examine after looking at each control structure in detail.

4.1 Statements and Blocks

C programs are built out of *statements*, which in turn may contain expressions. Indeed, one of the simplest statements is the *expression statement*, which consists of one expression followed by a semicolon. Most of the statements that we have seen in programs so far are in fact expression statements, such as these:

```
++i;
printf("hello, world\n");
n = 0;
```

Another simple statement is the *return statement*, which may appear with an expression, as in

```
return n+1;
```

or without an expression:

```
return;
```

Execution of the return statement causes a return of control to the calling function.

Also, C has a *null statement*, which consists of one lonely semicolon:

```
;
```

The null statement is the high-level equivalent of the "NO-OP" of assembler languages, except that the null statement generates no code at all. It is useful in contexts such as

```
while (getchar() != '\n')
    ;
```

which simply swallows characters until a newline is read.

C also has a *compound statement*, or *block*, formed by putting braces around any number of statements. Thus, in a C function, all the lines from the opening brace to its matching closing brace constitute a block, as in

```
hello.c:
    #include <stdio.h>
    main()
        {
        printf("hello, world\n");
        }
```

A statement's *syntax* (or *grammar*) tells what form the statement must have so that the compiler understands it correctly. We will describe both the syntax rules and the *readability format*, the form required for humans to understand it correctly. For the *compound statement*, or *block*, the rules look like this:

```
SYNTAX (Simplified)
    {stmt* }

READABILITY
    {
    stmt*
    }
```

In these rules, the large-type asterisk (*) means "repetition". Thus, the notation *stmt** means a *repetition* of zero or more *stmts* (statements).

The compiler, of course, ignores extra whitespace, so the indentation does not show in the syntax rule, only in the readability format. This is, of course, not the only possible readability format for compound statements. Consistency within your project or organization is the most important readability rule, and if your project already uses another format, then so should you. The main advantage of the readability format shown here is that all the components of a block are at the same level of indentation.

4.2 If

The simplest control statement of C is the if statement, which executes a statement if a certain expression is *true*. For example, this statement sets x to the absolute value of x:

```
if (x < 0)
    x = -x;
```

The if statement, as we have described it here, has this syntax:

```
if (expr) stmt
```

which means "the word if, followed by an open-parenthesis, followed by an expression, followed by a close-parenthesis, followed by a statement". The compiler has no need for whitespace here, so it is not mentioned in the syntax description. The corresponding readability format looks like this:

```
if (expr)
    stmt
```

This means "the word if, one space, an open-parenthesis, an expression, a close-parenthesis, a new line with one further tab-stop indent, and a statement". The symbols are the same as those in the syntax description, but the indenting is important for readability, as is the space following the word if.

Question [4-1] Which of these are valid if statements according to the syntax descriptions? Which agree with the readability format?

	VALID SYNTAX?	READABILITY FORMAT?
if (x < 0) y = x;	___	___
if (n) ;	___	___
if(c == EOF) done = YES;	___	___

The if statement can be understood as having three steps:

1.   After the keyword if there is an expression in parentheses. Evaluate the expression, to produce a single number.

2.   Interpret the resulting value of the expression, according to the *semi-Boolean* logic: zero means *false*, non-zero means *true*.

3.   If the expression value is *true*, execute the statement that follows the expression. If the value is *false*, skip that statement.

When drawn as a flow-chart, the logic of the if statement looks like this:

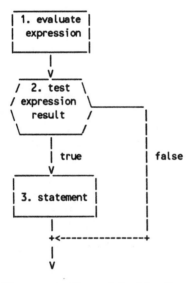

Side effects are allowed inside the expression. It is good C style to use them this way to avoid creating otherwise useless "temporary" variables. Thus,

```
if (scanf("%hd", &n) != 1)
    printf("bad n\n");
```

is better than

```
nread = scanf("%hd", &n);
if (nread != 1)
    printf("bad n\n");
```

if the variable nread is not needed for anything further.

4.3 If-else

The if statement can include an alternative to be executed if the condition is *false*. The syntax in this case is

```
if (expr) stmt else stmt
```

or, according to our readability rules,

```
if (expr)
    stmt
else
    stmt
```

Combining this syntax form with the one from the previous section, we want to show that the else clause is *optional*, for which we use *square brackets* [ ] in our syntax rules. Thus, for the if statement we have these rules:

SYNTAX
```
    if (expr) stmt [ else stmt ]
```

READABILITY
```
    if (expr)              if (expr)
        stmt                   stmt
                           else
                               stmt
```

Since an if statement is a valid possibility for the *stmt* of our rules, one if statement can be nested inside another. Some care is needed. The else will be associated with the most recent "un-else'd" if; the compiler again pays no attention to the indenting. We suggest the following uniform rule to avoid the confusion:

Whenever an if statement is nested inside another if statement, put braces around the nested statement.

Thus, this statement

```
/* nested if */
if (n > 0)
    {
    if (n % 2 == 0)
        printf("positive and even\n");
    }
else
    printf("not positive\n");
```

behaves differently from this statement

```
/* nested if-else */
if (n > 0)
    {
    if (n % 2 == 0)
        printf("positive and even\n");
    else
        printf("positive and odd\n");
    }
```

It would be a mistake to write

```
/* incorrect nesting */
if (n > 0)
    if (n % 2 == 0)
        printf("positive and even\n");
else
    printf("not positive\n");
```

because the compiler matches the else with the nearest "un-else'd" if.

Question [4-2] What does this if statement print, for each value of n:

```
if (n < 5)
    {
    if (n % 2 == 1)
        printf("A\n");
    else
        printf("B\n");
    }
else
    {
    if (n % 2 == 1)
        printf("C\n");
    else
        printf("D\n");
    }
```

```
n = 1   ____
n = 2   ____
n = 3   ____
n = 4   ____
n = 5   ____
n = 6   ____
n = 7   ____
```

4.4 Else-If

Whenever an if statement has nesting only inside its else clause, we can improve readability by formatting as though else if were one keyword. This emphasizes the *multiple choice* nature of the code. For example,

```
/* clear 3-way choice */
if (n > 0)
    printf("positive\n");
else if (n == 0)
    printf("zero\n");
else
    printf("negative\n");
```

This portrays the logic more clearly than slavish nesting with braces, such as this:

```
/* obscure 3-way choice */
if (n > 0)
    printf("positive\n");
else
    {
    if (n == 0)
        printf("zero\n");
    else
        printf("negative\n");
    }
```

Notice that we are not adding any new features to the syntax of the if statement; everything that follows the word else is syntactically one statement. We are just adding to the readability formats for the if statement:

SYNTAX
```
if (expr) stmt [ else stmt ]
```

READABILITY

```
if (expr)            if (expr)            if (expr)
    stmt                 stmt                 stmt
                     else                 else if (expr)
                         stmt                 stmt
                                          else if (expr)
                                              stmt
                                          else
                                              stmt
```

The else-if is an excellent format for an n-way choice, as in this children's game:

guess.c:

```
/* guess - guess a hidden number between 1 and 15, in 3 guesses
 */
#include "local.h"
main()
    {
    char line[BUFSIZ];   /* input line : string */
    bool found;          /* have I found it?  */
    short n;             /* how many guesses left : {0:3} */
    short range;         /* how much to adjust next guess : {1:4} */
    short try;           /* next number to try : {1:15} */
    metachar reply;      /* the user's reply */

    found = NO;
    n = 3;
    range = 4;
    try = 8;
    printf("Each time I guess, please answer\n");
    printf(" H if I'm high\n L if I'm low\n E if I guessed it\n");
    while (n > 0 && !found)
        {
        printf("I guess %d\n", try);
        if (getln(line, BUFSIZ) == EOF)
            error("Bye!", "");
        reply = line[0];
        if (reply == 'H' || reply == 'h')
            {
            try -= range;
            range /= 2;
            --n;
            }
        else if (reply == 'L' || reply == 'l')
            {
            try += range;
            range /= 2;
            --n;
            }
        else if (reply == 'E' || reply == 'e')
            found = YES;
        else
            printf("Please type H, L, or E\n");
        }
    printf("Your number is %d\nThanks for the game\n", try);
    exit(0);
    }
```

Since side effects are allowable in each condition, the else-if allows a sequence of actions to be performed until one gets the right result:

```
/* a series of attempts */
if (try1() == YES)
    printf("success on the first try\n");
else if (try2() == YES)
    printf("success on the second try\n");
else if (try3() == YES)
    printf("third try is a charm\n");
else
    printf("some days, nothing works\n");
```

One of the advantages of this vertical alignment of the else-if is that modification is clear and simple: adding another case or removing one is easy.

Question [4-3] If the guesser had four tries, how big a range could it handle? _____ Five tries? _____

4.5 Switch

C provides a special form of multiple-choice control structure for the situation in which all the choices are specific alternative values for one integer expression. This is the switch statement. It is constructed with the keyword switch, followed by an integer expression in parentheses, followed by a block (compound statement, enclosed in braces). Interspersed with the statements of the block are case labels, each of which precedes the statements to be executed when the expression has the value given by the label. At the end of each alternative section of code, there should be a break statement, which causes control to jump to the closing brace after the statements. Our previous example, guess.c, can be written equally well with switch or with else-if. We prefer switch in all such situations because it alerts the reader to a *mutually-exclusive* set of possibilities.

```
switch (reply)
    {
case 'H':
case 'h':
    try -= range;
    range /= 2;
    --n;
    break;
case 'L':
case 'l':
    try += range;
    range /= 2;
    --n;
    break;
case 'E':
case 'e':
    found = YES;
    break;
default:
    printf("Please type H, L, or E\n");
    break;
    }
```

There is a special case label — default — which stands for "none of the named cases". It is conventionally placed as the last case of the switch, but the compiler allows it to be placed anywhere. The order in which the cases appear does not matter, because the compiler ensures that they are all mutually-exclusive constant values. In other words, there cannot appear two instances of the same case label value.

After each case label, there may appear any number of statements, or *stmt**, in our syntax notation. Thus, these are the syntax and readability rules:

SYNTAX
    switch ⟨*expr*⟩ *block*

READABILITY
    switch ⟨*expr*⟩
        (
    case *const*:
        stmt
        break;
    case *const*:
    case *const*:
        stmt
        break;
    default:
        stmt
        break;
)

It is common and proper to attach multiple case labels to one statement, as is done in the pattern above. But a "flow-through" obtained by omitting a break is easily mistaken later for a careless (but common) bug. Therefore, if "flow-through" is really intended, insert a comment such as /* flow-through */ in place of the break. Avoid flow-through, except to prevent needless duplication of code lines.

4.6 While

The while statement repeats its statement body as long as the tested expression evaluates to a semi-Boolean *true* value, i.e., non-zero. The test is made each time before the body is executed, so that if it is *false* the first time it is tested, the body is never executed.

The flow-chart of the while statement shows that the tested expression is always evaluated one time more than the body.

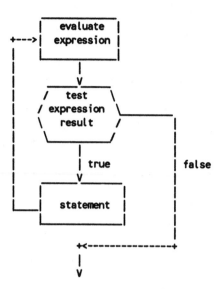

A loop of this form, where the first box is executed one time more than the second, is known in the programming-language literature as an $N + \frac{1}{2}$ time loop. In C, since the top box is only a single expression, whereas the second box can be a whole block of statements, the while loop might best be called an $N + \frac{1}{4}$ time loop. This form of loop is well suited to calling one function to get something, then executing a body which does something with it. For an example, let us re-visit the simple input-to-output copy program from Section 3.4, using the metachar defined-type and the exit(0) call:

```
copy3.c:
   /* copy3 - copy input to output
    */
   #include "local.h"
   main()
      {
      metachar c; /* input character */

      while ((c = getchar()) != EOF)
          putchar(c);
      exit(0);
      }
```

If this program is applied to a file of 100 bytes, it will call getchar 101 times. The first 100 calls will return a data byte; the 101-st call will return the EOF value. Thus, the test is evaluated 101 times, and the body is done 100 times. Some academic authorities like to code this loop in a different way:

```
c = getchar();
while (c != EOF)
    {
    putchar(c);
    c = getchar();
    }
```

We prefer the first program, because the latter style forces the *duplication of code*. The objection is not so much that the resulting program is larger (although that is true), but rather that duplication of code is a problem during maintenance. It is all too easy to make a change to one of the duplicated instances while overlooking the other. (Section 4.9 will address the special problems of nested loops.)

Summarizing syntax and readability:

SYNTAX
```
while (expr) stmt
```

READABILITY
```
while (expr)
    stmt
```

When coding a loop, you should be aware of a relationship known as the *loop invariant*, or the *typical picture of the loop*. This invariant is a relationship which

(a)   is always true, each time the loop is traversed; and

(b)   guarantees that the loop attains its goal when it terminates.

One can describe an invariant for any point during the execution of the loop, but the clearest place is just after evaluating the test and before executing the body, so we will henceforth assume this location. Thus, in the copy program, the invariant looks like this:

```
Already read:   __ __ __ __  ...  __
                                    c
Already written:__ __ __ __  ...
```

Or in words, "A series of one or more characters has already been read, and the last of them is in the variable c. The same series has been written, except for c, which has not been written".

To verify condition (a) above, that the invariant is always true, you can use *mathematical induction*. Prove that it is true the very first time, and then prove that if it was true for the first, second, ..., to n-th times, then it will be true after one more iteration to the n+1st time. In this case, our picture is obviously true the first time, when the series of characters contains only c. If it has been true for 1, 2, ..., n, then we have written a string of n characters. If the loop is then traversed one more time, c is now a new character, and the series of characters written is of length n+1. To write the induction out like this may seem tedious, but the mental processes that you go through in verifying a loop are really equivalent to this process.

Now, to verify condition (b) above, observe that when the loop terminates, c is equal to the EOF value. Thus the series of characters read and written contains every character of the input up to the EOF, which is the goal of the loop.

Strictly speaking, the invariant is required to be true only at one specific point. Programs are more readable, however, if the invariant is true throughout as much of the loop as possible. If we define the *domain of exceptions* as the portion of the loop in which the invariant does not hold true, our readability principle is to *minimize the domain of exceptions to the loop invariant.*

4.7 For

One way that C language assists you in achieving this readability principle is the for statement. This statement confines the primary manipulations of the loop invariant to one line of the listing. Consider this version of the function strscn, which searches a string s for the first occurrence of the character c. The function returns the subscript of this first occurrence, or the subscript of the terminating null character if there is no match. (The strscn function is not from the Standard C Library.)

```
/* strscn - return the index of c (or null-terminator) in string s
 */
#include "local.h"
uint strscn(          /* : returns (0:UINT_MAX) */
    char s[],         /* string to be scanned : string */
    char c)           /* char to be matched : (CHAR_MIN:CHAR_MAX) */
    {
    uint i;           /* loop index : (0:UINT_MAX) */

    for (i = 0; s[i] != c && s[i] != '\0'; ++i)
        ;
    return i;
    }
```

Compare the for loop above with this while loop:

```
i = 0;
while (s[i] != c && s[i] != '\0')
    ++i;
```

All those expressions which manipulate the loop variable are contained in the one line of the for controls, reducing the domain of exceptions.

The flow-chart of the for statement looks like this:

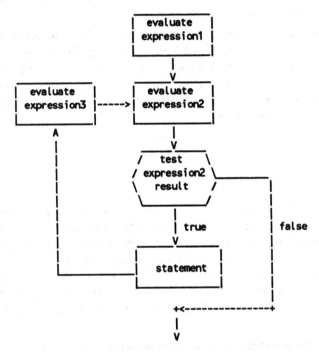

If the *expression1 (init)* is left blank, no initialization takes place. Similarly, if the *expression3 (step)* is left blank, no reinitialization takes place. And if the *expression2 (test)* is blank, the loop is executed "forever". In the header local.h, the symbol FOREVER is defined as

```
for (;;)
```

which is an "endless" loop. Thus, a "clock" program might have an outline like this:

```
FOREVER
    {
    wait 1 second
    print the time
    }
```

For a means of "breaking out" of an endless loop, there is the break statement. Execution of a break causes a jump to the next statement following the body of a for, switch, while, or do-while. Thus, in C, the true N + ½ time loop can be coded like this:

```
FOREVER
    (
    stmt*
    if (expr)
        break;
    stmt*
    )
```

Summarizing syntax and readability:

```
SYNTAX
    for (expr; expr; expr) stmt
```

```
READABILITY
    for (expr; expr; expr)             FOREVER
        stmt                               (
                                           stmt*
                                           if (expr)
                                               break;
                                           stmt*
                                           )
```

4.8 Do While

C provides a loop which tests *after* doing each iteration: the do-while loop. The flow-chart shows the unique form of this loop, which always performs its body of code at least once.

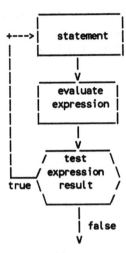

The do-while statement is desirable only if the problem dictates that the code must be done at least once — for example, in testing for an interactive reply to a prompt:

```
do
     {
     printf("Answer y or n: ");
     ans = getchar();
     while (getchar() != '\n')
          ;
     } while (ans != 'y' && ans != 'n');
```

Good programs have the property that they "do nothing gracefully", that is, each body of code is performed only if there is something for it to do. A program should not do crazy things when inputs are missing. Use do-while sparingly.

Summarizing syntax and readability:

SYNTAX
```
     do stmt while (expr);
```

READABILITY
```
     do
          {
          stmt*
          } while (expr);
```

4.9 Design of Control Structures

Before tackling a programming problem, it is useful to sketch your approach to the program. Such sketching is known as *logic design*, or simply *design*. In our opinion, the simplest approach to logic design is based on the idea of syntax. We have seen how syntax is used in defining the valid structures of C. Now we will apply it to the programming problems themselves.

First, consider the syntactic structure of *repetition*, one thing repeated over and over. For example, we often treat an input file as a repetition of one single character after another. In our syntax notation, we write this as

$$c^*$$

where *c* stands for one character. Our sketching tool for logic design is a *program outline* or *pseudo-code*, written with a mixture of real C constructs and verbal phrases that stand for code to be written later. The program outline that corresponds to the syntax c^* is this:

> *for each character c*
>   *process c*

This outline makes clear the structure of our program: do a certain processing for each character. If there are 100 characters to be processed, the body of the loop is done 100 times.

Further refinement of the outline is determined by the processing to be done. For example, if the characters are obtained by input from getchar, and if the processing consists of writing the character with putchar, the code for this outline becomes

```
while ((c = getchar()) != EOF)
    putchar(c);
```

Using the same program outline, if the characters are being taken from a string in memory, and the processing consists of printing their ASCII (or whatever) codes in decimal, we could translate the outline into this code:

```
for (i = 0; s[i] != '\0'; ++i)
    printf("%d\n", c);
```

You can see that these outlines are indeed just sketches. There is still some real programming work to the translation from outline to finished program. The outline simply serves to clarify the overall control structure of the program.

We thus have *Design Rule 1:*

1.   When the data being processed have the syntax of a *repetition* of things over and over, structure the program as a *loop*, whose body processes exactly one of the things.

One important point about loops: the simple N + ¼ time loop (which gets its data as part of the loop test) will not work in cases where a preceding part of the program has already read or produced the first data item for the loop. Often, a program must *read ahead* one item to know that the end of a loop is reached. Consider a simple tabulating program whose input consists of lines containing one account number and one entry for that account. The program's output is a series of lines which give the account number and the total of all entries for that account. The syntax of the input is

{ {*account entry*}* }*

This shows a repetition inside a repetition; the large braces { } are not C language braces, but a part of our syntax notation that *groups* everything inside them. An English translation of the syntax notation above is "a repetition of a repetition of *account*-followed-by-*entry*".

For those who like to work with a graphical notation, we can show the same information as a *syntax tree:*

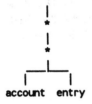

The repetition inside another repetition means that the program will have the structure of one loop nested inside another:

> *for all account numbers*
>   *zero the sum*
>   *for all lines with the same account number*
>   *add the entry to the sum*
>   *print the sum*

Or as a C program

```
nargs = scanf("%ld %lf", &account, &entry);
while (nargs == 2)
    {
    sum = 0.;
    this = account;
    while (nargs == 2 && this == account)
        {
        sum += entry;
        nargs = scanf("%ld %lf", &account, &entry);
        }
    printf("%ld %10.2f\n", this, sum);
    }
```

The inner loop must assume that the first line of each new account has already been read, because the new account number tells the program that all entries for the previous account have been processed — an example of "read-ahead logic".

Our second construct is a *sequence* of things, each being different in some way. In our syntax notation, a sequence is simply written as a list of the things one after another. Thus the syntax of *part1* followed by *part2* followed by *part3* is simply

   part1 part2 part3

and the syntax tree is

The corresponding program outline is the same list, written vertically:

   process part1
   process part2
   process part3

For an example, consider the problem of reading a text file which is all in lower case and selectively capitalizing the first letter of each word. (We will be rather general here about a "letter": any non-whitespace character will be called a letter. We will just be sure that "capitalizing" a non-alphabetic character does not alter the character.) Since we will treat the initial letter of a word in a different way from the other letters, the relevant syntax for a *word* is

$a\ a^{*}$

and its syntax tree is

where a stands for one non-whitespace character. The input file consists of a series of words separated by whitespace, so its syntax is

$w^{*}\ \{a\ a^{*}\ w^{*}\}^{*}$

("any amount of leading whitespace, followed by a repetition of these items: initial letter, repetition of more letters, repetition of whitespace") and its syntax tree is

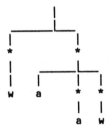

where w stands for one whitespace character. The corresponding program outline is this:

```
for each whitespace w
    copy w
for each word
    capitalize the initial letter
    for each succeeding letter a
        copy a
    for each whitespace w
        copy w
```

The body of our main loop is a *sequence* of three actions, some of which will themselves be loops. Since the program cannot know that it has reached the end of a word until a following whitespace is read, the loops must be coded with the read-ahead logic described above. That is, each loop must assume that its first case has already been read. The program thus looks like this:

```
c = getchar();  /* get the first char */
while (isspace(c))
    putchar(c), c = getchar();
while (c != EOF)
    {
    c = toupper(c);
    putchar(c), c = getchar();
    while (c != EOF && !isspace(c))
        putchar(c), c = getchar();
    while (isspace(c))
        putchar(c), c = getchar();
    }
```

This program illustrates our *Design Rule 2:*

2.   When the data being processed form a *sequence* of several different things, the program outline should contain a sequence of steps, each one of which processes one of the input items.

Our third design construct is a *choice* among several alternatives. Taking the same example as above, we might look at the file as containing two kinds of characters: those that should be capitalized and those that should not. Thus, the syntax of each character is simply

   $h \mid t$

where h is a "head" character to be capitalized, t is a "tail" character that should not be capitalized, and $\mid$ is a syntax notation for "choice". The syntax of the input file is thus

   $\{h \mid t\}^{*}$

and the syntax tree is

The program outline that corresponds to a *choice* is an if statement or a switch statement. The outline to process this input file (which consists of a choice inside a repetition) is thus

> *for each input character c*
> *if (c is a head character)*
> *output capitalized c*
> *else*
> *output c*

The corresponding program looks like this:

```
for (was_white = YES; (c = getchar()) != EOF; was_white = isspace(c))
    {
    if (!isspace(c) && was_white)
        putchar(toupper(c));
    else
        putchar(c);
    }
```

The handling of *choice* constructs is summarized by *Design Rule 3:*

3. When the data form a *choice* among one or more alternatives, the program outline should contain an if or switch construct, each alternative processing one of the choices.

    The capitalizing example has shown two different programs for the same problem, each arising from a different syntax view of the data. We prefer the second program, according to *Design Rule 4:*

4. Choose the design which results in the simpler program.

This does not mean that *choice* always gives simpler programs than *sequence;* the extra variables (such as was_white) can sometimes proliferate to an alarming extent. However, as a general rule, your first attempt should usually start by considering the data as a simple repetition of a single small thing: one character, one number, one line, etc. If the number of choices then looks overwhelming, look again at the data as being comprised of larger entities, and try again.

Exercise 4-1. Complete the first program fragment into a C program accnt.c and try it out.

Exercise 4-2. Complete the second or third program fragment into a C program cap.c and try it out.

4.10 Break and Continue

We have discussed the `break` statement in the context of the FOREVER loop, as a means of implementing the N + ½ time loop. Also, we have seen its use in the `switch` statement, where it terminates each of the alternative cases. The `break` statement is available within the `while`, `do-while`, `for`, and `switch`; it serves in each of these constructs as a jump to the end of the statement. Its effect is to immediately terminate execution of the loop (or `switch`).

Each time you code a `break`, you should question whether there is not a straightforward way to express the same logic without the `break`. Heavy use of `break` is often associated with the "step-at-a-time" thinking of beginning programmers. Consider this example, which looks for the first whitespace character in a string `s`:

```
/* misuse of break */
for (i = 0; i < BUFSIZ; ++i)
    {
    if (s[i] == ' ')
        break;
    else if (s[i] == '\n')
        break;
    else if (s[i] == '\t')
        break;
    }
```

A more professional approach is to state the looping condition in the test of the loop:

```
/* search for whitespace */
for (i = 0; i < BUFSIZ && s[i] != ' ' && s[i] != '\n' && s[i] != '\t'; ++i)
    ;
```

Or, generalizing the idea of whitespace,

```
/* search for whitespace */
for (i = 0; i < BUFSIZ && isspace(s[i]); ++i)
    ;
```

Note the null statement that forms the body of the loop; the loop control itself contains all that is needed.

The `continue` statement is similar to `break`, in that it causes a jump in the execution of a loop. However, `continue` jumps to the *next iteration* of the loop. In the `for` loop, it jumps to the *step* of the loop, the third expression on the `for` line. In the `while` and `do-while` loop, it jumps to the *test*.

As with the break, the continue is prone to abuse by beginners. Whenever it can be replaced by a single if test, it should not be used. Consider this bad example, which skips the processing of whitespace characters:

```
/* bad use of continue */
for (i = 0; s[i] != '\0'; ++i)
    {
    if (isspace(s[i]))
        continue;
    process the character s[i]
    }
```

The example is better coded with an if which says when to *do* something, rather than saying when *not to do* something:

```
/* process only the non-whitespace characters */
for (i = 0; s[i] != '\0'; ++i)
    {
    if (!isspace(s[i]))
        {
        process the character s[i]
        }
    }
```

Notice that continue has no relationship to the switch statement. A continue encountered inside a switch will jump to the next iteration of an enclosing loop, if there is one. Otherwise, the compiler will complain about the syntax error.

4.11 Goto

The goto statement, like the break and continue, is often associated with "one-step-at-a-time" thinking which misses the underlying syntax of the problem. Analyzing your problem into *repetition, sequence,* and *choice* structures will generally do away with the need for goto.

However, in some rare situations, the goto is the simplest solution to a programming problem. Furthermore, many C programs are themselves written by *other* programs, and goto is often needed by such program generators. The goto statement thus remains firmly entrenched in C language.

Syntactically, the goto statement is very simple, and the only readability rule is that it always deserves a comment explaining why it was necessary to use it:

SYNTAX
    goto *label*;

READABILITY
    goto *label*;   /* reason */

The label is an identifier followed by a colon, and it is prefixed to some statement inside the same function as the goto.

One situation commonly described as a candidate for goto is an error that is detected inside a deeply nested loop. Why "deeply nested"? Because a goto inside only one or two loops can easily be replaced by a new Boolean variable, e.g. found_error, like this:

```
/* error-handling using goto */
for (...)
    for (...)
        {
        ...
        if (some error is detected)
            goto fixit;
        ...
        }
...
fixit: repair the damage
```

Compare this with

```
/* error-handling using Boolean variable */
for (...; !found_error && ...; ...)
    for (...; !found_error && ...; ...)
        {
        ...
        if (some error is detected)
            found_error = YES;
        else
            ...
        }
if (found_error)
    repair the damage
```

While we are describing the handling of errors, we should mention that sometimes the responsibility for repairing the damage should rest with the calling function, and all the called function should do is to pass back an error indication:

```
if (some error is detected)
    return (-1);
```

And whenever a program is part of a real-time environment, errors must often be handled by a system-wide recovery facility:

```
if (some error is detected)
    syserr(code);
```

Such a facility could, for example, re-initialize the devices being controlled, ring a bell for the operator, and prompt for further commands. This "global" handling of exception conditions can be accomplished in C, but the details are beyond the scope of this book. If you need such facilities, consult with a senior programmer or the library documentation for your system.

At any rate, the `goto` is hardly the universal answer to the problem of handling errors.

CHAPTER 5: FUNCTIONS

5.1 Syntax and Readability

A *function* is an independent set of statements for performing some computation. Already you have seen many examples of the ways that you *use* functions; now you will learn how to *create* your own functions.

Each function that you create should do one specific, nameable task. For example, from mathematics we have the *power* function, which computes x raised to the power y:

$$x^y$$

As we saw in Section 3.17, in C the power function appears as

```
pow(x, y)
```

If we were going to write the pow function ourselves, we would need to attend to the *syntax* and *readability* rules for functions:

SYNTAX (Simplified)
function:
    [*type*] *name*(*param-list*) *block*

param-list:
    decl [*, decl*]*

READABILITY

```
/* comment              /* comment
 */                      */
type name(void)         type name(
    {                        type a1,    /* describe a1 */
    decl*                    type a2)    /* describe a2 */
                             {
    stmt*                    decl*
    }
                         stmt*
                         }
```

For example, a partial implementation of pow might look like this:

```
/* pow1 - return (positive) x to the power y
 */
double exp(double x);   /* declaration of exp function */
double log(double x);   /* declaration of log function */

double pow1(     /* : returns {>0:DBL_MAX} */
    double x,    /* base : {>0:DBL_MAX} */
    double y)    /* exponent : any */
    {
    return exp(log(x) * y);
    }
```

This function computes x^y by taking the natural log of x, multiplying the result by y, then taking the exponential function of the result. (If you are not familiar with the mathematical details, take our word for it, and continue undaunted. This over-simplified method would have too much round-off error for a good library, anyway.) We will address the components of the definition in the order they appear in the syntax:

1.   Type

2.   Name

3.   Parameters

4.   Block

(1) Type: If a function does not return any value, its type should be specified as void. If it does return a value, Standard C requires that this value must not be an array. The syntax shows that the *type* is optional; if none is specified, the compiler assumes int. However, in

our readability rules, the *type* is mandatory. (Careless use of int is a common portability problem, especially when it is the same size as long.) In the example of pow1, the *type* being returned is double.

In Section 3.14, we saw precise rules for the type of variable names in C. The same rules are important for function names. The type of the name pow1 is found by scratching the name off the definition line, and ignoring the whitespace, which leaves

        double(double,double)

(with the understanding that parameter names, such as x and y, have no role in determining the function type). Reading "double(double,double)" literally gives "double open-parenthesis double comma double close-parenthesis", but in more fluent C, this is read "function returning double and taking two double parameters". Just as with arrays, this shows the complementary relationship between declarations and usages:

pow1   has the type   double (double, double)

pow1(x, y)   has the type   double

(2) Name: The name of the function can be any C identifier. It should not start with underscore, because these are reserved to the compiler itself.

(3) Parameters: In Section 3.8, we saw that arguments are passed to a function in the *function-call* operation. In the definition of the called function which will receive those arguments, *parameters* are declared — these are local variables of the function, which will contain the argument values when they are passed. In the C language literature, there is a variety of names for arguments and parameters. In the *calling* program, within a function-call such as

        pow1(2., 3.)

the values in parentheses are known as *arguments, actual arguments,* or *actual parameters.* In the definition of the function, such as

        double pow1(double x, double y)

the names in parentheses are known as *parameters, formal parameters,* or *formal arguments.* We will refer consistently to *arguments* for function calls, and *parameters* for function definitions.

If the parameter-list consists of nothing but the word void, this means that this function accepts no arguments; it will be called with an empty argument-list, like

```
dummy();
```

(4) Block: A block consists of a left-brace, zero or more declarations, zero or more statements, and a right-brace. This completes the function definition. Notice that if *this* function calls *other* functions, it should be preceded by a *declaration* for each of these called functions, such as the declarations for `exp` and `log` shown above. However, declarations for functions are usually placed in headers, rather than being part of the source file. In the `pow1` example, it would be preferable to `#include` the `local.h` header, causing `<math.h>` to be `#include`'d; this would automatically provide declarations for `exp` and `log`.

Question [5-1] What is the type of each expression:

The type of `log(x)`   is _____

The type of `log`   is _____

The type of `exp`   is _____

The type of `exp(log(y) * y)`   is _____

The "smallest" function — the one that contains the minimal readable components — has a *type* of `void`, a *parameter-list* of `void`, and nothing between the braces:

```
void dummy(void)
   {
   }
```

Even though it does nothing except returning, it has its uses. For example, in building a large program it is sometimes useful to define dummy functions, or "stubs", to mark the place where further development will take place.

5.2 Argument Passing

As we saw in Section 3.8, function arguments are always passed *by value* in C. C compilers usually do this by copying the values into an *argument frame*, arranging for the called function to know where this argument frame is located in the memory. (By *argument frame*, we simply mean a sequence of the argument values, one after the other, in the memory.) This argument frame, although not a formal requirement of the language, is so widely used that we will show it in our diagrams. The following program, `powdem.c`,

```
powdem.c:
   /* powdem - demonstrate power function
    */
   #include "local.h"

   double pow1(double x, double y);     /* declaration of pow1 function */

   main()
      {
      short i;     /* loop index : {0:10} */

      for (i = 0; i < 10; ++i)
         printf("2 to the power %d equals %.0f\n",
             i, pow1(2., i));
      exit(0);
      }
   /* pow1 - return (positive) x to the power y
    */
   double pow1(     /* : returns {>0:DBL_MAX} */
      double x,     /* base : {>0:DBL_MAX} */
      double y)     /* exponent : any */
      {
      return exp(log(x) * y);
      }
```

produces the following output:

```
2 to the power 0 equals 1
2 to the power 1 equals 2
2 to the power 2 equals 4
2 to the power 3 equals 8
2 to the power 4 equals 16
2 to the power 5 equals 32
2 to the power 6 equals 64
2 to the power 7 equals 128
2 to the power 8 equals 256
2 to the power 9 equals 512
```

Notice that the powdem.c file contains the line

```
#include "local.h"
```

This line causes headers such as <math.h> to be #include'd, bringing declarations of the library functions into our program, including lines like

```
double exp(double);
double log(double);
```

Thus, the powdem.c file does not need to repeat these declarations. This, by the way, is the "modern" way to handle declarations for library functions; each library should be accompanied by its corresponding header with the necessary declarations.

In the powdem.c program, the arguments to pow1 are written as 2. and
i. Because the prototype for pow1 specifies double for both parameters,
the compiler will convert each argument value (as if by assignment) to
double. The second argument could have been explicitly written as
(double)i; we prefer brevity, and omit the cast. Each time pow1 is called,
the two values 2. and (double)i are copied into an argument frame (each
occupying eight bytes of storage, in most machines). The called function, pow1, receives some indication of where the values are located,
which we graphically indicate with "<-frame". On the first iteration,
when i equals zero, this looks like

```
                          <- frame
      |_____|
      |       2.         |
      |_____|
      |       0.         |
      |_____|
```

After the argument values are placed into the argument frame, the
called function is then invoked, receiving an indication of where the
argument frame is located.

Exercise 5-1. Remove the pow1 function from powdem.c, and change the
function-call to pow, so that the program will use the pow function from
the Standard Library. Compare its output with the output above.

5.3 Parameters and Automatic Variables

In the called function, the parameters are simply variables whose
storage consists of the argument locations *in the argument frame*. In
other words, the address of a parameter variable may be different each
time the function is called — the address is determined by the "frame"
indication received from the calling function. Thus, when our pow1
function is called as in the previous section, its parameter storage looks
like this:

```
                          <- frame
        |_____|
   x    |       2.         |
        |_____|
   y    |       0.         |
        |_____|
```

Notice that the names x and y have been added to the diagram. Parameter names are simply the names for specific locations in the argument
frame that was passed by the calling function. Each machine and compiler may have their own method of accessing these locations, using the
"frame" indication that was received from the calling function.

If the called function should *change* the value of a parameter, the calling function will never know it; once the called function returns, the argument frame is made available for re-use, or "trashed", in programmer vernacular. Thus, the called function can use the parameters just as it would use any other local variable.

Speaking of the local variables, let us look now at the way C language handles them. We will need a new example program, since powdem.c has no local variables other than its parameters. Consider, then, this version of the power function, named lpow, which accepts and returns long numbers. The algorithm is "brute-force": keep multiplying by lnum until n multiplications are complete.

```
/* lpow - power function (for long data)
 */
#include "local.h"
long lpow(          /* : returns {LONG_MIN:LONG_MAX} */
    long lnum,      /* base : {LONG_MIN:LONG_MAX} */
    long n)         /* exponent : {0:LONG_MAX} */
    {
    long p;         /* local ("auto") result : {LONG_MIN:LONG_MAX} */

    p = 1;
    for ( ; n > 0; --n)
        p *= lnum;
    return p;
    }
```

Besides the parameters lnum and n, we see a local variable named p. In C, such local variables are known as auto ("automatic") variables, so named because C "automatically" creates storage for them each time their function is entered. Expanding our notion of "frame", our picture of the local storage for lpow looks like this:

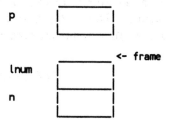

Thus, the storage for p is "private" storage for the lpow function, just as is the storage for the parameters lnum and n. It is given to lpow when the function is entered, and it is "trashed" when lpow returns.

Exercise 5-2. Write a demonstration program `lpowd.c` to exercise the `lpow` function. Do not forget to declare

```
long lpow(long lnum, long n);
```

C language has a keyword for "automatic" variables — they can be explicitly declared as `auto`, as in

```
auto long p;
```

You will probably never see this keyword in an actual C program, since the compiler understands `auto` as the default for all local variables.

Returning for a moment to the parameters of a function, let us examine the syntax checking that the compiler performs on function calls. If we have caused `<math.h>` to be `#include`'d (perhaps via `local.h`), then prototypes such as

```
double pow(double, double);
```

will be visible after the `#include`. If the program later contains

```
xyz = pow(a, b, c);
```

the compiler will diagnose this as a "wrong number of arguments" syntax error. If the program contains

```
xyz = pow(1., "2");
```

the compiler again complains, because `"2"` is a string constant, hence an array, and arrays cannot be assigned to arithmetic scalars such as the second parameter of `pow`.

In order to obtain this syntax checking from the compiler, you must be sure that a prototype is always visible before every function call:

Be sure that headers have been `#include`'d for all the library functions that you call.

For programs that consist of only one source file (which is all we have seen so far), every function except `main` should be declared by a prototype at the top of the file.

5.4 Array Arguments

This simple picture of argument passing becomes more complicated when an argument is an array. Consider the string "hello", a constant of type char[6]. Supposing that it is located at address 1400, it looks like this in memory:

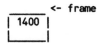

```
1400      | 104 | 101 | 108 | 108 | 111 |   0 |
          |_'h'_|_'e'_|_'l'_|_'l'_|_'o'_|_'\0'_|
```

When we pass "hello" as an argument, the argument frame does not receive the contents of the array. Instead, the *address* of the initial element of the array is passed. Thus, in order to call

        strlen1("hello")

the compiler will generate this argument frame:

```
  _____    <- frame
| 1400 |
|_____|
```

Now consider what happens in the strlen1 function:

```
/* strlen1 - return length of string s
 */
#include "local.h"
uint strlen1(              /* : returns {0:UINT_MAX} */
    char s[])              /* input : string */
    {
    uint i;                /* loop index : {0:UINT_MAX} */

    for (i = 0; s[i] != '\0'; ++i)  /* search for terminating null */
        ;
    return i;
    }
```

The crucial point to notice is that the declaration of the parameter s looks like an an array of characters, but it really is not. s is a variable that holds the *address* of the initial element of the array. The C terminology for such a variable is "character pointer", and s could equivalently be declared as

        char *s;

(The type char * means "pointer to char".) When strlen1 runs through its loop, it will look successively at s[0], s[1], and so forth. Since s contains the value 1400, C understands that s[0] means "the character at address 1400", s[1] means "the character at address 1401", and so forth. In other words, the code performs with the same result as if s were in fact an array of characters; each one is tested for equality with the null character '\0' and the loop terminates when '\0' is found.

For a slightly larger example, consider the strncpy1 function:

```
/* strncpy1 - copy n bytes from s2 to s1
 */
#include "local.h"
void strncpy1(
    char s1[],  /* target : string */
    char s2[],  /* source : string */
    uint n)     /* max number of chars to copy : {0:UINT_MAX} */
    {
    uint i;     /* loop index : {0:UINT_MAX} */

    for (i = 0; i < n && s2[i] != '\0'; ++i)
        s1[i] = s2[i];
    for ( ; i < n; ++i)
        s1[i] = '\0';
    }
```

The strncpy1 function copies n characters from one array (the "source") to another (the "target"). If the source has a null-terminator in the first n characters, the target will be "null-padded" — extended with null characters. If the source string has n or more non-null characters, the target will *not* be null-terminated (i.e., it will not have the "string" property).

The parameter storage for strncpy1 looks like this:

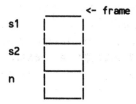

Question [5-2] Assume the following machine state just before calling

    strncpy1(save, line, 4)

VARIABLE	ADDRESS	STORAGE			
line	800	97	98	99	0
		'a'	'b'	'c'	'\0'
save	1800	119	120	121	118
		'x'	'y'	'z'	'w'

What does the parameter storage look like when strncpy1 is entered?

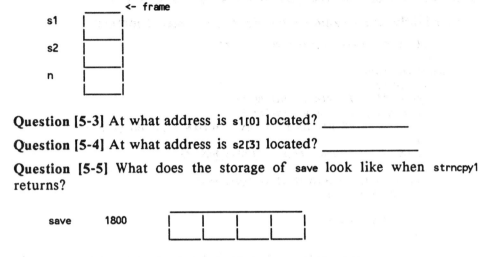

Question [5-3] At what address is s1[0] located? _____

Question [5-4] At what address is s2[3] located? _____

Question [5-5] What does the storage of save look like when strncpy1 returns?

Exercise 5-3. The Standard Library provides a function

```
int strncmp(s1, s2, n)
```

which looks at no more than n characters of the strings to determine the comparison result. Write and test your own version, to be called strncmp1.

C language has full access to all the data storage of your program — this allows it to *replace assembler code* in many engineering applications. But it also can lead to bugs and portability problems when the programmer does not understand what C is doing. For an example, consider the dump function, which prints n bytes of memory as hexadecimal numbers.

```
dmpdem.c:
    /* dmpdem - demonstrate dump function
     */
    #include "local.h"
    #define LINESIZE 16
    #define BYTEMASK 0xFF

    void dump(char s[], uint n);

    main()
        {
        char msg[16];
        double d = 100.;

        strncpy(msg, "testing 1 2 3\n", sizeof(msg));

        /* case 1 - quite proper */
        dump(msg, sizeof(msg));

        /* case 2 - ok, but output will vary with machine */
        dump((char *)&d, sizeof(d));

        /* case 3 - non-portable, may cause hardware error */
        dump((char *)0x40, 4);
        exit(0);
        }
/* dump - print memory bytes
 *        (Warning - some usages may be non-portable)
 */
void dump(
    char s[],       /* byte address to be dumped : non-NULL */
    uint n)         /* number of bytes to dump : {0:UINT_MAX} */
    {
    uint i;         /* byte counter : {0:UINT_MAX} */

    for (i = 0; i < n; ++i)
        {
        if (i % LINESIZE == 0)
            printf("\n%8.8X: ", &s[i]);
        printf(" %2.2X", s[i] & BYTEMASK);
        }
    printf("\n");
    }
```

The parameter s is understood by dump to be the address of some byte
(char) in the memory, and n is the number of bytes to be printed. The
function blindly prints s[0], s[1], etc., using a format which will divide
the printout into lines of sixteen bytes. (The bit-and with BYTEMASK
ensures that a non-negative byte value is passed to printf.) The usages of
dump can be divided into several cases, as the main program shows.

(1) When dump is applied to an array of characters no larger than the parameter n specifies, its usage is error-free and portable. The bytes of the array are printed one-by-one.

(2) When dump is applied to data other than char data, the internal representation of such data may be different on different machines, and the printouts could look different. The argument is not the same type as dump expects, and the (char *) cast is necessary.

(3) When dump is applied to an arbitrary *numerical address*, the program could "bomb out" with hardware errors on some machines (from trying to reference non-existent or inaccessible memory locations), and the usage is certainly *not portable*. This latter type of programming is only to be used when you are quite sure that a non-portable program is needed for one particular machine.

The need for explicit casts (such as the (char *) here) is often a tip-off that something non-portable is going on. Without making it an inflexible rule, we suggest:

> For each cast that appears in the program, question whether it performs a portable operation.

Speaking of portability, there are some unusual environments in which an array could have even more bytes than can be counted in an unsigned int (for example, the PC "huge" memory model). Standard C therefore provides a defined-type named size_t. This is almost always defined as unsigned int, but in some environments it is unsigned long.

Some of the library functions of Standard C have arguments or returned values that count the number of bytes in a (possibly very large) array; these are declared using the size_t type:

```
size_t strlen(const char s[]);
char *strncpy(char s1[], const char s2[], size_t n);
int strncmp(const char s1[], const char s2[], size_t n);
```

Furthermore, size_t is the type of the value produced by the sizeof operator, so in the "huge" environment mentioned above, sizeof always returns an unsigned long result. The definition of size_t is in the Standard header <stddef.h> (included automatically by our "local.h").

These declarations also introduce the keyword const. The declaration const char s[] says that s designates an array of *unchanging* characters. Thus, these declarations state that strlen will not modify the string it is given, strncpy will modify only the first string, and strncmp will not modify either string.

5.5 Recursive Functions

As we have seen, each function receives its own frame when it is entered, and this frame is given back when the function returns control. Thus it is easy for a function to *call itself*, thus becoming a *recursive* function.

The most familiar example of a recursive function is the factorial function:

n! *equals* n x (n-1)!   *if n > 0;*

    equals 1   *otherwise.*

Here is a program containing a factorial function:

```
fact.c:
    /* fact - demonstrate factl function
     */
    #include "local.h"
    ulong factl(ulong n);
    main()
        {
        ulong result;    /* returned from factl : {1:ULONG_MAX} */

        result = factl(3);
        printf("3! = %lu\n", result);
        exit(0);
        }
    /* factl - return n! (n factorial)
     */
    ulong factl(
        ulong n)         /* : {0:12} for portability */
        {
        if (n <= 1)
            return (1);
        else
            return (n * factl(n - 1));
        }
```

The function definition line

```
    ulong factl(
        ulong n)
```

says that the function will return a ulong number, that its name is factl, and that it has one ulong parameter, n. The crucial part of the function body is the expression

```
factl(n - 1)
```

which calls the `factl` function from within itself, passing an argument which is one less than the value passed in the parameter `n`.

We will now trace the execution of the expression `factl(3)` in the main program. The value 3 is placed into an argument frame, and the function `factl` is called. Its parameter `n` has the value 3:

```
                _____  <- frame for factl(3)
    n          |     3 |
               |_____|
```

The function in turn executes the expression

```
factl(n - 1)
```

thus placing 2 into another argument frame, and calling `factl` again.

```
                _____  <- frame for factl(2)
    n          |     2 |
               |_____|

                _____  <- frame for factl(3)
    n          |     3 |
               |_____|
```

The process is repeated once again to place the value 1 into another argument frame and to call `factl` again.

```
                _____  <- frame for factl(1)
    n          |     1 |
               |_____|

                _____  <- frame for factl(2)
    n          |     2 |
               |_____|

                _____  <- frame for factl(3)
    n          |     3 |
               |_____|
```

This time, the function returns the value 1 and control returns to the computation of

```
2 * factl(1)
```

giving the result 2. This result is returned into the computation of

```
3 * factl(2)
```

giving the result 6, which is the last return from `factl`. The value 6 is thus assigned to `result`.

In mathematical terms, what has just transpired is the computation of 3! like this:

```
3! equals 3 * 2!
2! equals 2 * 1!
1! equals 1, so
2! equals 2, so
3! equals 6
```

Exercise 5-4. In Section 3.20, you wrote a function maxulng which returns the largest positive ulong number available on your machine. On the assumption that double variables can hold values much larger than ulong variables, write a program facmax.c to determine the largest value of n such that factl(n) is less than the largest ulong number on your machine.

Exercise 5-5. Using the result of the previous exercise, modify the factl function for "defensive programming". That is, the function should examine its parameter n, and return 0 if a meaningful result cannot be produced.

5.6 Initializing Automatic Scalars

In the declaration of a scalar automatic variable, each variable may have an initializer attached to it. The initializer is written with an equal-sign and a value which becomes the initial value of the variable. Consider the following simple program:

```
inits.c:
    /* inits - initialization examples
     */
    #include "local.h"
    main()
        {
        char c = 'x';
        short i = 1;
        short j = i * 2;

        printf("%d %d %c\n", i, j, c);
        exit(0);
        }
```

Question [5-6] What does inits print?

Each initializer applies to only one variable. We suggest that initialized declarations should each have a line of their own; it is very easy to falsely interpret this declaration (which initializes only n2)

```
long n1, n2 = 0;
```

to mean

```
long n1 = 0;
long n2 = 0;
```

The initialization is performed by instructions that are executed each time the function is entered. Furthermore, these instructions are performed in the same sequence that the declarations appear in the program. Consider this program:

```
recpt1.c:
    /* recpt1 - receipt example #1
     */
    #include "local.h"
    short receipt(void);
    main()
        {
        printf("First = %d\n", receipt());
        printf("Second = %d\n", receipt());
        exit(0);
        }
    short receipt(void)
        {
        short number = 1;

        return number++;
        }
```

Question [5-7] What does recpt1 print?

Because the receipt function initializes its number to 1 each time the function is entered, the function would not work very well as a "take-a-number" dispenser. Before we discuss how to correct this behavior, we must discuss the different *storage classes* of the C machine.

5.7 Storage Class and Internal Static

The memory of the computer is organized by C into three areas, conventionally known as the *text, data* and *dynamic segments*. The relative location of these segments may vary in different environments, but we can picture them like this:

```
 _____
|        |
| text   |     contains the machine instructions
|        |     for the program
|_____|
|        |
| data   |     contains variables which remain in
|        |     fixed locations -- the "static" storage
|_____|
|        |
| dynamic|     contains automatic variables, parameters, and
|        |     function-call bookkeeping; changes as
|_____|     functions are called and returned
```

So far, all the variables we have seen have lived in the dynamic segment: the automatic variables of the `main` function and of other functions, and the parameters of functions.

C language administers these variables as a *stack*. A stack, in computing parlance, is a data structure with a "top" and a "bottom". A data item can be added at the top, which is called *pushing* the item onto the stack, and makes the stack larger. Or an item can be removed from the top, which is called *popping* the stack, and makes the stack smaller. In most C implementations, when a function is called, the frame for that function is *pushed* into the next space in the stack area. Thus, in this little program

```
stack1.c:
    /* stack1 - stack example 1
     */
    #include "local.h"
    void f1(short n);
    void f2(short n);
    main()
        {
        f1(1);
        exit(0);
        }
    void f1(
        short n)
        {
        f2(n + 1);
        }
    void f2(
        short n)
        {
        printf("%d\n", n);
        }
```

by the time the printf function is called, the stack looks something like
this:

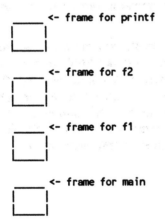

And each time a function returns, its frame is *popped* off the stack; the
space is thus made available for re-use in the next function call. These
operations are done automatically by the code that C language generates;
in other words, they are not anything that *you* have to program.

Now we want to consider the data segment, the region for variables which remain in fixed locations. These variables stay put while
functions are called and return. Variables can be placed into the
(fixed-location) data segment by being declared as static. For example,
the declaration

```
static short number;
```

will place the short integer named number into the (fixed-location) data segment. Syntactically, the keyword static is known as a *storage class*. (Another storage class keyword is auto, the default for local function variables, which we saw in Section 5.3.) The first variety of static variables is *internal static*. The internal static variables are declared inside a function block, just like the automatic variables. They are like automatic variables in that they are known only to the block in which they are declared, but they live in the data segment.

The initialization of static variables is different from that of automatic variables; initialization is done only once, when the program is loaded into the machine. Thus, in our "receipt" example from Section 5.6, we can place the receipt number in static storage and it will keep its value between calls upon the function. The program would look like this:

```
recpt2.c:
    /* recpt2 - receipt example #2
     */
    #include "local.h"
    short receipt(void);
    main()
        {
        printf("First = %d\n", receipt());
        printf("Second = %d\n", receipt());
        exit(0);
        }
    short receipt(void)
        {
        static short number = 1;

        return number++;
        }
```

Question [5-8] What is the output of recpt2?

5.8 Separate Compilation and Linkage

So far, all our programs have been created as one source file. A source file may contain any number of separate functions, so it is certainly possible to write any C program this way. But there are several practical reasons for programmers to create programs that are split into several source files:

1.   As we are debugging and revising a program, it is operationally easier if each re-compilation processes only one part of a large program.

2.   Once we have written and debugged a function, we do not need to keep re-compiling it as we work on other functions in the program.

We can compile a source file to produce *object code*, and by a process known as *linking*, we can combine its functions with other functions in other source files. The linking process is done by a tool known as a *linker*, or a *linkage editor;* the linker stitches together the code from several object-code files (or "object files" for short) into a single executable program.

The linker also stitches our program together with functions whose object code has been collected into a *library* (or *object library*). This is the mechanism by which our programs are combined with the code for functions such as strlen or printf. The linker searches a pre-existing library (supplied with the compiler), looking for the names of any functions which are not found in our program itself.

Given this background, let us look in more detail at the steps the compiler goes through to compile a program such as our simple recpt2 example. Using the UNIX compiler as an example, when we give the command

```
cc -o recpt2 recpt2.c
```

most compilers accomplish five successive phases:

1.   The preprocessor is invoked, to do any #define or #include requests.

2.   The pre-processed program is compiled into a "parse tree", a relatively machine-independent representation of our program.

3.   The parse tree is converted into a human-readable assembler-code file, which specifies the actual machine instructions comprised by our program.

4.   An assembler is invoked to convert the assembler code into actual numeric machine instructions, and the result is an object file.

5.   The linker combines this object code with the object code in the compiler-provided libraries, to produce an executable program.

We can tell the compiler to stop after the production of object code with a compile-command flag such as -c. Suppose we break our recpt2 program into two files. One file contains the main program:

```
recpt3.c:
    /* recpt3 - receipt example #3
     */
    #include "local.h"
    short receipt(void);
    main()
        {
        printf("First = %d\n", receipt());
        printf("Second = %d\n", receipt());
        exit(0);
        }
```

And a second file contains the receipt function:

```
    /* receipt - deliver a unique receipt number
     */
    #include "local.h"
    short receipt(void)
        {
        static short number = 1;

        return number++;
        }
```

Notice that *each* of the files must contain any #include directives that are needed; they are not remembered from any other files compiled.

A sequence of commands to compile these two files separately and then link them together would look like this:

```
cc -c recpt3.c
cc -c receipt.c
cc -o recpt3 recpt3.o receipt.o
```

Each of the first two commands compiles one source file into object code. On UNIX systems, the object file is given a name ending in the suffix .o. (On some other systems, the suffix is .obj .)

The third command does nothing more than to *link* these two object files together, along with any library functions — printf, in this case — to produce an executable program called recpt3.

Now that we have separated the compilation of receipt.c from the linking of it with the main program, we could make further changes to the main program recpt3.c, then re-compile and re-link without compiling receipt.c again. In fact, we can combine the compile and link together like this:

```
cc -o recpt3 recpt3.c receipt.o
```

which will compile recpt3.c and link it together with receipt.o (as well as with the library). The compiler determines which steps are necessary by looking at the suffix of the file name: files ending in .c are to be compiled, whereas files ending in .o (or .obj, etc.) are only to be linked.

A large program of hundreds or thousands of lines is typically written in a number of separate source files, with compile and link accomplished in the manner that we have just seen.

Now that you have seen these procedures for separate compilation of functions, when we show the code for a C function, we will portray it as it would look in a source file of its own, including its own #include and #define lines for whatever symbols it needs.

5.9 External Static Storage

If a C source file contains declarations of static variables appearing *before* any functions, then these variables will be visible in all the functions in the file. Such variables are known as *external static* variables — external, because their declaration appears outside any function.

One common reason for using external static variables is to allow two or more functions in one file to share a variable, without requiring the programmers of other files to keep track of its name. A mundane reason for hiding its name from other files is simply to avoid the book-keeping chore of remembering the name. In large programs another reason is more important: by *hiding* the name from other files, we can be sure that all accesses to this variable must go through the functions in its file — it becomes a *resource* administered by that file.

For a simple example of an external static variable, we introduce a *pseudo-random number generator*. This is a function which produces a series of numbers that appear to be chosen at random — they jump around randomly in value. Of course, they are not *really* random, and serious statistical analysis is beyond our scope. But for programs that roll dice, shuffle cards, or print unpredictable replies, a simple pseudo-random generator will serve. Here is a C source file containing an external static variable (named rnum) and two functions that access this variable:

```
/* rand1.c - generate random numbers with srand1 and rand1
 */
#include "local.h"
static ulong rnum = 0;
/* srand1 - set random seed
 */
void srand1(
    short n)
    {
    rnum = n;
    }
/* rand1 - produce random number
 */
short rand1(void)
    {
    rnum = rnum * 0x41C64E6D + 0x3039;
    return (short)(rnum >> 16) & 0x7FFF;
    }
```

These two functions, rand1 and srand1, both access the external static variable rnum. The function rand1 uses it to generate a new random number. The function srand1 sets it to the new "seed" (initial random value). Only these two functions can see the variable rnum; any other functions will have to call rand1 or srand1 to have any effect on rnum.

Each time rand1 is called, it will return a new random number, which is a short integer bit-and'ed with 0x7FFF. Thus there are 32,768 possible numbers that it can return. However, rand1 will produce 2^{32} numbers before it starts repeating itself; this measure is known as the *period* of the random number generator.

Most often, we do not actually want a number between 0 and 32,767, but would rather choose the low and high limits ourselves. Here is another source file, nfrom.c, which contains one function, nfrom. This function returns a number between low and high, inclusive.

```
/* nfrom - return a number between low and high, inclusive
 */
#include "local.h"
#include "lpclib.h"
short nfrom(
    short low,  /* low limit : {SHRT_MIN:SHRT_MAX} */
    short high) /* high limit : {low:SHRT_MAX} */
    {
    short nb = high - low + 1;  /* : {1:SHRT_MAX} */

    return rand1() % nb + low;
    }
```

Here we are grouping six functions into a little library, and providing a header lpclib.h for using these functions:

```
/* lpclib.h - header for library for "Learning to Program in C"
 */
void error(char s1[], char s2[]);
short rand1(void);
void srand1(short n);
short nfrom(short low, short high);
void remark(char s1[], char s2[]);
uint strscn(char s[], char c);
```

We needed the #include "lpclib.h" in nfrom.c because it calls rand1 and needs its prototype. It is not really necessary to #include "lpclib.h" inside rand1.c, but it would be more consistent to do so; the compiler can be sure that the function prototypes in lpclib.h agree with the function definitions.

Question [5-9] Suppose a program were to call

```
nfrom(1, 10)
```

and rand1() were to return 1003. What would nfrom return? _____

Question [5-10] Suppose a program were to call

```
nfrom(1, 6)
```

and rand1() were to return 3605. What would nfrom return? _____

Now for a main program to exercise these functions. Let the numbers 0 through 51 stand for the different playing cards in a deck. For example, 0 could stand for "Ace of Spades", 1 could stand for "Two of Spades", and so forth through Spades, Hearts, Diamonds, and Clubs. To shuffle a deck of 52 cards, we call nfrom once for each card, selecting the card randomly from the remaining cards. The program looks like this:

shuf52.c:

```
/* shuf52 - shuffle a deck of 52 cards and print result
 */
#include "local.h"
#include "lpclib.h"
#define NCARDS 52
void shuffl(short deck[]);
main()
    {
    short cards[NCARDS];      /* the deck : each {0:NCARDS-1} */
    short i;                  /* loop index : {0:NCARDS} */

    for (i = 0; i < NCARDS; ++i)
        cards[i] = i;
    shuffl(cards);
    for (i = 0; i < NCARDS; ++i)
        {
        printf("%2d ", cards[i]);
        if (i % 13 == 12)
            putchar('\n');
        }
    putchar('\n');
    exit(0);
    }
/* shuffl - permute the cards
 */
void shuffl(
    short deck[])            /* array of cards : each {0:NCARDS-1} */
    {
    short t;                 /* temporary for swap : {0:NCARDS-1} */
    short i;                 /* index for loop over cards : {0:NCARDS-1} */
    short j;                 /* index for swap : {0:NCARDS-1} */

    for (i = 0; i < NCARDS - 1; ++i)
        {
        j = nfrom(i, NCARDS - 1);
        t = deck[j], deck[j] = deck[i], deck[i] = t;
        }
    }
```

Here are some commands to compile and execute the program:

```
cc -c nfrom.c
cc -o shuf52 shuf52.c nfrom.o
shuf52
```
                                                                                (output)

```
 0 49 40 21 46 12 43 38 30 34  1 44 31
 3 10 27 20 35 32 25 36 28 47 33 18 23
16 39 24 13  7 19 42 15  5 45  8  2  6
41 22 17  9  4 50 14 48 37 26 11 51 29
```

It is often convenient to make an *object library* containing functions in object-code form. We could, using the UNIX "archiver" ar as an example, create a library to contain the object-files error.o, rand1.o, nfrom.o, remark.o, and strscn.o, like this:

```
ar c lpclib.a error.o rand1.o nfrom.o remark.o strscn.o
```

and we could then compile our shuf52.c program using this library:

```
cc -o shuf52 shuf52.c lpclib.a
```

If we wish to replace a function in a library, the command looks like this:

```
ar r lpclib.a nfrom.o
```

5.10 Initializing Arrays

Arrays in static storage, like static scalars, may be initialized on their declaration. The initialization takes place when the program is loaded. There are no machine instructions in the object program to do the initialization; the object file contains the actual data values for the array. Here is an example:

```
static short digits[10] = {0, 1, 2, 3, 4, 5, 6, 7, 8, 9};
```

The list of initializers must be enclosed in braces, and is separated by commas.

A shorthand is provided for initializers consisting of character values: The initializer may be written as a string of characters enclosed in double-quotes. Example:

```
static char msg[6] = "hello";
```

Remember, a character string always includes a '\0' null terminator at the end. Thus, the previous declaration is completely equivalent to this one:

```
static char msg[6] = {'h', 'e', 'l', 'l', 'o', '\0'};
```

But take notice: Standard C allows the array bound to exactly equal the number of non-null characters in the initializer string, as in

```
static char msg[5] = "hello"; /* valid in Standard C, no null terminator */
```

in which case the array is not null-terminated. (Some compilers will warn about this situation; we suggest you avoid using this special case.)

Aside from this special case, it is invalid syntax if the initializers exceed the number of elements.

If the array bound is greater than the number of initializers, the extra elements are initialized to zero. If no bound is given, the bound is taken to be the number of initializers. A final convenience: the last initializer is allowed to have a trailing comma.

Question [5-11] What are the initial values?

```
static char st[5] = "std";
```

```
static char s[2] = "ab";
```

```
static short a[5] = {1, 2, 3};
```

```
static short b[] = {1, 3, 5, 7,};
```

It is also permissible to initialize automatic arrays. The initializers must follow the same rules as for static arrays, but the initialization will be performed each time the function is entered.

Exercise 5-6. Write a program bingo.c that will randomly generate cards for the game of BINGO. The general format looks like this:

```
| B | I | N | G | O |
|___|___|___|___|___|
|   |   |   |   |   |
|___|___|___|___|___|
|   |   |   |   |   |
|___|___|___|___|___|
|   |   |X X|   |   |
|   |   |X X|   |   |
|___|___|___|___|___|
|   |   |   |   |   |
|___|___|___|___|___|
|   |   |   |   |   |
|___|___|___|___|___|
```

The B column contains non-duplicate numbers from 1 to 15; I, from 16 to 30; N, from 31 to 45; G, from 46 to 60; and O, from 61 to 75.

Exercise 5-7. Write a program `dice.c` that will roll two 6-sided dice ten thousand times and will tabulate how many times each result is obtained.

5.11 Two-dimensional Arrays

C language allows arrays of more than one dimension; we will describe here the two-dimensional form. These arrays are also known as *rectangular arrays*, because their contents form a rectangle:

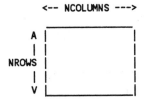

The following declaration creates space for a two-dimensional array of short integers:

```
short a[NROWS][NCOLUMNS];
```

The total storage space occupied by the array `a` is

```
NROWS x NCOLUMNS x sizeof(short)
```

which, in our Typical Environment, is

```
NROWS x NCOLUMNS x 2
```

The declaration for a two-dimensional array of characters is similar, except that you must remember the extra space for a null terminator if each row is to be treated as a character string:

```
    char s[NROWS][NCOLUMNS + 1];
```

The declaration can contain an initializer:

```
char sampler[35][61] =
    {
    "LOVELOVELOVELOVELOVELOVELOVELOVELOVELOVELOVELOVELOVELOVELOVE",
    "L                OVELOVELOVELOVELOVELOV        LOVELOVELOVE",
    "LOV        ELOVELOVELOVELOVELOV                    LOVELOVE",
    "LOVE        VELOVELOVELOVELOVEL                        VELOVE",
    "LOVE        VELOVELOVELOVELOVE            LOVEL      ELOVE",
    "LOVE        VELOVELOVELOVELOV          VELOVELO    LOVE",
    "LOVE        VELOVELOVELOVELOV          OVELOVELOV  LOVE",
    "LOVE        VELOVELOVELOVELOV          LOVELOVELOV LOVE",
    "LOVE        VELOVELOVELOVELOV          ELOVELOVELO LOVE",
    "LOVE        VELOVELOVELOVELOV          VELOVELOVEL LOVE",
    "LOVE        VELOVELOVELOVELOV          OVELOVELOVE LOVE",
    "LOVE        VELOVELOVELOVELOVEL V      LOVELOVELOV LOVE",
    "LOVE        VELOVELOVELOVELOVE  V      LOVELOVELO  LOVE",
    "LOVE        VELOVELOVELOVELOV   V      OVELOVEL    LOVE",
    "LOVE        VELOVELOVELOVEL     VE                 ELOVE",
    "L                           VELOV          LOVELOVE",
    "L                           VELOVELOV    LOVELOVELOVE",
    "L           VELOV                                        E",
    "L           VELOV                                        E",
    "LOVE        VELOVELOVELOV  VELOVELOVE      VELOVELOVELO   E",
    "LOVEL       ELOVELOVELO   OVELOVELOVE      VELOVELOVELOVE E",
    "LOVEL       ELOVELOVELO   OVELOVELOVE      VELOVELOVELOVEL E",
    "LOVELO      LOVELOVEL     LOVELOVELOVE     VELOVELOVELOVELO E",
    "LOVELO      LOVELOVEL     LOVELOVELOVE     VELOVELOVELOVELOVE",
    "LOVELOV     OVELOVE       ELOVELOVELOVE    VELOVEL VELOVELOVE",
    "LOVELOV     OVELOVE       ELOVELOVELOVE            VELOVELOVE",
    "LOVELOVE    VELOV         VELOVELOVELOVE   VELOVE  VELOVELOVE",
    "LOVELOVE    VELOV         VELOVELOVELOVE   VELOVEL VELOVELOVE",
    "LOVELOVEL   ELO           OVELOVELOVELOVE  VELOVELOVELOVELO E",
    "LOVELOVEL   ELO           OVELOVELOVELOVE  VELOVELOVELOVEL  E",
    "LOVELOVELO  L             LOVELOVELOVELO   VELOVELOVELOVE   E",
    "LOVELOVELO                LOVELOVELOVELOVE VELOVELOVELO    E",
    "LOVELOVELOV               ELOVELOVELOVE                    E",
    "LOVELOVELOV               ELOVELOVELOVE                    E",
    "LOVELOVELOVELOVELOVELOVELOVELOVELOVELOVELOVELOVELOVELOVELOVE"
    };
```

(Thanks to the artist Robert Indiana and the author David H. Ahl. Typing this initializer is truly a labor of love.)

We see that there are 35 rows in this array, each containing 60 data characters plus the null terminator that the compiler appends to each string.

The data is stored in *row-major order*, which means that each row forms an array of items in the memory. In C, each row is itself a one-dimensional array, and can be used in contexts where an array is allowed. For example, to print this array we could use this loop:

```
for (i = 0; i < 35; ++i)
    printf("%s\n", sampler[i]);
```

Each of the individual elements of a two-dimensional array is accessed using two subscripts like this

```
sampler[i][j]
```

The following program accepts an input string from the user, and substitutes each character of the string for a character of the sampler array, thus printing the sampler with the user's string:

```
prsam.c:
    /* prsam - print sampler
     */
    #include "local.h"
    #include "lpclib.h"
    #define NROWS 35
    #define NCOLUMNS 60
    main()
        {
        char sampler[NROWS][NCOLUMNS + 1] =
            {
            "LOVELOVE ... LOVELOVE",
                /* et cetera, with the rest of the array */
            };
        short i;            /* row index for sampler : {0:NROWS} */
        short j;            /* column index for sampler : {0:NCOLUMNS} */
        short len;          /* length of s : {1:BUFSIZ-1} */
        char s[BUFSIZ];     /* user's message : string */

        printf("Enter a string:");
        if ((len = getln(s, BUFSIZ)) == EOF)
            error("Bye!", "");
        printf("\n");
        s[--len] = '\0';
        if (NCOLUMNS < len)
            len = NCOLUMNS;
        for (i = 0; i < NROWS; ++i)
            {
            for (j = 0; j < NCOLUMNS; ++j)
                if (sampler[i][j] != ' ')
                    sampler[i][j] = s[j % len];
            printf("%s\n", sampler[i]);
            }
        exit(0);
        }
```

Exercise 5-8. Enter and test the prsam.c program. (This may be the only program in the book that does useful things for your younger relatives.)

In Section 5.7, we saw that C maintains a "stack" for functions, in the "dynamic" memory segment. If you wish to create your own stack for use by a program, you cannot make use of C language's own stack mechanism.

However, it is easy to create your own stacks using external static storage. You need two functions — one to do the pushing and one to do the popping — and a shared data structure.

Consider the puzzle called "Towers of Hanoi". There are three vertical pegs onto which are slid disks of varying sizes — five such disks, for example. One may move a disk onto another peg only if all the disks on that peg are larger than it is. Initially, all the disks are on peg number one:

The object is to move them to peg number three. Each stack of disks is like a programming "stack", as described above, since we can add or remove disks only on the top of each stack. We can represent the three pegs and the disks that are upon them by a two-dimensional array called pegs:

```
static short pegs[3][NDISKS] = {0};
```

This declaration makes use of the special property of C initializers that fills all uninitialized elements to zero; thus all the elements of pegs are initialized to zero. (Note that the puzzle may have any number of disks, specified by NDISKS, but must have 3 pegs — the unmodifiable constant appears as is.) We also need an array ndisks to keep track of the number of disks on each peg:

```
static short ndisks[3] = {0};
```

Making provision for "defensive programming", we will include tests for the validity of requested push and pop operations. We also provide a dumppg ("dump pegs") function to show the state of our pegs. The real work of "pushing" takes place in one powerful statement:

```
pegs[i][ndisks[i]++] = disk;
```

"The next available space on pegs[i]" is given by the element ndisks[i], and the ++ postfix increment causes this number to be incremented after use; thus it is ready for the next operation. The entire statement therefore "pushes" the new disk number into the appropriate space. The "popping" operation is similarly performed by one powerful statement:

```
return pegs[i][--ndisks[i]];
```

In this case, the "next available space" number — ndisks[i] — is decremented before use, to give us the subscript of the "most recently used space", while leaving the number ready for the next operation.

pegs.c:

```
/* pegs.c - three functions (push, pop, dumppg) for Towers of Hanoi
 */
#include "local.h"
#include "pegs.h"    /* for NDISKS, push, pop, dumppg */
static short pegs[3][NDISKS] = {0};
static short ndisks[3] = {0};
/* push - put disk onto peg
 */
void push(
    short i,     /* which peg : {0:2} */
    short disk) /* which disk : {0:NDISKS-1} */
    {
    assert(0 <= i && i <= 2);
    pegs[i][ndisks[i]++] = disk;
    }
/* pop - remove disk from peg
 */
short pop(
    short i)         /* which peg : {0:2} */
    {
    assert(0 <= i && i <= 2);
    assert(ndisks[i] >= 1);
    return (pegs[i][--ndisks[i]]);
    }
/* dumppg - print status of disks and pegs
 */
void dumppg(void)
    {
    short i;    /* index over pegs : {0:3} */
    short j;    /* index over disks : {0:NDISKS} */

    for (i = 0; i < 3; ++i)
        {
        for (j = 0; j < NDISKS; ++j)
            {
            if (j < ndisks[i])
                printf("%d", pegs[i][j]);
            else
                printf(" ");
            }
        printf("    ");
        }
    printf("\n");
    }
```

To go along with pegs.c we also provide a header pegs.h which declares the functions available in pegs.c and any necessary defined constants (such as NDISKS). In modern programming terms, a set of one or more files such as pegs.c is known as a *resource monitor*, or *package*. And an accompanying header such as pegs.h is the *public interface* for the package — it defines what the user is allowed to see about the package.

```
/* pegs.h - interface for pegs package
 */
#define NDISKS 5
void push(short i, short disk);
short pop(short i);
void dumppg(void);
```

In pegs.c we have introduced the use of assert. Look for example in the push function:

```
assert(0 <= i && i <= 2);
```

This simply computes the specified test and continues on if the test is *true* (non-zero). But if the test is *false* (zero), then assert generates a diagnostic message and terminates the program. It is a handy way for a package such as pegs.c to protect itself from being invoked with invalid arguments. The Standard header <assert.h> defines assert; this is automatically included by our "local.h". In Section 5.18 we will see how, once debugging is completed, all the occurrences of assert can be "turned off" so that they generate no code.

Exercise 5-9. Compile pegs.c to produce an object file pegs.o. Write a program tower.c which solves the Towers of Hanoi problem, for any specified number NDISKS. Compile tower.c separately from pegs.c and use the linker to combine them into an executable program. Hint: consider a recursive function

```
move(n, p0, p1)
```

which moves an entire pile of n disks from peg p0 to peg p1.

5.12 External Variables

External names are made linkable to any source file that references them; the linker arranges that all references to an external name will refer to the same location in storage. There are two kinds of external names: *external variables* and *external functions*.

The external variables all reside in the static storage (the data segment); automatic variables cannot be external.

External variables behave just like the external static variables that we saw in Section 5.9, except that they are linkable to all source files, not just the one in which they are declared.

The *definition* (or *"def"*, for brevity) of an external variable initializes it with an initial value. External definitions should be placed at the front of the source file that they appear in, before any functions. For example, a `char` array named `screen` could be given an external definition like this:

```
char screen[24][80] = {0};


/*
 * (now appear any functions in the file)
 */
```

This definition establishes the variable `screen`, initializes it to all zeroes, and makes it linkable to any function that references it.

A *reference declaration* (abbreviated *ref-declaration* or *"ref"*) of an external variable is a request to link with the storage that is created by its definition. A ref-declaration does not reserve any storage by itself; somewhere in one of the object files being linked together there must be a definition of the variable. A ref-declaration may appear either inside or outside a function, and it begins with the keyword `extern`, as in

```
void fn(void)
    {
    extern char screen[24][80];
```

Unlike a definition, an external ref-declaration does *not* contain an initializer. Programs are easier to maintain if all external ref-declarations are kept either inside functions or inside the public interfaces of packages.

We are deliberately showing no code examples of external variables. The techniques shown in the previous section eliminate all need that the introductory programmer might otherwise have for external variables. An excess of external variables has often been a feature of hard-to-maintain computer systems.

Turning now to external *functions*, we should point out that all the functions we have seen so far are, in fact, external. That is, their names are made linkable to the linker; there may be any number of ref-declarations, but there may be only one definition. The *definition* of a function is just the technical name for the text of the function itself — this is what *defines* the function. A *ref-declaration* for a function is like any other declaration — a "sandwich" of *type* and *name* — except that the keyword `extern` will be assumed if no storage class is given explicitly. Thus these two declarations are equivalent:

```
extern short pop(void);

short pop(void);
```

Both of them declare the name pop to have the type short(void) (i.e., function with no parameters that returns short) and to have the storage class extern.

What other storage class might a function have? Although we did not mention it in Section 5.9, a function may have the storage class static attached to its definition. If so, the function can be called only by other functions *in the same source file* — it becomes a "private resource" of the "package" that it belongs to. Whatever its storage class, a function is always located in the *text* segment, referring back to the classification shown in Section 5.7.

5.13 Register Storage Class

We say good-bye for the moment to the static variables and take another look at the automatic variables and the function parameters. These are the variables that come into being when their function is entered and disappear when it returns. These variables can be placed in the actual hardware registers of the computer by declaring them to have register storage class. You simply put the keyword register on their declarations, they are placed in registers, and the program runs faster.

It sounds so simple — what is the catch? Well, to begin with, each machine is limited in the number of registers available for such variables. Many C machines have only three such registers available, but the number varies. Secondly, only certain data types can be placed in registers: char, short, int, with their unsigned versions, and the *pointer* variables that we have seen as array parameters. Finally, programs may not take the *address* (&) of a register variable — for example, we cannot read into a register with scanf.

5.14 Scope, Linkage, and Duration

The *scope* of a name consists of all those parts of the file which can "see" the name. In other words, it consists of all those places where the use of the name would produce a valid reference. There are four varieties of scope:

1. *File scope:* For names declared *outside* a function, the scope is the rest of the file — from the end of the declaration to the end of the file. If such declarations are placed at the front of the file, as we have suggested, this allows all the functions in the file to see the name.

2. *Block scope:* For names declared *inside a function*, the scope is the rest of the block — from the declaration to the end of the block. This limited scope of local variables means that a programmer does not need to worry about inadvertently using a name that has been used inside some other function.

3. *Prototype scope:* For dummy names declared inside a prototype — such as x in

    ```
    double sqrt(double x);
    ```

    the scope extends only to the end of the prototype. In other words, the name disappears outside the prototype.

4. *Function scope:* Labels are visible anywhere inside the same function. (Good code contains very few labels anyway, so this is almost irrelevant.)

    The *linkage* of a name determines whether different declarations of the name will refer to the same thing or not. Automatic, and internal static, variables can have only one declaration; they have *no linkage*. External static variables will be linkable only within their source file; they have *internal linkage*. Non-static ("global") external variables will be published to the linker and linked together across source files; they have *external linkage*. For an external-linkage variable to be linkable in a source file other than the one containing its definition, that source file must contain an extern declaration for the variable.

    The names of functions have external linkage by default. It is therefore not necessary to add the keyword extern to function declarations.

    These rules explain all the intricacies of variable scope and linkage, but an example is still useful. Here are two source files containing three functions and declaring six variables. The scope of each variable is indicated at the left of each line; if a variable name appears on a line, it means that the line is in the scope of that variable. The two scopes for a refer to the same storage, because a has external linkage.

Scope
```
        x.c:
            #include "local.h"
            short a = 2;
a           static short b = 3;
ab          main()
ab              {
ab              short c = a + b;
abc
abc             xsub(c);
abc             }
ab          xsub(
ab              short d)
ab d            {
ab d            short e = 7 * d;
ab de
ab de           ysub(e);
ab de           }


        ysub.c:
            #include "local.h"
            ysub(
                short f)
    f           {
    f           extern short a;
a   f
a   f           printf("%d\n", a + f);
a   f           }
```

Question [5-12] What does the program x print?

5.15 Summary of Initialization

We have seen that there are two categories of data storage: "dynamic" storage for automatic, parameter, and register variables; and "static" storage for internal static, external static, and external variables. We have also seen two categories of variables: scalars and arrays.

To begin with, parameters can never have initializers. This leaves us with four rules for initialization of variables:

A.   *Internal static, external static, external:*

A.1   *Scalars:* May be initialized to constants, such as

```
static short a = 10;
```

A.2   *Arrays:* May be initialized to a list of constants (if needed, the compiler pads with zeroes):

```
static short ar[100] = {0};
static char msg[] = "help!";
```

B.   *Automatic and register:*

B.1   *Scalars:* May be initialized to expressions, such as

```
short a = 10;
register short b = a + 1;
```

B.2   *Arrays:* May be initialized, following the same rules as for static arrays.

Question [5-13] In this incorrect sample program, which lines have invalid initializers?

```
noinit.c:
    /* noinit - some invalid initializers
     */
    #include "local.h"
    short a = 0;
    short b = a + 1;
    short c[5] = {4, 3, 2, 1};
    main()
        {
        short d = a + 2;
        short e[3] = {1, 2, 3};
        static short f = d + 1;
        static short g[2] = {4, 5, 6};

        printf("initializers\n");
        }
```

5.16 Empty Brackets: Three Cases

There are three cases in which C allows the abbreviation of empty brackets on an array name, such as a[]. Unfortunately for the learner, this abbreviation means three completely different things in the three cases.

(1) When empty brackets appear on the declaration of a function parameter, they mean that the parameter contains the *address* of the initial element of the array which is passed to the function. (Indeed, C behaves the same way even if you do put a number inside the brackets; the number is just disregarded.) For example,

```
void fn(
    short a[])
```

says that the parameter a contains the address of the initial element of an array of short integers.

(2) When empty brackets appear with an array initializer, they mean "take the array bound from the number of initializers". Thus in this example

```
short a[] = {012, 034, 056};
```

the size of array a is specified as three, by the compiler's counting the initializers.

(3) When empty brackets appear on an extern ref-declaration, they mean "the array bound will be specified by the *definition* of the array (which appears elsewhere)". For example,

```
extern char msg[];
```

says that the size of msg will be specified by its definition, somewhere else.

There can never be any confusion about which rule is applicable to a specific instance of empty brackets because parameters can never be initialized and cannot be external variables, and ref-declarations can never have initializers. (Only *definitions* have initializers.)

These three cases are worth memorizing.

5.17 Macros with Parameters

The C preprocessor provides for macro (i.e., #define) definitions with parameters. For example, in local.h we find these lines:

```
#define ABS(x)      (((x) < 0) ? -(x) : (x))
#define MAX(x, y)   (((x) < (y)) ? (y) : (x))
#define MIN(x, y)   (((x) < (y)) ? (x) : (y))
```

When a program has read these definitions, a line such as

```
len = MIN(len, 10);
```

will be rewritten by the preprocessor into

```
len = (((len) < (10)) ? (len) : (10));
```

This is known as "in-line replacement", because MIN has produced code directly in the program that invokes it — there is no function call-and-return overhead. Thus macros with parameters, or (as we shall refer to them) *macro functions*, can sometimes be used effectively to make a program run faster.

Macro functions have the advantage of being *generic* — they can accept data of any type. For example, ABS can be applied to any type of numeric data, integer or floating-point.

Macro functions, however, have an important restriction on their use: their arguments should, in general, not contain any side effects. If we were to write ABS(++n) the generated code would look like

```
(((++n) < 0) ? -(++n) : (++n))
```

thus incrementing n twice.

Macro functions are typically trickier to write correctly, relative to ordinary functions. In particular, each occurrence of a parameter in the replacement text needs to be parenthesized, as does the entire replacement text. If we wrote the following incorrect version of ABS,

```
#define ABS(x) x < 0 ? -x : x
```

then the expansion of

```
ABS(n + 1) + m
```

would be

```
n + 1 ? - n + 1 : n + 1 + m
```

where the missing parentheses are sorely needed.

As a general rule, you should get your program working correctly first without defining any macro functions. Then introduce them later, if you need the speed advantage.

5.18 Conditional Compilation

The preprocessor can provide for parts of a program to be compiled *conditionally*. For example, our local.h header contains the lines

```
#ifndef LOCAL_H
#define LOCAL_H
  ...
#endif  /* LOCAL_H */
```

This says that if the symbol LOCAL_H has *not* already been #define'd, then process all the lines up to the #endif line. If, on the other hand, the symbol already has been #define'd (presumably by previous inclusion of local.h), the following lines should be skipped.

Another form of conditional compilation uses #ifdef:

```
#ifdef TRYMAIN
  ...
#endif /* TRYMAIN */
```

will compile the enclosed statements only if the symbol TRYMAIN *has* been #define'd. This provides a useful technique for attaching a simple test driver to each separately-compilable source file. Consider this packaging of our factl factorial function:

```
factl.c:
    /* factl - return n! (n factorial)
     */
    #include "local.h"
    ulong factl(
        ulong n)     /* : {0:12} for portability */
        {
        if (n <= 1)
            return (1);
        else
            return (n * factl(n - 1));
        }
    #ifdef TRYMAIN
    main()
        {
        assert(factl(0) == 1);
        assert(factl(3) == 6);
        assert(factl(12) == 479001600);
        exit(0);
        }
    #endif /* TRYMAIN */
```

In UNIX environments, we can cause the symbol TRYMAIN to be #define'd
by adding the flag -DTRYMAIN to our compile command:

```
cc -o factl.x -DTRYMAIN factl.c
```

This will compile the main function as well as factl, producing an executable test program, factl.x. If factl.x runs successfully, it prints nothing
and returns a successful-return code; if it fails, it prints a message and
returns a failure code. This allows it to be used in an automated test
procedure.

   The assert capability is provided by a macro function in the Standard header <assert.h>. In that header, the actual definition of assert is
conditional upon the symbol NDEBUG, something like this:

```
#ifdef NDEBUG
#define assert(x)   /* nothing at all */
#else
#define assert(x)   /* ... complicated definition ... */
#endif
```

The net result of this is that, during an ordinary compilation such as

```
cc -c pegs.c
```

the assert macro produces the full expansion; but if we compile with the
flag -DNDEBUG ("define NDEBUG") —

```
cc -c -DNDEBUG pegs.c
```

— then all the occurrences of assert are made to produce no code whatever, saving time and space in the final production version of the program.

Of course, there would be no purpose in "turning off" the assert's in the factl.c test driver; the debugging code is all that we want. Once the factl.c program has been successfully tested, we should re-compile without the -DTRYMAIN flag, to produce an ordinary object file for the factl function.

Other varieties of #if are available:

```
#if  constant-expression
```

will evaluate the given constant expression and compile the following lines only if it is *true*.

With all varieties of #if, the line #else may appear on a later line; in this case, the lines following #else will be compiled only if the #if, #ifdef, or #ifndef line evaluated *false*.

In Standard C, the construct

```
#if defined(NAME)
```

is equivalent to

```
#ifdef NAME
```

Standard C also has the directive #elif ("else if"), so a multiple-choice is easy to write:

```
#if    defined(TYPE1)
    /* ... */
#elif defined(TYPE2)
    /* ... */
#elif defined(TYPE3)
    /* ... */
#else
    /* ... */
#endif
```

Exercise 5-10. For each header that you have created (e.g., lpclib.h and pegs.h), enclose the header in a "#ifndef ... #endif" wrapper.

CHAPTER 6: SOFTWARE DEVELOPMENT

6.1 The Software Development Life Cycle

We now step back from the learning of C language to consider the overall process by which software comes into being. Each of our programming exercises has already been specified in enough detail that the intended program is clearly defined. This is not so in the typical real application. The coding of a program is only a small fraction of the total expense of software. The overall sequence of activities from birth to death of a program is known as the *software development life cycle*, and we now turn our attention to this sequence.

Weighty volumes have been written about this life cycle, and it is not our intention to supersede them. We wish merely to outline the process so that the beginner may have some appreciation of it. Here is our outline of the software development life cycle:

1. *Analysis:* getting enough information about the intended function of the software so that expected benefits can be compared with expected costs.

2. *Design:* outlining the approach to the problem in sufficient detail to verify that the software can achieve the expected benefits and can be produced within the expected costs.

3. *Implementation:* converting the design into working software.

4.   *Maintenance:* (after delivery) enhancing the software's function and repairing previously undetected errors.

Unfortunately for pedagogic simplicity, these phases do not always follow one another so neatly as the outline implies. Often, information gained about the problem in one phase requires going back to an earlier phase and revising its product. This reality is known as the *iterative* approach to development. After we describe the work done in each phase we will discuss some approaches to iterative development. First, a look at each phase.

6.2 Analysis

The goal of analysis is to determine what function the software is to perform and to evaluate the economic viability of proceeding further.

In our discussion, we will assume that one individual is doing all the steps in the life cycle, an assumption that is true only in the smallest projects or cottage industries. As this individual proceeds through the phases, he or she will wear various "hats"; in this phase, the role is known as the *analyst* or *systems analyst*.

Some other individual plays the role of *user* or *system user* — the person who will ultimately make use of the software.

The first step in analysis is very important: establishing a good working relationship with the user. A cheerful, confident, empathetic analyst will succeed where a sullen, hesitant, self-centered person would fail. Studies have shown the the difficulty of the interface between the analyst and the user is *four times* more important in software productivity than *any* other single factor (Walston and Felix [1977]).

The analyst needs to get information from the user about what is wanted. As an analyst, you should be aware that the user will often have a *premature packaging* of the system, often based on a previous generation of technical knowledge. The important motto here is *first what, then how*. This means, first determine what functions the software is supposed to perform (analysis), then determine how those functions will be implemented (design, implementation).

It may be important to *broaden the space of alternatives*. The user may start with only one specific idea, possibly including premature packaging. One strategy is to present a *menu of alternatives:* do not present just one approach to the problem, but rather a set of alternative approaches, each with its own benefits and costs.

Clarity of communication between analyst and user is important. Often the user's verbal formulations mean different things to user and analyst. One means of sharpening the communication is to present *specific examples*, small cases worked out in complete detail. There is almost always a small paper-and-pencil model that can be created to make the system tangible. Detailed pictures of sample inputs and outputs are necessary; sometimes similar small pictures are also needed for internal data.

The final product of the analysis phase is a *specification* (or *spec*) which is tangible, concise, useful documentation.

The spec should be the first in a series of documents which are useful in understanding what the software does. One useful strategy here is to cast the spec into the form of a *user manual*, which can serve as the rough outline for the eventual manual which will be delivered with the software. In addition, it may be useful to produce a rough draft of *training materials* as part of the spec — it is often during the process of training users that the problems of the software first become known. Since you are familiar by now with the library manual for your C compiler, we will use that format in our discussions of specifications.

In this chapter, we will follow the development of a real program through all the phases of the life cycle. We have chosen a project that was a real-world undertaking for us recently — a portable Blackjack program that could be used no matter which operating system the office was using at the time. The "menu of alternatives" can be described like this:

1. *Buy an existing package.* Estimated cost: $200 for video-game hardware using existing TV set. "Too expensive", says the user, "and it ties up my TV".

2. *Port existing software from one operating system.* "Cannot even present it to the user because of licensing restrictions", says the analyst, "and besides, it would not serve the purposes of a programming book!"

3. *Copy the design of existing software and re-program:* Estimated cost: 1 day design, 3 days programming. "Sounds good", says the user, "but the other program does not play Atlantic City rules".

4. *Use existing software as a guideline and design from scratch:* Estimated cost: 2 days design, 3 days programming. "That's my choice", says the user.

One advantage in programming something with an existing design or specification is that the uncertainties of analysis are drastically reduced. To be specific about this program, the structure of the game is given almost entirely by the rules of the game. Herewith, the rules:

The object of this card game is to have the total point value of the cards dealt to you exceed the point value of the Dealer's hand without going over 21. If you draw cards that total more than 21, your hand is "busted" and you automatically lose. If your first *two* cards total 21, you have a Blackjack that automatically wins. If, however, both you and the Dealer have a Blackjack, it is a standoff.

The dealer starts the game by dealing two cards face up to each Player. The Dealer takes one card face up. The Dealer's second card is dealt face down and placed underneath the first card. Each card assumes the value of the card shown. Kings, Queens, and Jacks count as 10. The Ace counts either as 1 or 11, whichever you choose. If you feel satisfied with your hand after receiving the first two cards, you "stand" and do not draw additional cards. If you feel you need additional cards to beat the Dealer, you gesture one at a time for additional cards (called "hits") until you decide to stand. A Dealer must draw on any point total of 16 or less and must stand on any point total of 17 or more. If a Dealer busts, all Players win who have not busted. Otherwise, the Dealer pays all hands that exceed the Dealer's point total, takes all bets that are less and leaves ("pushes") all bets that equal the Dealer's point total. A Dealer's Blackjack (two-card point total of 21) beats a Player's three-card point total of 21. All winning bets are paid two-to-one, except a winning Blackjack which is paid 3 to 2.

SPLITTING PAIRS: If your first two cards are a pair with the same numerical value, you may split them into two hands provided that the bet on the second hand equals the original bet. Once the hands are split and the wager placed, you play out the first hand until satisfied. Only after the first hand is complete may you act on the second hand. A split hand may not be split again if another pair of cards with the same identical value is formed. Also, if the split pair are Aces, you are limited to a one card draw on each hand. In those instances where the Dealer subsequently gets a Blackjack, you lose the money wagered on the first bet only.

DOUBLING DOWN: After receiving the first two cards, you may elect to wager an additional amount not to exceed the value of the original bet. In any Double Down, you draw only one additional card. If the Dealer gets a Blackjack, the Dealer collects only the amount of the original wager.

INSURANCE: If the Dealer's first card is an Ace, you may elect to take insurance by placing a bet on the insurance line not greater than one-half of the original bet. The insurance bet is a wager that the Dealer will get a Blackjack with his second card. In other words, you are betting the Dealer will draw a 10, Jack, Queen, or King. Insurance pays 2 to 1 if the Dealer draws a Blackjack, but loses in all other instances.

SHUFFLING: The cards are dealt from a "shoe" containing four full decks. A yellow "shuffle" card is inserted towards the rear of the shoe, and when the shuffle card is reached, the cards are shuffled at the end of the current hand.

Further discussion produces a first draft of a manual page, which completes the analysis phase.

bj   USER MANUAL   bj

NAME
bj - play Blackjack

SYNOPSIS
bj

DESCRIPTION
bj deals Blackjack for one player, loosely based on Atlantic City rules. The bet is specified by the player on each hand (since variable betting is essential to winning at Blackjack).

Player Blackjack (21 in two cards) wins 3-for-2, except that player and dealer both Blackjack is a "push" (no money exchanged). All other bets win even money.

If dealer shows Ace, player may take "Insurance". If dealer subsequently shows Blackjack, player wins even money, otherwise loses.

If player's first two cards are equal value, player may "Split Pair" into two hands, placing a bet on the second hand that is equal to the original bet. If the original pair were Aces, not further hits can be taken. Otherwise, the player takes hits on the first hand until satisfied (or "busted") and then may take hits on the second hand. If the dealer subsequently wins with Blackjack, only the original bet is lost.

After receiving the first two cards, player may "double down", wagering an additional amount equal to the first bet. One hit is given at this time, and no more may be taken. (Our simplification: split pairs cannot double-down.)

- Player "busted" (over 21) loses.
- Dealer Blackjack beats anything but Blackjack.
- Dealer "busted" wins for every hand not busted.

Otherwise, dealer pays all hands exceeding dealer total, takes all bets below dealer's total, and "pushes" all ties.

Dealer will announce each shuffle. The machine deals and keeps the score.

The game can be terminated by typing the EOF character or the INTERRUPT character (both of which vary with operating system).

6.3 Design

In the context of the software development life cycle, there are three aspects of software design: *logic design* (which we discussed in Section 4.9), *data design* (choosing the right data representations), and *packaging design* (selecting the overall package to be delivered). These three design processes proceed in parallel, or more accurately, in an iterative manner.

On a larger project, an extra phase for *structural design* may be needed (Yourdon and Constantine [1978]). In such a case, the type of design we are describing here is known as *detail design*. For the small problems that we are tackling now, no such distinction is needed.

Three important considerations will be addressed during the design process: *error-handling* (making sure the program behaves correctly in the face of errors outside of itself), *portability* (making sure that the program can be run in an appropriate variety of environments), and *documentation* (keeping a useful written record of what was produced).

The overall task of design is to refine the problem into pieces, each one of which is something that you are sure the programmer can implement.

The general strategy is known as *top-down design*, or *design by refinement*. We start with the specification — a general idea of what is needed — and proceed to refine the software into ever-smaller pieces. As was the case with our simple design examples in Section 4.9, our first step is to choose the basic repetition. We can consider a session to be a series of shuffles, a series of hands, or a series of transactions (bet, take card, etc.). Since a player may leave at the end of any hand, a "shuffle" is too big a unit. And a "transaction" is too small a unit — the structure of the game is lost. We will thus consider the game to be a repetition of hands, or

   *hand**

Setting aside for a moment the complications of split pairs, shuffling, doubling down, and insurance, each hand is a sequence of events:

   *deal hit** *hit-dealer** *outcome*

or in words, this sequence: dealing the cards, a repetition of hits, a repetition of hits for the dealer, and an outcome. Taking the bet from the player can be considered part of the major loop control — no bet, no game! (The repetition of hits for dealer could repeat *zero* times, because if dealer has 17 or more, or if all player hands are busted, the dealer takes no hits.) Thus, the whole game has the syntax

{*deal hit* hit-dealer* outcome*}*

or as a syntax tree,

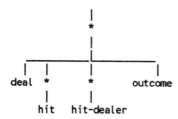

The program outline so far looks like this:

for each hand
    deal the cards
    while (player can hit and player asks for hits)
        hit player
    while (dealer can hit)
        hit dealer
    score the outcome

Shuffling is easy to add to this structure: as the first step of each hand before dealing, shuffling takes place if the shuffle point has been reached. Insurance is easy to add: after the deal, insurance bets are taken if the dealer shows an Ace. Adding shuffling and insurance to our syntax, the syntax now reads

{[*shuffle*] *deal* [*insur*] *hit* hit-dealer* outcome*}*

or as a tree,

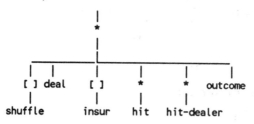

Question [6-1] Write the program outline of this revised syntax.

We look next at "doubling down". After insurance, our first query to the player must allow for more alternatives than simply "yes" or "no" to the first hit; it must allow for him to ask to double down. We will add a *query* just after the optional insurance.

Splitting pairs adds a loop around the taking of hits; two hands are played separately if player asks to split pairs. The syntax thus becomes:

{[*shuffle*] *deal* [*insur*] *query* {*hit**}* *hit-dealer** *outcome*}*

or as a tree,

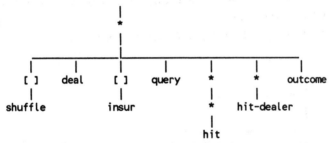

Our final program outline looks like this:

```
for each hand
    if (deck is low on cards)
        shuffle cards
    deal the cards
    if (dealer shows Ace)
        offer insurance
    query — split pair, double down?
    for each hand of player
        while (player can hit and asks for hit)
            hit player
    while (dealer can hit)
        hit dealer
    score the outcome
```

Question [6-2] Using this syntactic approach, it is fairly easy to modify the design to accommodate multiple players. Do so.

Exercise 6-1. Use your modified design to program bj for multiple players.

We now turn to the question of *error-handling*. There are several general strategies for handling errors:

1. *Ignore errors.* Simply proceed as if no error had happened. This strategy can only be used when errors do not affect the integrity of the program or its results.

2. *Complain about the error and quit.* This strategy can be used only in an interactive environment where the user is available on-line to re-enter the command.

3. *Complain and prompt for correct values.* This strategy also assumes an interactive user, but is more "friendly" in that the program does not exit.

4. *Change the erroneous values to acceptable values, and proceed.* An error message may also be produced.

In our bj program, we can assume an interactive user as the almost universal environment, so method 3 will be our choice in general.

Our next concern is *portability*. In this problem, we could lose portability if we succumbed to the temptation to use "bells and whistles" (fancy features of marginal usefulness) such as reverse-video or cursor-control characters. If we stick to simple line-by-line printing of ordinary characters we can maximize the range of target environments.

With regard to *documentation,* there are many formats to choose from. The ones that we will use are useful for a wide variety of problems:

1. *Manual pages* for each separately-callable function, or package of functions. These give the information necessary for a programmer to make use of the functions.

2. *Internals-manual pages* for each function or package. These give the information that a maintenance programmer would need to understand and modify the code. A program outline (pseudo-code) should be given for the high-level functions.

After the design of the main program flow, we look for the capabilities that will be required at the next level — the "vice-president" functions of our program tree. Wherever possible, we will collect them into "packages", as described in Section 5.11. We prefer for the main program not to concern itself with the implementation details of the data.

Some details must nonetheless be attended to. We will at various times refer to the Dealer, or Player's first hand, or Player's second hand. Our solution will be no less general if we simply assign numbers to the different hands:

```
0   dealer
1   player's first hand
2   player's second hand
```

Within a hand, the cards must also be numbered. We will follow zero-origin conventions by starting the numbers with 0.

We also have a basic question to answer regarding data type. "Cash" is of the essence in this problem, but should it be recorded in double, long, or short data? To be sure, double is the only convenient way to handle 3-for-2 splits of $1 bets, but our audience may be forgiving if we round everything to even dollars — particularly if we make the minimum bet $2. And short may run faster on small processors, but when a user can play $1000 as cheaply as $2, the action can exceed $32,767 very quickly. Our choice is to defer the question by defining our own data type, CASH, which we will define as long, but you can change it to another type if you desire. We must also be sure to #define two strings CASHIN and CASHOUT with the formats for scanf and printf.

A first pass through the pseudo-code suggests this set of functions:

```
bool deklow(void);      /* is deck low on cards */
void shuffl(void);      /* shuffle cards */
void deal(void);        /* deal the cards */
short val(int h, int n);  /* tell value of hand h, card n */
bool takes(char s[]);   /* prompt message s, return YES or NO */
short query(void);      /* query -- split pair, double down? */
bool hit(int h);        /* hit hand h, return "can hit again?" */
CASH outcom(/*...*/);   /* score the outcome, return net result */
```

In grouping these functions into packages, we consider the information to which they need access. Some of them are concerned with the deck of cards, some of them with the hands of the dealer and player, and some with the terminal interaction. We thus have our first draft for the packages. The "deck package", deck.c:

```
bool deklow(void);      /* is deck low on cards */
void shuffl(void);      /* shuffle cards */
```

The "hand package", hand.c:

```
void deal(void);        /* deal the cards */
short val(int h, int n);  /* tell value of hand h, card n */
bool hit(int h);        /* hit hand h, return "can hit again?" */
CASH outcom(/*...*/);   /* score the outcome, return net result */
```

And the "terminal package", terminal.c:

```
bool takes(char s[]);   /* prompt message s, return YES or NO */
short query(void);      /* query -- split pair, double down? */
```

One final packaging observation: if you are working on a system that has directories, it will be useful to collect all files relating to bj into a directory devoted to that purpose. On systems like UNIX, the name of a file in that directory — bj.c, for example — would look like bj/bj.c.

With these first-level interfaces determined, we are ready for another draft of the top-level outline; it appears here in the form of a question.

Question [6-3] Write a more detailed outline for the main program, bj.c. Note any new functions that you discover in the process, and note all data that the top-level program needs to administer. Hand-simulate some simple cases for each function to determine if it has the information it needs. Do not include any miscellaneous printf calls that may be needed, but consider whether new functions are needed for printing results.

After this re-draft, we discover that we need to revise our package definitions: To the "deck package", deck.c, we add

```
void opndek(void);        /* initialize the deck */
```

To the "hand package", hand.c, we add

```
bool allbst(void);        /* are all player's hands busted */
short score(int h);       /* tell point value of hand */
short split(void);        /* split the player's pair if allowed */
```

Now we want to iterate on the design once more, to determine other functions that may be needed, as one package may need hitherto undiscovered functions within another package. The outcom function, for example, still needs a determination of its interface. It will need to know the scores of the various hands, of course, but that information is available directly from the hand package. In addition to the numerical scores, it needs to know if each hand is a "natural" Blackjack, for which we add another function to the hand package:

```
bool isbj(int h);         /* is hand a "natural" 2-card blackjack? */
```

It also needs to know the amount of the bet, whether player took insurance or doubled down, and the number of hands in play, all of which is known by the main function. Its interface thus looks like this:

```
CASH outcom(CASH bet, int tophand, bool isinsur, bool isdbl);
```

No further changes to the interfaces are needed. This set of notes defining each of our "packages" will serve as the rough draft for the manual page for each package. Now we are ready for implementation.

6.4 Implementation: Writing the Programs

Since we have already completed an analysis and a design for our problem, we are now left with the tasks that belong strictly to the implementation phase. These are the issues we will deal with:

1. Translation into code: This should be easy, given a good design.

2. Efficiency of execution time and space: Wherever possible without compromising a clean design, we want the program to be as fast and as small as possible.

3. Desk-checking (hand-simulation): details that were previously overlooked can show up at this stage.

4. Editing the program (using correct layout from the start): Do not rely on automatic formatters or "beautifiers".

5.   Creating test cases: some rules for thorough but economical testing.

6.   Documenting: leaving an understandable record of what was done.

7.   Packaging: converting a program into a product.

8.   Demonstration and acceptance test: clearly showing the user what was accomplished.

9.   Delivery and celebration: satisfaction in a job well done.

In this section, we will discuss the first step; the other steps will wait for the following section.

(1) Translation into code. Often, while training programmers to write readable code, we have remarked that the examples that programmers see in programming textbooks are vastly undercommented, since the *book text* surrounding the programs is, in fact, one large set of comments. We depart from the practice here, in an attempt to give a realistic example of how a program like this might be documented in practice. Our preference is for documentation in the separate *internals-manual pages* mentioned in Section 6.1, and the description of the bj program will be given in this form. Thus, the remainder of this discussion on "Translation into Code" will be presented in the form of internals-manual pages to give information useful to the maintainer. The listings of the programs themselves are given along with the appropriate manual page.

Pretend, then, that your first working assignment as a maintainer of already-written C programs is to understand this program that has just been presented to you. Sit back, relax, and enjoy.

Internals manual for bj.h

The header bj.h is the "project-wide standard header" for all parts of the bj project. Each component of bj will begin with

    #include "bj.h"

and will receive all the declarations and definitions that are used throughout the bj project. Besides including bj.h, each component will also include its own interface header and the interface headers of any other sub-project components that it makes use of.

The CASH type is defined here — long, in this implementation. The defined constants CASHIN and CASHOUT specify how it should be read by scanf and written by printf.

The constant DEALER is defined as 0, and its value cannot be altered. The player's hands appear herein by the actual values 1 and 2.

Symbolic constants are provided for the various requests of the player — "no reply", "double down", "split pair", "insurance", "hit".

MSGLIM (set here to 5) controls printout of messages. When a set of messages are to be printed, if they have all been printed MSGLIM times already, they are then printed in a highly abbreviated format.

```
 1 /* bj.h - header for blackjack
 2  */
 3 #ifndef BJ_H
 4 #define BJ_H
 5
 6 #include "local.h"
 7 #include "lpclib.h"
 8
 9 #define CASH long          /* currency : dollars */
10 #define CASHIN "%ld"       /* input format for CASH data */
11 #define CASHOUT "%ld"      /* output format for CASH data */
12
13 #define DEALER 0           /* which hand is dealer; not modifiable */
14 #define NONE 0             /* no reply */
15 #define DBLDN 1            /* reply: double down */
16 #define SPLIT 2            /* reply: split pair */
17 #define INSUR 3            /* takes: insurance */
18 #define HIT   4            /* takes: hit */
19 #define MSGLIM 5           /* when to start abbreviating in query */
20 #endif /* BJ_H */
```

Internals manual for bj.c

The program outline for `bj.c` is as follows:

> *for each hand*
>   *if (deck is low on cards)*
>   *shuffle cards*
>   *deal the cards*
>   *if (dealer shows Ace)*
>   *offer insurance*
>   *query — split pair, double down, first hit?*
>   *for each hand of player*
>   *while (player can hit and asks for hit)*
>   *hit player*
>   *while (dealer can hit)*
>   *hit dealer*
>   *score the outcome*

The main loop continues until a bet of zero dollars is received from `get-bet`. `query` combines the query for "hit", "split", and "double down", because the repetitive prompting for separate responses can become tiresome. The main program takes an appropriate action to each response.

`getbet` returns 0 on `EOF`; if `EOF` is received at any other time during the hand, the game ends abruptly by error exits in the `takes` and `query` functions.

bj.c:

```
 1 /* bj - blackjack
 2  *       Permission is hereby granted to reproduce and use bj
 3  */
 4 #include "bj.h"
 5 #include "deck.h"
 6 #include "hand.h"
 7 #include "terminal.h"
 8 main()
 9    {
10    CASH action;    /* how much money has crossed the table */
11    CASH bet;       /* amount of player's current bet per hand */
12    CASH result;    /* net result of this hand, plus or minus */
13    CASH standing;  /* how much has player won or lost */
14    bool canhit;    /* can player's hand take hit? */
15    bool isdbl;     /* did player take DBLDN? */
16    bool isinsur;   /* did player take insurance? */
17    short hand;     /* current hand number : {1:2} */
18    short reply;    /* player's reply : {NONE, DBLDN, SPLIT} */
19    short tophand;  /* how many hands is player playing : {1:2} */
20
21    printf("Copyright (c) Plum Hall Inc, 1989\n");
22    /* permission to copy and modify is granted, provided that
23     * this printout and comment remain intact
24     */
25    printf("\nWelcome to the Blackjack table\n");
26    action = standing = 0;
27    opndek();
28    while ((bet = getbet()) != 0)
29       {
30       tophand = 1;
31       isinsur = isdbl = NO;
32       if (deklow())
33          shuffl();
34       deal();
35       if (val(DEALER, 0) == 11)
36          isinsur = takes("i");
37       reply = query();
38       if (reply == SPLIT)
39          tophand = split();
40       else if (reply == DBLDN)
41          {
42          hit(1);
43          printf("\n");
44          isdbl = YES;
45          bet *= 2;
46          }
47
48
49
50
```

Internals manual for bj.c (continued)

The loop over player hands is actually traversed only once unless the player has split. If he has split, a message announces which hand is in play.

The determination of canhit is a somewhat complicated but straightforward consequence of the rules. If player doubled down, his hand has already been hit once and player can receive no further hits. If player split Aces, no hits are allowed. Hit will tell whether further hits are allowed.

The "Bust" message is printed immediately instead of waiting for the outcome because it must be made clear to player that first hand has busted before proceeding to second hand. All other outcome messages are printed by outcom.

To achieve consistency in formatting of messages, the convention throughout is that each function that prints a message will ensure that it is terminated with a newline. show and hit functions are an exception to this convention, so that the dealer's hand can be printed all on one line.

After all hands are completed, outcom prints a description of the outcome and returns the net CASH outcome to the main program. The action and standing are printed after each hand.

bj.c:
```
 51            for (hand = 1; hand <= tophand; ++hand)
 52                {
 53                if (tophand == 2)
 54                    printf("Hand %d:\n", hand);
 55                canhit = !isdbl;
 56                canhit &= !isbj(1);
 57                canhit &= (reply != SPLIT || val(1, 0) != 11);
 58                while (canhit && takes("h"))
 59                    {
 60                    canhit = hit(hand);
 61                    printf("\n");
 62                    }
 63                if (score(hand) > 21)
 64                    printf("Bust\n");
 65                }
 66            printf("Dealer has ");
 67            show(DEALER, 0);
 68            printf(" + ");
 69            show(DEALER, 1);
 70            if (!allbst())
 71                while (score(DEALER) < 17)
 72                    hit(DEALER);
 73            printf(" = %d\n", score(DEALER));
 74            result = outcom(bet, tophand, isinsur, isdbl);
 75            action += ABS(result);
 76            standing += result;
 77            printf("action = ");
 78            printf(CASHOUT, action);
 79            printf(" standing = ");
 80            printf(CASHOUT, standing);
 81            printf("\n");
 82            }
 83        printf("\nThanks for the game.\n");
 84        exit(0);
 85        }
```

Internals manual for deck

deklow returns YES if the deck has reached the point for shuffling, otherwise returns NO.

opndek initializes the deck. It calls the Standard Library function time to get some form of system time. This is only used to set the random seed to an unpredictable value, using my_srand. Then, opndek shuffles once, with the new seed now controlling which numbers the my_rand function will give to nfrom. Next, opndek calls the Standard Library function getenv("BJTEST") ("get environment BJTEST") and checks whether the returned pointer is pointing to the string "YES". If so, it sets the system_test flag, which will cause certain inputs to come from canned scripts instead of from randomly-chosen cards. How does the environment variable BJTEST get set? It depends upon the system. On MS-DOS systems, the (testing) user would enter something like SET BJTEST=YES. On UNIX systems, the user would enter something like

```
$  BJTEST=YES  bj
```

shuffl shuffles the cards and prints the message "Shuffle".

These functions make no interpretation of the cards in the deck; any scheme of assigning short integers to cards will work equally well with these functions. Thus, they could deal Bridge, Pinochle, or Blackjack equally well.

The size of the deck is compiled into deck.c, which must therefore be recompiled to change deck size.

Any source file which calls these functions should have a

```
#include "deck.h"
```

in order to include this "package interface" header:

```
1 /* deck.h - interface for deck package
2 */
3 #ifndef DECK_H
4 #define DECK_H
5 bool deklow(void);
6 void opndek(void);
7 void shuffl(void);
8 int tkcard(void);
9 #endif /* DECK_H */
```

```
 1 /* deck - deck package
 2 */
 3 #include "bj.h"
 4 #include "deck.h"
 5 #define DECKSIZE  52              /* how many cards in one deck */
 6 #define NCARDS    6 * DECKSIZE    /* total number of cards in play */
 7 #define SHUFMIN   NCARDS - DECKSIZE /* first possible shuffle point */
 8 #define SHUFMAX   NCARDS - 36     /* last possible shuffle point */
 9 static bool system_test = NO;     /* system-test, canned input sequences? */
10 static short deck[NCARDS] = {0};  /* the deck */
11 static short nc = 0;              /* subscript of next card : {0:NCARDS-1} */
12 static short shufpt = 0;          /* shuffle point : {SHUFMIN:SHUFMAX} */
13 /* deklow - is deck at or past shuffle point?
14 */
15 bool deklow(void)
16    {
17    return shufpt <= nc;
18    }
19 /* opndek - initialize the deck
20 */
21 void opndek(void)
22    {
23    short i;
24    short low;
25
26    for (low = 0; low < NCARDS; low += DECKSIZE)
27        for (i = 0; i < DECKSIZE; ++i)
28            deck[i + low] = i;
29    srand1(time(0));
30    shuffl();
31    if (getenv("BJTEST") != NULL && strcmp(getenv("BJTEST"), "YES") == 0)
32        system_test = YES;
33    }
34 /* shuffl - shuffle the deck
35 */
36 void shuffl(void)
37    {
38    short t;         /* temporary for swap */
39    short i;         /* index for loop over cards */
40    short j;         /* index for swap */
41
42    for (i = 0; i < NCARDS - 1; ++i)
43        {
44        j = nfrom(i, NCARDS - 1);
45        t = deck[j], deck[j] = deck[i], deck[i] = t;
46        }
47    shufpt = nfrom(SHUFMIN, SHUFMAX);
48    nc = 0;
49    printf("Shuffle\n");
50    }
```

Internals manual for deck (continued)

tkcard returns, as a short integer, the next card from the deck.

If this is a system-test execution, the value of the next card is taken from the input stream. To be sure that the inputs are properly synchronized, each system-test card value must have the letter c first. The value returned is card-1, because the actual deck values are zero-origin. (See the table in hand.c.)

```
51 /* tkcard - take a card
52  */
53 int tkcard(void)
54     {
55     int card;
56
57     if (system_test)
58         {
59         if (scanf("c%d", &card) == 1)
60             {
61             getchar();
62             printf("card=%d\n", card);
63             return card-1;
64             }
65         else
66             error("expected card","");
67         }
68     else
69         {
70         if (NCARDS <= nc)
71             shuffl();
72         return deck[nc++];
73         }
74     }
```

Internals manual for hand

al lbst returns YES if all player hands are "busted", and NO otherwise.

deal gives two cards to player and two to dealer. It produces a message
in this format:

```
The dealer shows 5H
You have 2D + 9S
```

To use the "hand package", you should #include this header:

```
1 /* hand.h - interface for hand package
2 */
3 #ifndef HAND_H
4 #define HAND_H
5 bool allbst(void);
6 void deal(void);
7 bool hit(int which_hand);
8 bool isbj(int which_hand);
9 CASH outcom(CASH bet, int tophand, bool isinsur, bool isdbl);
10 int score(int which_hand);
11 void show(int which_hand, int which_card);
12 int split(void);
13 int val(int which_hand, int which_card);
14 #endif /* HAND_H */
```

```
 1 /* hand - hand package
 2 */
 3 #include "bj.h"
 4 #include "hand.h"
 5 #include "deck.h"
 6 static char spots[13][3] =
 7     {"A", "2", "3", "4", "5", "6", "7", "8", "9",
 8     "10", "J", "Q", "K"};
 9 static char suits[4][2] = {"S", "H", "D", "C"};
10 static short hands[3][12] = {0};    /* three hands */
11 static short ncards[3] = {0};       /* how many cards in each hand */
12 static short tophand = 0;           /* how many player hands active */
13 /* allbst - are all player's hands busted?
14 */
15 bool allbst(void)
16     {
17     if (score(1) <= 21 || (tophand == 2 && score(2) <= 21))
18         return NO;
19     else
20         return YES;
21     }
22 /* deal - initialize the hands
23 */
24 void deal(void)
25     {
26     hands[1][0] = tkcard();
27     hands[DEALER][0] = tkcard();
28     hands[1][1] = tkcard();
29     hands[DEALER][1] = tkcard();
30     ncards[DEALER] = ncards[1] = 2;
31     tophand = 1;
32     printf("The dealer shows ");
33     show(DEALER, 0);
34     printf("\nYou have ");
35     show(1, 0);
36     printf(" + ");
37     show(1, 1);
38     printf("\n");
39     }
40
41
42
43
44
45
46
47
48
49
50
```

Internals manual for hand (continued)

hit gives another card to hand h, and prints a message (without newline) in this format:

    + KD

isbj returns YES if hand h is a "Blackjack" — 21 in two cards and NO otherwise. Player's hand can never be BJ if player has taken "double down" or "split pair".

outcom determines the outcome of the hand and computes the net cash result; positive result is a win for player, negative is a loss. In all cases except "Bust", the outcome is announced by one or more messages.

score tells the Blackjack value of hand 1. Since val always reports 11 for Aces, score must keep track of the number of Aces found in the hand. If the score exceeds 21 and the hand contains Aces, the score is lowered by 10 for each Ace, as many times as necessary.

```
51 /* hit - add a card to a hand
52  */
53 bool hit(
54     int h)      /* which hand */
55     {
56     hands[h][ncards[h]] = tkcard();
57     printf(" + ");
58     show(h, ncards[h]);
59     ++ncards[h];
60     if (21 < score(h) || h == DEALER && 17 <= score(h))
61         return NO;
62     else
63         return YES;
64     }
65 /* isbj - is hand a "natural" 2-card blackjack?
66  */
67 bool isbj(
68     int h)      /* which hand */
69     {
70     if (h == DEALER)
71         return ncards[DEALER] == 2 && score(DEALER) == 21;
72     else if (h == 1)
73         return tophand == 1 && ncards[1] == 2 && score(1) == 21;
74     else
75         return NO;
76     }
77 /* score - tell blackjack value of hand
78  */
79 int score(
80     int h)      /* which hand */
81     {
82     short aces = 0; /* number of aces in hand */
83     short i;        /* card counter */
84     short sum = 0;  /* accumulated value of hand */
85
86     for (i = 0; i < ncards[h]; ++i)
87         {
88         sum += val(h, i);
89         if (val(h, i) == 11)
90             ++aces;
91         }
92     for (i = aces; 0 < i; --i)
93         if (21 < sum)
94             sum -= 10;
95     return sum;
96     }
97
98
99
100
```

Internals manual for hand (continued)

show prints the two- or three-letter representation of a card. The current implementation maps integers and cards as follows:

AS – 0	AH – 13	AD – 26	AC – 39
2S – 1	2H – 14	2D – 27	2C – 40
3S – 2	3H – 15	3D – 28	3C – 41
4S – 3	4H – 16	4D – 29	4C – 42
5S – 4	5H – 17	5D – 30	5C – 43
6S – 5	6H – 18	6D – 31	6C – 44
7S – 6	7H – 19	7D – 32	7C – 45
8S – 7	8H – 20	8D – 33	8C – 46
9S – 8	9H – 21	9D – 34	9C – 47
10S – 9	10H – 22	10D – 35	10C – 48
JS – 10	JH – 23	JD – 36	JC – 49
QS – 11	QH – 24	QD – 37	QC – 50
KS – 12	KH – 25	KD – 38	KC – 51

In other words, for a given card value v, the spots are given by v % 13 and the suit is given by v / 13.

split splits hand 1 into two hands if possible, and prints a message in this format:

```
Hand 1: 4S + 2D
Hand 2: 4H + 7C
```

If the hand cannot be split, split returns 1, otherwise 2.

val reports the value of card i from hand h, according to Blackjack interpretation:

```
Ace      = 11
2-10     = card-spot value
J,Q,K    = 10
```

```
101 /* show - print a card
102 */
103 void show(
104     int h,  /* which hand */
105     int i)  /* which card */
106     {
107     printf("%s", spots[hands[h][i] % 13]);
108     printf("%s", suits[hands[h][i] / 13]);
109     }
110 /* split - split the players pair if allowed
111 */
112 int split(void)
113     {
114     if (val(1, 0) != val(1, 1))
115         return 1;
116     hands[2][0] = hands[1][1];
117     hands[1][1] = tkcard();
118     hands[2][1] = tkcard();
119     ncards[2] = 2;
120     printf("Hand 1: "); show(1, 0); printf(" + "); show(1, 1);
121     printf("\n");
122     printf("Hand 2: "); show(2, 0); printf(" + "); show(2, 1);
123     printf("\n");
124     tophand = 2;
125     return 2;
126     }
127 /* val - tell value of card n of hand h
128 */
129 int val(
130     int h,  /* which hand */
131     int i)  /* which card */
132     {
133     short n;     /* spots value of card */
134
135     n = (hands[h][i] % 13) + 1;
136     if (n > 9)
137         return 10;
138     else if (n == 1)
139         return 11;
140     else
141         return n;
142     }
```

Internals manual for hand (continued)

outcom does not need to see the hands directly; it uses the functions isbj and score to learn of the hand values. It therefore is in a source file of its own, outcom.c.

outcom makes use of a static (i.e., internal to the file outcom.c) function, prmsg, to print the outcome messages and to add the delta (change) to value. If player has two hands in play, prmsg will report which hand is being announced; this is why h and tophand are being passed to prmsg.

The "insurance" bet is scored separately from the other outcomes. The "Blackjack" outcomes can be scored without reference to the number of hands in play, since Dealer Blackjack wins the same amount regardless and player Blackjack can only take place with one hand in play. (A score of 21 on a split pair does not count as a Blackjack.) The other outcomes require looking at each player's possible two hands. Each outcome prints the appropriate message and computes the result. Exception: The "Bust" message has already been printed, because with two hands in play, the player had to be notified immediately if hand 1 busted.

The outcom function returns the accumulated value.

```
1 /* outcom - print outcome of hand(s)
2  */
3 #include "bj.h"
4 #include "hand.h"
5 static CASH value = 0;
6 static void prmsg(int h, int tophand, char s[], CASH delta);
7 /* outcom - print outcome of hand and compute result
8  */
9 CASH outcom(
10     CASH bet,       /* amount of player's bet */
11     int tophand,    /* how many player hands : {1:2} */
12     bool isinsur,   /* player took insurance? */
13     bool isdbl)     /* is player DBLDN? */
14     {
15     short h;        /* which hand */
16
17     value = 0;
18     if (isinsur && isbj(DEALER))
19         prmsg(1, 1, "Insurance wins\n", bet / (isdbl ? 4 : 2));
20     else if (isinsur)
21         prmsg(1, 1, "Insurance loses\n", -bet / (isdbl ? 4 : 2));
22     if (isbj(DEALER) && !isbj(1))
23         prmsg(1, 1, "Dealer BJ beats all but BJ",
24             -bet / (isdbl ? 2 : 1));
25     else if (isbj(DEALER) && isbj(1))
26         prmsg(1, 1, "Both BJ: push", 0);
27     else if (isbj(1))
28         prmsg(1, 1, "Your BJ wins 3 for 2", (3 * bet) / 2);
29     else
30         {
31         for (h = 1; h <= tophand; ++h)
32             {
33             if (21 < score(h))
34                 value -= bet;   /* "Bust" message printed already */
35             else if (score(DEALER) == score(h))
36                 prmsg(h, tophand, "Push", 0);
37             else if (score(DEALER) < score(h) || 21 < score(DEALER))
38                 prmsg(h, tophand, "Win", bet);
39             else
40                 prmsg(h, tophand, "Lose", -bet);
41             }
42         }
43     return value;
44     }
45
46
47
48
49
50
```

Internals manual for hand (continued)

prmsg must identify which hand is being reported, if two hands are in play (i.e., a split pair). In any event, it prints the message and adds the delta to value.

The rest of the source file contains a test driver. It would, of course, be possible to contrive input sequences that would test each of the possible outcomes. (See the discussion of getenv("BJTEST") in the internals manual for deck.) But development and testing may sometimes be simplified by adding test drivers that can be given unambiguous tables of test data directly.

Therefore, this driver simply reads input lines containing nine integers that determine the test to be performed. The static function echoln reads the input line and echoes it to the output. The sscanf function extracts the integers from the input line; if the line was not properly formatted, the test driver simply takes an error exit. (Test drivers are usually designed for simplicity of programming, not for "user-friendliness".) Calling outcom will produce its printout of the outcome. Then the driver prints the result that was returned from outcom.

```
51 /* prmsg - print appropriate message
52 */
53 static void prmsg(
54     int h,              /* which hand : {1:2} */
55     int tophand,        /* how many hands : {1:2} */
56     char s[],           /* message : string */
57     CASH delta)         /* change of value (+ | -) */
58     {
59     if (tophand == 2)
60         printf("On hand %d, ", h);
61     printf("%s\n", s);
62     value += delta;
63     }
64 #ifdef TRYMAIN
65 static short bj[2] = {0};    /* isbj, for each hand */
66 static short sc[3] = {0};    /* hand scores, for testing */
67 static int echoln(char line[], int size);
68 main()
69     {
70     char line[BUFSIZ];      /* line of test input */
71     short len;              /* returned value from input fn */
72     short ibet;             /* players bet, as short int */
73     short ins;              /* isinsur? */
74     short toph;             /* tophand */
75     short dbl;              /* isdbl? */
76     CASH result;            /* return from outcom */
77
78     FOREVER
79         {
80         printf("%-8s %-8s %-8s %-8s %-8s %-8s %-8s %-8s %-8s\n",
81             "bet", "toph", "ins", "dbl",
82             "bj[0]", "bj[1]", "sc[0]", "sc[1]", "sc[2]");
83         len = echoln(line, BUFSIZ);
84         if (len == EOF)
85             break;
86         if (9 != sscanf(line, "%hd %hd %hd %hd %hd %hd %hd %hd %hd",
87             &ibet, &toph, &ins, &dbl,
88             &bj[0], &bj[1], &sc[0], &sc[1], &sc[2]))
89             error("outcom input error", "");
90         result = outcom(ibet, toph, ins, dbl);
91         printf("outcom() = ");
92         printf(CASHOUT, result);
93         printf("\n");
94         }
95     }
96
97
98
99
100
```

Internals manual for hand (continued)

This test driver section contains dummy versions of score and isbj. In order to make the execution of outcom totally self-contained and driven by its input file, we must replace the usual methods of score and isbj. Accordingly, these two little functions just return the appropriate value that was read on the line of input data. The names score and isbj have already been declared (in the header hand.h) to be external function names, so these little functions are also external (i.e., not static).

```
101 /* score - dummy version for testing
102 */
103 int score(
104     int h)  /* which hand */
105     {
106     return sc[h];
107     }
108 /* isbj - dummy version for testing
109 */
110 bool isbj(
111     int h)  /* which hand */
112     {
113     return bj[h];
114     }
115 /* echoln - get and echo an input line
116 */
117 static int echoln(
118     char line[],
119     int size)
120     {
121     short len;
122
123     if ((len = getln(line, size)) != EOF)
124         printf("%s", line);
125     return len;
126     }
127 #endif /* TRYMAIN */
```

Internals manual for terminal

getbet prompts the user for a bet and reads one line of input. On EOF, getbet returns 0. If the input forms a valid number between MINBET and MAXBET, inclusive, the numerical result is returned as a CASH data item. Otherwise, a more explicit prompt is printed, and the process is repeated by reading another line of input. This protocol is more long-winded than a simple scanf, but the extra logic is important for avoiding unpleasant surprises for the user.

getbet is part of the terminal package, because it deals with the user interface. But it does not share any internal static data with the other functions (takes and query), so it appears in a source file of its own.

To use terminal, be sure to #include this header:

```
1 /* terminal.h - interface for terminal package
2 */
3 #ifndef TERMINAL_H
4 #define TERMINAL_H
5 CASH getbet(void);
6 bool takes(char s[]);
7 int query(void);
8 #endif /* TERMINAL_H */
```

```
1 /* getbet - get the player's bet
2 */
3 #include "bj.h"
4 #define MINBET 2
5 #define MAXBET 1000
6 CASH getbet(void)
7     {
8     char line[BUFSIZ];  /* input line : string*/
9     short retn;           /* return from getln and sscanf */
10    CASH bet;             /* player's bet */
11
12    printf("\n\nYour bet (amount): ");
13    FOREVER
14        {
15        retn = getln(line, BUFSIZ);
16        if (retn == EOF)
17            return 0;
18        retn = sscanf(line, CASHIN, &bet);
19        if (retn != 1 || bet < MINBET || MAXBET < bet)
20            printf("Number from %d to %d please: ",
21                MINBET, MAXBET);
22        else
23            return bet;
24        }
25    }
```

Internals manual for terminal (continued)

query prompts the user for a variety of choices:

```
d        Double down
s        Split pair (if appropriate)
h        Hit
RETURN   None
```

One line of input is read, and if the initial character matches one of these possibilities, the coded value of the reply is returned:

```
NONE    = no selection, empty line
DBLDN   = double down
SPLIT   = split pair
HIT     = hit
```

If input is EOF, query takes an immediate exit via error("Bye!", "").

takes prints the prompt for one designated action — either

```
i        Insurance
```

or

```
h        Hit
```

and returns YES if the user selects the prompted action; otherwise the return is NO. On EOF, takes exits via error("Bye!", "") in the ask function.

```
1 /* terminal - terminal package
2 */
3 #include "bj.h"
4 #include "hand.h"
5 #include "terminal.h"
6 #define NMSGS 4                        /* number of messages */
7 #define LENMSG 15                      /* max length of message */
8 #define MSGNUM(c) strscn(qchar, (c))   /* which message does c stand for? */
9 static bool askedhit = NO;             /* was player already asked re hit? */
10 static bool wanthit = NO;             /* did player want a hit */
11 static char qchar[NMSGS+1] = "dsih";  /* table of message abbreviations */
12 static char qmsg[NMSGS][LENMSG+1] =   /* table of message strings */
13     {
14     "Double down",
15     "Split pair",
16     "Insurance",
17     "Hit",
18     };
19 static short nmsg[NMSGS] = {0};        /* how many times was each msg presented */
20 static int ask(char[]);               /* internal function to ask questions */
21 /* query - get players response for DBLDN, SPLIT, HIT
22 */
23 int query(void)
24     {
25     short ret;        /* return from ask() */
26
27     if (val(1, 0) == val(1, 1))
28         ret = ask("dsh");        /* double? split? hit? */
29     else
30         ret = ask("dh");         /* double? hit? */
31     askedhit = (ret != SPLIT);
32     wanthit = (ret == HIT);
33     if (wanthit)
34         ret = NONE;
35     return ret;
36     }
37 /* takes - get a YES or NO reply to question
38 */
39 bool takes(
40     char s[])
41     {
42
43     if (askedhit && strcmp(s, "h") == 0)
44         {
45         askedhit = NO;
46         return wanthit;
47         }
48     return ask(s) != NONE;
49     }
50
```

Internals manual for terminal (continued)

ask has one parameter, s, a character string which lists the alternatives available. For example,

    ask("dh")

allows for d ("double down") or h ("hit"). The pseudo-code (i.e., program outline) looks like this:

> *First, assume that messages can be brief*
> *slen = how many choices are there*
> *for each possible message*
> >   *j = its message-number*
> >   *if not yet past message-limit,*
> > >   *then not brief yet*
>
> *if brief,*
> >   *print brief message summary*
>
> *FOREVER*
> >   *if not brief,*
> > >   *display all choices*
> >   *read input line into ans*
> >   *if EOF,*
> > >   *bye-bye*
> >   *convert input to lower case*
> >   *if newline,*
> > >   *return NONE*
> >   *for each possible choice,*
> > >   *if match to c,*
> > > >   *return message-number plus one*
> >   *(otherwise) be verbose,*
> >   *(and loop for another try)*

The loop terminates when the player has entered a proper reply.

```
51 /* ask - get a choice among alternatives
52 */
53 static int ask(
54     char s[])
55     {
56     bool isbrief;              /* is prompt brief? */
57     char ans[BUFSIZ];          /* player's reply line : string */
58     char c;                    /* player's one-char answer */
59     short i;                   /* index over chars of s */
60     short j;                   /* index over chars of qchar */
61     short slen;                /* length of s */
62
63     isbrief = YES;
64     slen = strlen(s);
65     for (i = 0; i < slen; ++i)
66         {
67         j = MSGNUM(s[i]);
68         if (++nmsg[j] <= MSGLIM)
69             isbrief = NO;
70         }
71     if (isbrief)
72         {
73         for (i = 0; i < slen; ++i)
74             printf("%c?", s[i]);
75         printf("\n");
76         }
77     FOREVER
78         {
79         if (!isbrief)
80             {
81             printf("Type\n");
82             for (i = 0; i < slen; ++i)
83                 printf("%c      For %s\n",
84                     s[i], qmsg[MSGNUM(s[i])]);
85             printf("RETURN For None\n");
86             }
87         if (getln(ans, BUFSIZ) == EOF)
88             error("Bye!", "");
89         c = tolower(ans[0]);
90         if (c == '\n')
91                 return NONE;
92         for (i = 0; i < slen; ++i)
93             if (s[i] == c)
94                     return 1 + MSGNUM(c);
95         isbrief = NO;
96         }
97     }
```

6.5 Implementation: The Latter Phases

In the previous section, we saw the full program documentation for the case study program, bj.c. The writing of the program was item (1) on our list of implementation phases. The other phases continue below.

(2) Efficiency of execution time and space: In most environments, the execution time of the program will be determined by the output speed of the terminal. Saving a microsecond here or there would give no real payoff. On the other hand, if one wanted to adapt this program into a totally automated player — for example, to use in testing an automated strategy for Blackjack — time efficiency could become more important. We have found that this program spends about two-thirds of its CPU time doing output. Of the remaining time, about half is spent calling, executing, and returning from the val function.

Exercise 6-2. Modify hand.c and hand.h so that val is implemented as a macro. Hint: you will need to add an extern declaration of hands, which must be made external in hand.c.

Regarding space efficiency, the size of the program is often determined by how much of the function library it calls. In this case, the function printf would be the first to examine. With its code space of 3000 to 5000 bytes on most systems, this would be the first candidate for replacement. The simple conversions done here could be accomplished by a much simpler function. However, we will leave the program as is, in the interests of simplicity.

(3) Desk-checking (hand-simulation): In the normal course of producing a program, you should write it first on paper before entering at the terminal. Very few people can sit at a terminal and create a perfect program at the keyboard. And before entering it, check it first with a little hand-simulation. As you are reading·this, take a small test case and simulate the computer's handling of it.

(4) Editing the program (using correct layout from the start): Having completed our desk-checking, we are ready to enter the program. At this point, it is important to be clear about the standard that we are using for the layout of the code. All the examples in this book have been presented in a certain layout format that we recommend. However, what is most important is that you adhere closely to whatever standard is followed by the other people on your project. Uniformity within a project is often a more attainable goal than uniformity within an entire organization, especially as programmers gain familiarity with

the language and the problems of maintaining it. Naturally, we recommend Plum [1989] *C Programming Guidelines (Second Edition)*, but in any case, get the layout right when you enter the code. Do not rely on beautifiers or formatters to do the work for you. They cannot handle tabulated comments, carefully-organized initializers, etc. Good layout is a visible sign of clear thinking, and the discipline is useful.

After we enter the program, we are ready to compile. If we can document our compilation process with an automated facility such as a make file, batch file, command procedure, etc., it will be easier for maintainers to follow in our footsteps.

(5) Creating test cases: There are good materials on the subject of testing, such as Myers [1979], or Gelperin and Hetzel [1988], and we will only summarize some of the important methods.

Having spent all this time working to make the program correct, we now play devil's advocate and try to determine data cases that have the best probability of finding errors in it. Even if our current program passes all these tests successfully, they still remain useful as a *regression test*, a collection of cases that should be tried whenever a change is made to the program or to its environment (such as compiling it for another computer). To allow convenient regression testing, we should package our tests as commands that can be run without interaction with the terminal.

Our first technique for choosing test cases is *equivalence partitioning* — finding which classes of input are treated equivalently by the program. For example, if the hit function were to give incorrect results for a score of 20 in hand number 1, there would be no point testing it upon a score of 19, since the program behaves equivalently in both cases. To determine the equivalence classes, we use the specs from analysis and design, as well as the program itself. Each time a choice is specified (in C, an if, switch, for, or while) there is some value that is typical of a *true* test, and one typical of a *false* test. If we have done our work right, any particular data values that we choose for each of these cases will be as good as any other representative value. In other words, supplying two different tests for each case will be wasted effort. We will therefore usually prefer the least amount of data for each alternative.

Before we choose specific test cases, however, we should turn to our second testing method: *boundary-value analysis* — choosing data values that bracket each limit of the program. Each case that we choose by this method will also belong to one of the equivalence classes that we identified previously so such cases will do double duty in our testing.

Applying this analysis to outcom, we identify one case for

score(1) == 21

This will serve as a specific value for one equivalence class. Choosing the bracketing value that is numerically closest to our first case gives

score(1) == 22

We can use this as part of another equivalence class. In similar fashion, the bracketing values for score(2) are also 21 and 22. Thus, our boundary-value analysis has supplied us with specific values to satisfy several of the equivalence classes that we determined earlier. Any other boundary-value cases we find will also be added to the test set, increasing the total number of cases.

A third testing criterion is *every-expression coverage* — being sure that all the code is executed by some test. This coverage should be assured by the combination of methods that we have already employed. Notice, however, that the converse is not true — just because each piece of the code is executed does not mean that our test coverage exercises all the limits of the program.

Question [6-4] Apply these three methods to designing test cases for the outcom function in outcom.c.

	bet	toph	ins	dbl	bj[0]	bj[1]	sc[0]	sc[1]	sc[2]
1	__	__	__	__	__	__	__	__	__
2	__	__	__	__	__	__	__	__	__
3	__	__	__	__	__	__	__	__	__
4	__	__	__	__	__	__	__	__	__
5	__	__	__	__	__	__	__	__	__
6	__	__	__	__	__	__	__	__	__
7	__	__	__	__	__	__	__	__	__
8	__	__	__	__	__	__	__	__	__
9	__	__	__	__	__	__	__	__	__
10	__	__	__	__	__	__	__	__	__

Question [6-5] Predict what values outcom should give for each of your test cases. Compile outcom.c with the symbol TRYMAIN defined, to obtain the test driver for outcom. Run the driver, using your file of test cases as input. Compare the output with your predictions.

(6) Documentation: Since we have emphasized documentation as we worked through each phase, very little is left to be done. Our criteria for detailed documentation are determined largely by our expectations for the maintenance environment. In the typical industrial situation, the program will eventually be maintained by novice programmers who have little familiarity with the intricacies of the program. Thus, any points which required extra care or scrutiny in the implementation deserve a note somewhere for the benefit of the maintainers. This is especially true if the code contains unavoidable hardware or environment dependencies. Whenever an internals manual is part of standard procedure, it is probably better to keep all such comments there, as we have done. Otherwise, the code itself deserves much more liberal commenting than we have employed.

(7) Packaging: Since we have proceeded so far according to a very careful recipe, little more remains in the way of packaging.

Our program is split into separate source files. We did not blindly create one file per package; functions have been combined into a single source file only when there is data that they must share.

Our compiling procedures are captured in a make file or similar automated procedure.

And finally, the manual pages are completed.

If the project were larger, an entire library, directory, tape, or diskette might be required. The collection presented here would be appropriate for a small to medium sized internal project.

The package is ready.

(8) Demonstration and acceptance test: A test case should be chosen which is representative of the function that the program is expected to perform. Our testing methodology did not require such a case; it was directed only to the revealing of errors, and many of the cases generated may be rather oddball examples. In the case of the Blackjack program, demonstration is easy — sit down and try it. But for some other systems, demonstration and acceptance test must be carefully attended to.

(9) Delivery and celebration: No further lessons should be needed for the last phase!

6.6 Maintenance

Under the category of "maintenance", we are grouping both "enhancement" (adding new features and changing old ones) and "bug-fixing" (correcting errors in the original product).

In our case study, each of you who use this case-study problem will be playing the role of maintainer, so a few suggestions may be of value.

An important technique in maintenance is the discipline of *versions*. When changes are being made daily, it becomes hard to know what new symptoms have been created by recent work. Develop a regular cycle of version integration, so that you always have a system with known behavior to fall back on. At the very least, this implies that you will preserve one copy of the original product that you are maintaining.

A second technique is *regression testing*. Set up whatever programs and procedures you need so that the testing of a version can be totally automated from stored test data. Then, when changes are made, you have a procedure to insure that the new changes have not broken something which was previously working. In the Blackjack example, this was illustrated in the tkcard function, in which the "system-test" version simply accepts card values supplied from an input file.

Under the earlier topic of "packaging", we suggested the importance of *automating your compilation procedures*. The value is even greater during maintenance. If you have make, use it always. If not, create your own automated procedures. Running the regression test should be part of the automated procedures also.

An organized procedure for *tracking user feedback* is often helpful. Any "modification request" (or "MR", for short) can be given an identifying number and logged in a record-keeping system. (Apropos of user feedback, in the back of this book you will find a form for sending your comments to the publisher, to assist in our own maintenance procedures.)

CHAPTER 7: POINTERS

7.1 Basics

We have already brushed up against pointers in their disguise as array parameters. In the general case, a pointer variable holds the *address* of another variable. This implies that pointer variables (which point to a data object) are big enough to hold one address, typically 2 or 4 bytes, as we have seen.

For example, consider this portion of a program:

```
short i, j;     /* i, j are both short integers */
short *p;       /* p is a pointer-to-short */

i = 123;
p = &i;
j = *p;
```

In a declaration, the symbol * means "pointer to" —

```
short *p;
```

means that p has the type short * (verbalized as "short star", and meaning "pointer to short"). A variable with the type short * can be assigned the address of a short, as in

```
p = &i;
```

Continuing with this example, let us assume that the storage of the three variables looks like this (with hypothetical two-byte addresses):

```
i    1200  |         |
           |_____|
j    1202  |         |
           |_____|
p    1204  |         |
           |_____|
```

After the two assignments,

```
i = 123;
p = &i;
```

the storage will look like this

```
i    1200  |   123   |
           |_____|
j    1202  |         |
           |_____|
p    1204  |   1200  |
           |_____|
```

Each variable is an *object*, some bytes of memory into which a *value* can be stored. In our diagrams, each *object* is a box, and its *value* is written inside that box. If we look at the value in the box named p, we will find the value 1200, which is the address of the variable i.

In an expression, * means "the indirect object" — i.e., "the storage pointed-to". In other words, *p is an object (a "box" of short size), which is currently located at address 1200. Thus, in the example above,

```
j = *p;
```

means "copy a short integer from location 1200 into location 1202" — from 1200 (the location of *p) into 1202 (the location of j).

The object j is a short-size box located at 1202:

```
j    1202  |         |
           |_____|
```

The object *p is a short-size box currently located at 1200:

```
i    1200  |   123   |    (which is *p)
           |_____|
```

If we change the value of p, we change the location of *p —

```
p = &j;
```

creates this picture:

```
j    1202  ┌───────┐      (which is now *p)
           │       │
           └───────┤
p    1204  │ 1202  │
           └───────┘
```

Thus, we obtain the same net result from saying

```
p = &i,  j = *p;
```

as from saying

```
i = j;
```

The address-of operator can only be applied to *lvalues*, and we need now to be very precise about this. An lvalue is an expression that designates the location of an object. The simplest form of lvalue is the name (i.e. identifier) of a variable (which could have any data type). If we declare

```
int i = 1;
```

then the name i is an lvalue expression. Another form of lvalue expression is a subscript expression; if we declare

```
int a[10] = {0};
```

then any subscript expression such as a[i] is an lvalue expression.

So we could apply the address-of operator to the name of a variable (as in &i), or to a subscript expression (as in &a[i]).

The other expressions that we saw in previous chapters are *not* lvalue expressions; the expression i - 5 and the expression a[2] > 1 produce result values, but they do not designate a location, and they are not lvalues.

There is one category of lvalue whose address can *not* be taken: a variable declared to have register storage class, as in

```
register int regvar = 2;
```

Such a variable has a *location* (e.g. in machine register N), but it might not have a numerical *address* in the memory space.

Question [7-1] Which of the following are *invalid?*

____	p = &i;	____	p = &a[i];
____	p = &(i + 1);	____	p = &regvar;
____	p = &++i;	____	p = &a[regvar];

We saw in Section 3.9 that assignment, increment, and decrement require an lvalue operand. Actually, the lvalue has to be a *modifiable lvalue*. The const keyword plays a role here. If we declare

```
static const char messages[3][6] = {"WASH", "RINSE", "SPIN"};
```

we have told the compiler that these strings will never be modified, that they could safely be stored in read-only memory (or *ROM*), and that we will never attempt to increment, decrement, or assign to any of the characters in messages. So const objects are not modifiable.

Array names are also non-modifiable lvalues. The name of the array does designate a location, but C prohibits incrementing, decrementing, or assigning to an array name:

```
a = 0;      /* very bad syntax */
a[i] = 0;   /* just fine */
```

To summarize: The address-of operator can be applied to any lvalue except for register variables. The increment, decrement, and assignment operators can be applied to any lvalue except for array names and lvalues that designate const objects.

7.2 Declaring and Using Pointers

In C, each pointer variable is declared to point to a particular type of data, and this type pointed-to is part of the type of the pointer. In these declarations,

```
short *pi;
short *pj;
short t;
long *pl;
double *pd;
const char *pcc;
```

we are declaring the following types:

pi	has the type	short *	(pointer to short)
pj	has the type	short *	(pointer to short)
t	has the type	short	
pl	has the type	long *	(pointer to long)
pd	has the type	double *	(pointer to double)
pcc	has the type	const char *	(pointer to const char)

In a declaration, such as

```
short *pi;
```

the symbol * means "pointer-to"; in an expression, such as

```
j = *pi
```

the symbol * means "indirect", or "the thing pointed to". Each pointer is pointing to its own kind of data, but the pointer itself only occupies the amount of memory that is needed to hold one address. A pointer variable is itself an lvalue — it has a location in the memory and can be assigned to. But the *indirect object* (or *"the thing pointed to"*) of a pointer is also an lvalue — *pi is a short integer somewhere in the machine. The *type* of the indirect object can be determined several ways, equivalently. One way is to remove one asterisk from the type of the pointer — if pi has the type short *, then the indirect object, *pi, has the type short. Alternatively, we can read directly from the declaration of pi: scratch out the expression *pi from the declaration

```
short *pi;
```

and what do you have? Simply, short. Thus, a pointer declaration makes two statements simultaneously.

```
short *pi;
```

says that pi has the type short * (pointer to short), and that *pi has the type short. This is not accidental — the complementary relationship between the declaration type modifiers and the corresponding expression operators is one of the fundamental principles of C.

C language allows several declarations in the same statement, so long as all the variables have the same "base type". Thus,

```
short *pi, *pj, t;
long *pl;
double *pd;
```

means the same as the first five declarations given earlier. However, our style suggests separate lines for each declaration, to provide space for comments.

Since the indirect object of a pointer is an lvalue, it can be assigned into and incremented just like a variable. All these statements are legal and sensible for the variables declared above:

```
*pd += *pi;
pi = &t;
*pi = *pl;
pj = pi;
*pj /= 3;
++pj;
++*pj;
```

Question [7-2] Assuming the following initial configuration of memory, and assuming two-byte addresses, after this series of statements is executed, what is the resulting configuration of memory?

7.3 Pointers as Function Parameters

We have seen that C functions are always called by passing the *value* of each argument, making C a *call-by-value* language. The one apparent exception to this rule concerned arguments which are arrays, but as will be explained shortly, the *value* of an unsubscripted array name is the *address of the initial element*. Thus, even for an array argument, a "value" is passed, but this value is the address of something.

Using pointer values, it is also possible to pass the address of any scalar item of data also.

In the discussion of scanf, we have seen how to pass the address: simply add the & address-of operator to the name, as in

```
scanf("%lf", &x);
```

What has not yet been shown is how you can write a function that will accept an address argument.

The function that receives the address argument will need to declare its parameter as a *pointer* variable. For example, a swap function for interchanging two short integers would look like this:

```
/* swap - interchange two short integers
 */
#include "local.h"
void swap(
    short *pi,
    short *pj)
    {
    short t;

    t = *pi, *pi = *pj, *pj = t;
    }
```

In the calling program, if we wished to swap the values of n (located at address 800, say) and m (located at address 900), we would write

```
swap(&n, &m);
```

At the time that swap is entered, the memory would look like this:

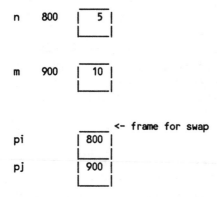

Question [7-3] At the time that swap is entered, what is the value of *pi? _____ What is the value of *pj? _____

Question [7-4] At the time the swap returns, what is the value of *pi? _____ What is the value of *pj? _____

When a parameter points to memory that is never modified by the function, that parameter should be declared to point to a const type. First of all, this is simply good documentation. More importantly, it is a syntax error to assign the address of a const object to a pointer not declared to point to const. In other words, this is a syntax error:

```
const short serial_number = 123;
short new_number;
short *pnumber;

pnumber = &serial_number;   /* syntax error */
```

And so if we had some function such as this trivial copy_short —

```
void copy_short(
    short *pi,
    const short *pj)
    {
    *pi = *pj;
    }
```

— we could safely call copy_short(&new_number, &serial_number) which copies from the constant to the non-constant, but it would be a syntax error to invoke copy_short(&serial_number, &new_number).

Think of it like this: A function has to be especially careful with its use of the address of const memory. Any inadvertant modification could cause a hardware error or destroy a table that the rest of the program depends upon. Such addresses can only be handed to pointers which promise that they will be appropriately careful; they are explicitly declared to be safe for use with const objects.

7.4 Pointers and Arrays

C language has a very close relation between arrays and pointers. There is one important difference between them to bear in mind at all times. An *array* always consists of a "fat" amount of memory, enough space to hold all the elements of the array. The array q declared like this

```
short q[100];
```

reserves several hundred bytes of memory — 100 times the size of a short integer. On the other hand, a *pointer* always has a "skinny" storage — only enough storage to hold one address. So the pointer variable pq declared like this

```
short *pq;
```

itself only contains a few bytes.

However, if the address of the initial element of some array is assigned to pq, then we can access the array storage using the pointer variable. Thus, after we execute

```
pq = &q[0];
```

the initial element of the array can be accessed as *pq — the "thing pointed to" by pq. A picture may help:

```
pq    600   | 700 |
            |_____|


q     700   |   5 |   q[0]
            |_____|
            |  10 |   q[1]
            |_____|
              ...
            | 495 |   q[99]
            |_____|


i     800   |     |
            |_____|
```

Question [7-5]
In the following example, what value will be given to i? _____

```
pq = &q[1];
i = *pq;
```

In this next example, what value will be given to i? _____

```
pq = &q[0];
i = *pq;
```

Hold your hats now, because we come to one of the fundamental secrets of C language. Mastering the rest of this section entitles you to consider yourself a *real* C programmer.

One convenience that C provides is that when an integer is added to a pointer, the language automatically *scales* the integer, multiplying it by the number of bytes in the indirect object of the pointer (by the "size of the thing pointed to"). Thus, if short integers are two-byte integers on our machine, and pq contains 700 as it does above, then pq + 3 equals 706. And pq + 10 is actually 720. Therefore, in C, if one puts a subscript on a pointer, as in pq[n], it is defined to mean the same thing as *(pq + n). In other words, any reference to pq[n] means the same thing as "the object located at address pq + n" (where the pointer-addition involves scaling for size). (Using the word "bytes" is overly-specific; some machines also have "word pointers", and their arithmetic is scaled by words.)

In any event, this formula is true for any pointer, and is worth memorizing:

pq[n]   *means*   *(pq + n)

We have hinted several times at a related fact of C language, and state it outright — the *value* of an unsubscripted array name is the *address of the initial element of the array.* Thus, earlier where we wrote

```
pq = &q[0];
```

we could equally well have written

```
pq = q;
```

Why? Because q (with no subscript) *means* &q[0] — the two expressions are equivalent. Furthermore, since addresses are *pointer values*, any time we add an integer to an address value, C will scale the integer just as we saw above. To be specific for the example picture above, &q[0] has the value 700, and the expression q + 5 has the value 710. Since addition is scaled in this case, we can write the "indexing formula" like this:

&q[n] *means* &q[0] + n *means* q + n

Obviously, if the addresses are equal, then the things at the addresses are the same thing. Therefore,

*(&q[n]) *means* *(q + n)

But this roundabout´ expression *(&q[n]) is simply q[n] — "the thing at the address of q[n]" is simply q[n]. Thus we finally have the important identity

q[n] *means* *(q + n)

We have derived, for any array q, the same relationship that we showed earlier for the pointer pq. Thus, we can use the subscription operator [] on either arrays or pointers, and equally well use the indirection operator * on either:

q[n]   *means* *(q + n)

pq[n] *means* *(pq + n)

Work this through until you understand it, and then memorize it. You will need to know it.

7.5 Functions using Pointers

If a pointer is assigned the value 0 (the actual number zero), it becomes a *null pointer* — i.e., not pointing at any valid data. In the header <stdio.h>, the name NULL is defined as some sort of zero, and we will use the name NULL for null-pointer values, rather than an actual 0. The C compiler makes sure that no variables will be allocated into machine location 0, so there is no chance that the address of some variable would be mistaken for the null pointer. If a function is defined to return a pointer value, it can return a null pointer to mean "there is no returned value". Consider, for example, the strchr function.

The function strchr searches a string to find the first occurrence of a specific character, and returns the address of that occurrence. If the character is nowhere to be found in the string, strchr returns a NULL value. Here is our version of strchr, called strchr1, written with subscripts:

```
/* strchr1 - return pointer to first occurrence of char c in string s
 *   subscripted version
 */
#include "local.h"
char *strchr1(
    const char s[],        /* : string */
    int c)                 /* target character : {CHAR_MIN:CHAR_MAX} */
    {
    size_t i = 0;

    while (s[i] != '\0' && s[i] != c)
        ++i;
    return s[i] == c ? (char *)&s[i] : NULL;
    }
```

And here is the corresponding version using pointers:

```
/* strchr2 - return pointer to first occurrence of char c in string s
 *   pointer version
 */
#include "local.h"
char *strchr2(
    const char s[],        /* : string */
    int c)                 /* target character : {CHAR_MIN:CHAR_MAX} */
    {
    while (*s != '\0' && *s != c)
        ++s;
    return *s == c ? (char *)s : NULL;
    }
```

Notice that both functions are declared to return data of type `char *`; this means that the function will return the address of a `char`. Both functions declare that the parameter `s` has the type `const char []`. As we saw in Section 5.4, this means the same thing as `const char *`, namely "pointer to a `const char`". Many people declare all pointer parameters with the `*` form, but we prefer a different convention of style — use `char *` to mean a pointer to a *single* `char`, and `char []` to mean a pointer to the initial element of an *array* of `char`. (Or, as here, a `const char []` means a pointer to the initial element of an array of `const char`.)

In `strchr1`, the value returned is `&s[i]` if the character is found. If the character is not found, `NULL` (defined in `<stdio.h>`) is returned.

Turning now to `strchr2`, the parameter `s` is again declared as `const char []`, but we will be processing it explicitly as a pointer. The `while` loop keeps running as long as `*s` (the indirect object of `s`, "the thing that `s` points to") is not the null character and is not equal to the target character `c`. The body of the loop consists simply of `++s;` which increments `s` by the size of the data that it points to — namely, one byte. The function returns either the current value of `s` or else `NULL`, depending whether `*s` is equal to `c`.

Exercise 7-1. Write and test the function

```
char *strrchr1(const char s[], int c)
```

which, like the Standard Library's strrchr function, returns a pointer to the *rightmost* occurrence of c in string s.

Consider now the function strcpy2, which, like strcpy in the Standard Library, passes back its first argument as the returned value.

```
/* strcpy2 - copy characters from s2 to s1
 */
#include "local.h"
char *strcpy2(
    register char s1[],         /* : non-NULL */
    register const char s2[])   /* : string */
    {
    char *s0 = s1;

    while ((*s1++ = *s2++) != '\0')
        ;
    return s0;
    }
```

The declaration

```
register char s1[];
```

means the same thing as

```
register char *s1;
```

— a pointer to char, allocated into a register (if possible). The pointer s1 will be used for modifying the storage that it points to; it points to non-constant characters. The declaration

```
register const char s2[];
```

means the same thing as

```
register const char *s2;
```

— a pointer to const char, again allocated into a register if possible. The pointer s2 will not be used for modifying the storage that it points to; it points to constant characters.

Let us next unpack the declaration

```
char *s0 = s1;
```

The *type* of s0 is char *, and s1 is the *initial value* that is assigned to s0. In other words, the address contained in the pointer s1 is copied into the pointer s0 when the function is entered. The function would behave the same if the initialization were performed by an assignment:

```
char *s0;
s0 = s1;
```

In other words, it is s0 that is being initialized, not *s0. The while loop assigns one character (*s2) into the location pointed-to by s1, incrementing both pointers in the process. The loop stops when the null character has been copied. The value returned is s0, which was created solely to be returned.

Why does the Standard Library function strcpy return its first argument? For only one purpose: to allow embedding the function-call into another expression. For example, this allows writing

```
strcat(strcpy(name, prefix), suffix);
```

instead of

```
strcpy(name, prefix);
strcat(name, suffix);
```

Actually, the latter form looks much clearer to us.

7.6 Pointer Arithmetic

We have seen that when adding a pointer and an integer, C will *scale* the integer by the size of the pointer's indirect object. To be consistent with this scaled version of arithmetic, when a pointer is subtracted from another pointer, the difference is *divided by* the size of the indirect object. Thus, the pointers should have the same type, and if the results are to mean anything, both pointers should reference data within the same array. For example:

```
double x[10];
double *pa, *pb;
int diff;

pa = x;
pb = pa + 3;
diff = pb - pa;
printf("%d", diff);
```

will print the value 3.

Two pointers (of the same type) may be compared with each other. If the comparison is done by <, <=, >, or >=, the results are portable only if the two pointers are referencing data within the same array. Any pointer may be meaningfully compared for "equal" or "not equal" to NULL (or to any integer constant of value zero).

7.7 Arrays of Pointers

We can declare an *array of pointers;* the array will contain nothing but pointers. For example,

```
short *aptr[10];
```

declares that `aptr` is an array of 10 pointers to `short` integers. Take a moment to unpack the type of `aptr` directly from the declaration. Just as in expressions, the `[]` binds more tightly than the `*`, so the declaration says that `aptr[n]` (that is, `aptr` *sub* anything) has the type `short *`. Thus, `aptr[0]`, `aptr[1]`, etc., all have the type `short *`. And therefore, `aptr` is an array of pointers.

An array of pointers-to-`char` is a handy way to represent a *table*. For example,

```
char *cities[] =
    {"NY", "PHILA", "BOS", "LA", NULL};
```

creates an array of five pointers-to-`char`. Its representation in memory might look like this:

```
cities:
cities[0]  1000    | 1100 |
                   |_____|
cities[1]  1002    | 1103 |
                   |_____|
cities[2]  1004    | 1109 |
                   |_____|
cities[3]  1006    | 1113 |
                   |_____|
cities[4]  1008    |   0  |
                   |_____|


           1100    | N | Y | \0 |
                   |___|___|____|

           1103    | P | H | I | L | A | \0 |
                   |___|___|___|___|___|____|

           1109    | B | O | S | \0 |
                   |___|___|___|____|

           1113    | L | A | \0 |
                   |___|___|____|
```

Question [7-6] Write the *type* and *value* of each expression:

	type	value
cities[1][1]	_____	_____
&cities[1][1]	_____	_____
*cities[1]	_____	_____

An array of pointers is sometimes known as a "ragged array", because each pointed-to row may be of different size. (Contrast this with the "rectangular array" described in Section 5.11, where each row is of the same size.) A ragged array is useful in cases where a table contains data of widely varying sizes.

7.8 Command Line Arguments

One common use of ragged arrays is to provide arguments to the main function. So far, we have only seen main defined as a function with no parameters:

```
main()
```

but it is more generally defined with two parameters:

```
main(
    int argc,        /* number of arguments */
    char *argv[])    /* argument strings */
```

An "argument count" is passed in argc, and argv is a pointer to a "ragged array" of strings.

If, for example, our program is named cmd, to execute it from the keyboard we could type

```
cmd a1 a2
```

and the program might receive some data looking like this (assuming hypothetical two-byte addresses):

```
argc    1400       | 3 |
                   |___|
argv    1402       | 1440 |
                   |_____|


argv[0] 1440   | 1662 |      1662    | c | m | d | \0 |
               |_____|             |___|___|___|____|
argv[1] 1442   | 1666 |      1666    | a | 1 | \0 |
               |_____|             |___|___|____|
argv[2] 1444   | 1669 |      1669    | a | 2 | \0 |
               |_____|             |___|___|____|
argv[3] 1446   |  0   |
               |_____|
```

The declaration of argv deserves some attention. First, notice that because argv is a function parameter, the square brackets are converted to the "pointer" asterisk by the compiler, so the declaration

```
char *argv[];
```

means the same as

```
char **argv;
```

namely, "pointer to pointer to char". We prefer the [] form, to indicate that the pointer is to the initial element of an array. In any case, if we look at the storage pointed to by argv, we will find an array of pointers-to-char, each one pointing to the first character of a null-terminated string. In most environments, argv[0] is the name of the command itself. In all Standard C environments, argv[1] points to the first argument string, argv[2] points to the second argument string, and so forth. The last element of the argv array — argv[argc] — is always a null pointer (value 0).

In any operating system, the work of creating this argument vector must be done by the operating system itself and any start-up instructions executed before main is called. In a UNIX system, most of this work is done by the operating system; in other environments, the program may contain several hundred bytes of instructions to set up argv before main is called.

A simple example program for command arguments is the echo1 program, which simply prints out its arguments. The last argument to be printed is followed by a newline; each of the others is followed by a space.

```
echo1.c:
    /* echo1 - print command-line arguments
     */
    #include "local.h"
    main(
        int argc,
        char *argv[])
        {
        int i;

        for (i = 1; i < argc; ++i)
            printf(i < argc-1 ? "%s " : "%s\n", argv[i]);
        exit(0);
        }
```

Question [7-7] If we execute echo1 with the command

    echo1 abc xyz 123

how many pointers are passed in the array that argv points to? _____ What is the value of argc? _____

Exercise 7-2. A common convention for command-line arguments is that an argument whose initial character is + or - is called a *flag argument* (or *flag*, for short) and is optional. We have seen such flags earlier as the -c option of the cc command. Generally, such flags must appear before any non-flag arguments, so the common form for invoking a command is

   cmd [*flags*] *args*

Modify the program echo1.c to produce echo2.c which accepts an optional flag -n. If this flag appears, the output line should not have a newline at its end.

Exercise 7-3. Write program echo3.c which accepts no flags, but if the last argument ends with the two characters \c, the output line will not have a newline at its end.

A main function which uses no command-line arguments can be defined with main() as we have been doing, or with main(void), using the precise function-definition syntax shown in Section 3.8. We will henceforth prefer the latter, so that the absence of parameters will be consistently indicated with void.

To be even more precise, the type returned by main is int; we could actually terminate main with a "return 0;" instead of an "exit(0);". (We like exit better, because it can be used anywhere.)

CHAPTER 8: STRUCTURES

8.1 Basics

A structure is a collection of data items, whose types may differ, grouped together for ease of manipulation. There are several forms of structure declaration, but the format that we describe here is recommended, based upon our consulting experience.

First, we declare a structure *template* — a representation of memory layout, which will be named by a structure *tag* name. For an application example, consider the definition of some "task" to be done. We give it a character-string description, and specify the time that the task is planned to start, the time that it actually does start, and the time that it finishes. We will represent "time" values as long integers, being noncommittal for now as to whether the units are years, days, sixtieths of a second, or whatever.

```
typedef long TIME;

struct task
    {
    char *desc;
    TIME plan;
    TIME start;
    TIME finish;
    };
```

The keyword struct is followed by a *tag* name (task, in this case) which can be used later to *declare* a variable to have this template —

```
struct task t;
```

declares one instance of the structure. Thus, t is a variable that has storage in the memory, whereas the tag task has no storage. The tag serves merely to name the "shape" or template for a structure. After

declaring the template named task, the words struct task constitute a
data type that can be used analogously with any other data type. Thus,

```
struct task ti, tj, tk;
```

declares three variables, each having the type struct task.

Question [8-1] What is the size of ti on a machine with 2-byte
addresses? With 4-byte addresses?

	2-byte machine	4-byte machine
sizeof(ti)	_____	_____

From this example, you see that the actual memory layout of a
specific structure may be different on different machines. Portable
code should never depend upon the actual byte-by-byte layout of structure members — let the compiler keep track of that.

Another issue for portability is the possibility of "holes" within a
structure, a consequence of *alignment requirements* of computer
hardware. On many machines, multi-byte data must be located at an
address that is divisible by two or four. If such data appears in a structure, and the previous structure member has not occupied all the space
to the next evenly-divisible address, the structure will contain a "hole"
— an unused, unoccupied space of one or more bytes. All the more reason not to write programs that embody assumptions about the actual
numeric values of member offsets.

We generally prefer to put the declarations of templates into
headers and to give each template a name in capital letters:

```
/* task.h - header for TASK structure
 */
typedef long TIME;         /* makes  TIME  a synonym for  long */
typedef struct task TASK;  /* makes  TASK  a synonym for  struct task */
struct task                /* and what is a  struct task ... */
    {
    char *desc;
    TIME plan;
    TIME start;
    TIME finish;
    };
```

This creates the same template as before, but we can now use the name
TASK as a data type, as in

```
TASK ti, tj, tk;
```

8.2 Members

The individual components of a structure can be referenced using the "dot", or *member*, operator:

```
ti.desc     has the type char *
ti.plan     has the type TIME
ti.start    has the type TIME
ti.finish   has the type TIME
```

The expression *structure.member* is an *lvalue* — it can be used anywhere that a variable name is allowed. Thus we can write

```
ti.start = 0;
```

or

```
tj.desc = "Write manuals";
```

The member names of each structure are unique to that structure; they may be used in other structures, or as variable names, without any conflict between the uses. Each member name defines a *type* and an *offset*:

```
Members of struct task:
```

Name	Type	Offset (2-byte machine)	Offset (4-byte machine)
desc	char *	0	0
plan	TIME (long)	2	4
start	TIME (long)	6	8
finish	TIME (long)	10	12

8.3 Initialization

Structure initialization is similar to array initialization, except that the data types being initialized may be different for each member. We could, for example, write

```
TASK vacation = {"leave for Hawaii", 1984, 0, 0};
```

(presumably treating the plan member as a "years" variable). As with arrays, if there are fewer initializers than members, the remaining members are initialized to zero.

Question [8-2] Write a short program vacat.c containing the above declaration for vacation. In the program, assign the value 1983 to the members start and finish. Print the resulting values of all members, using printf.

8.4 Nested Structures

One structure may be "nested" inside another. If, for example, we wished to record our TIME values as days and minutes, we could create a new template like this:

```
/* task2.h - header for TASK structure (using days and mins)
 */
typedef struct time TIME;
struct time
    {
    short days;
    short mins;
    };
typedef struct task TASK;
struct task
    {
    char *desc;
    TIME plan;
    TIME start;
    TIME finish;
    };
```

Now each of the TIME variables in a TASK is itself a structure, containing the members days and mins. If we declare a variable to be a TASK, as in

```
TASK t2;
```

we can now reference t2.plan.days, t2.plan.mins, and so forth.

8.5 Arrays of Structures

We could reserve storage for an array of five TASK structures with a declaration like this:

```
TASK tt[5];
```

which means the same as

```
struct task tt[5];
```

The following program will read input values for the structures in tt
and then print the resulting contents.

```
loadtt.c:
    /* loadtt - read data into the task table
     */
    #include "local.h"
    #include "task.h"    /* the original header: TIME == long */
    #define TSIZE 5
    int main(void)
        {
        TASK tt[TSIZE];              /* task table */
        char tstring[TSIZE][21];     /* string storage */
        short i;                     /* index for printing */
        short n;                     /* number of successful reads */
        short ret;                   /* returned value from scanf */

        n = 0;
        FOREVER
            {
            tt[n].desc = tstring[n];      /* desc gets the addr of nth tstring */
            ret = scanf("%20s%ld%ld%ld",  /* read structure members */
                tt[n].desc, &tt[n].plan, &tt[n].start, &tt[n].finish);
            if (ret == EOF)
                break;
            else if (ret != 4)
                error("Data error", "");
            else if (++n >= TSIZE)
                break;
            }
        for (i = 0; i < n; ++i)
            printf("%20s %8ld %8ld %8ld\n",
                tt[i].desc, tt[i].plan, tt[i].start, tt[i].finish);
        exit(0);
        }
```

Exercise 8-1. The following header task3.h has revised the declaration
of a TASK such that the storage for each desc member is a character array
included in the structure tt.

```
/* task3.h - header for TASK structure
 */
#define DSIZE 20
typedef long TIME;
typedef struct task TASK;
struct task
    {
    char desc[DSIZE+1];
    TIME plan;
    TIME start;
    TIME finish;
    };
```

Revise the loadtt.c program to use this revised declaration.

8.6 Pointers to Structures

A structure is an lvalue; you can take the address of a structure, assign into a structure, pass a structure as a function argument, and return a structure from a function:

&t	*address of* t
t1 = t2	*assign one structure to another*
t1 = f(t2)	*structure argument and structure return*
t.plan	*member* plan *of structure* t
sizeof(t)	*size of* t

These are the only operators allowed upon structures. For example, you cannot directly add one structure to another —

t1 + t2	*invalid syntax*

— but you could define a function which performs the addition, member-by-member, and get back a structure result.

When a structure is passed to a function, a copy of the entire structure is passed. Often it is more efficient to pass the *address* as an argument. In the called function, the argument needs to be declared as a pointer to a structure. For example, the declaration

    TASK *ptask;

declares that ptask has the type TASK * ("pointer to TASK"). To access the members of a structure that ptask points to, we use the "arrow" -> operator, as in

    ptask->start

Using structure pointers, we can write a function gettask and revise our loadtt program to use this function.

```
gettt.c:
    /* gettt - read data into the task table (using gettask function)
     */
    #include "local.h"
    #include "task3.h"              /* revised to include storage for desc */
    #define TSIZE 5
    short gettask(TASK *);          /* function to get one TASK */
    int main(void)
        {
        TASK tt[TSIZE];             /* task table */
        short i;                    /* index for printing */
        short n;                    /* number of successful reads */

        n = 0;
        while (n < TSIZE && gettask(&tt[n]) == 4)
            ++n;
        for (i = 0; i < n; ++i)
            printf("%20s %8ld %8ld %8ld\n",
                tt[i].desc, tt[i].plan, tt[i].start, tt[i].finish);
        exit(0);
        }
    /* gettask - get one TASK
     */
    short gettask(
        TASK *ptask)
        {
        return scanf("%20s%ld%ld%ld",
            ptask->desc, &ptask->plan, &ptask->start, &ptask->finish);
        }
```

Exercise 8-2. Write a program runtt.c which will accept lines of data like those read by gettt but if the desc agrees with an existing TASK, the various TIME members are updated in place. The resulting structure should be printed out in sequence by the plan member of each entry.

EPILOG

As this book goes to press, the new ANSI/ISO C Standard is in the final stages of ratification. An interesting observation from our consulting experience is that C programs are, in general, more easily ported to new environments than programs written in some other languages with a formal standard, such as Pascal. We have a possible explanation: C has a more realistic fit to real processors and systems, so there is less need for system-dependent extensions. This empirical suitability of C for modern computing has been well demonstrated in practice. There is a great future for Standard C.

Some people, of course, turn to the end of a book just to see how it comes out. If, however, you have completed the prevous chapters and done the questions and exercises, you now have the power of C language at your command. In particular, you have access to the entire data space available to your running program, which is essential in many engineering and systems programming applications.

As for the instructions that you prepare for the computer, the control structure of C provides just the facilities that are needed for readable programs. Well-constructed C programs will be easily understood by the people who maintain your programs in years to come.

To do operations beyone the repertory of C's operators and control structures, you can make use of the libraries provided by your vendor or your organization. Now is a good time for a detailed study of your manuals. Also, the Plum Hall intermediate book *Reliable Data Structures in C* will guide you through reliable use of pointers, structures, and files. You now know enough C to make full use of these capabilities; the time you spend with the manuals will be well repaid in programming skill.

And when you begin to dream C programs, you will know you have made the language your own.

APPENDIX A: C LANGUAGE REFERENCE

The following pages constitute a "pocket guide" to Standard C. They are not meant to replace the syntax reference that came with your compiler, but rather to serve as a guide to writing readable C programs according to the rules described in this book. Some of the more baroque possibilities of C syntax are deliberately omitted. (See, for example, Plauger and Brodie [1989] for full syntax rules.)

Each rule in Appendix A cites the appropriate section in the book; turn to that section for greater detail on syntax and usage.

The rules shown here use this syntax notation:

Symbol	Meaning	Usage
*	repetition	$stmt^*$ means "zero or more $stmt$s"
[]	option	$[stor\text{-}cl]$ means "an optional $stor\text{-}cl$"
|	choice	$h \mid t$ means "either h or t"
{}	grouping	$\{h \mid t\}^*$ means "a repetition of choices between h and t"

10.1 Programs

SECTION   READABILITY

A *source file* IS:

5.   program   /* comment
                  */
                 #include <std-file>
                 #include "local-file"
                 #define *ID* const

                 *data-definition**

                 *function**

A *data-definition* IS:

5.12   *decl* (external, with initializer)

A *function* IS:

5.1   *function*   /* comment
      with   */
      params   *type name*(
                        type a1,   /* describe a1 */
                        type a2)   /* describe a2 */
                        {
                        *decl**

                        *stmt**
                        }

5.1   *function*   /* comment
      without   */
      params   *type name*(void)
                        {
                        *decl**

                        *stmt**
                        }

10.2 Declarations

SECTION		READABILITY

A *decl* IS:

2.1	scalar (uninitialized)	*sc-type name* [, *name*]*;
2.1	scalar (initialized)	*sc-type name* = *expr*;
3.14	array (uninitialized)	*sc-type name*[*constant*];

5.15	array
	(initialized)
		sc-type name[*constant*] =
		{
		constant, [*constant*,]*
		};

5.13	*function* *decl*	*sc-type name*();
7.5	array param (pointer)	*sc-type name*[];
7.1	pointer	*sc-type *name*;
7.7	array of pointers	*sc-type *name*[*constant*];

8.1	structure
	template
		typedef struct *structyp STRUCTYP*;
		struct *structyp*
		{
		decl*
		};

8.1	structure (uninitialized)	*STRUCTYP name*;

8.3	structure
	(initialized)
		STRUCTYP name =
		{
		constant, [*constant*,]*
		};

8.5	array of structures	*STRUCTYP name*[*constant*];
8.6	pointer to structure	*STRUCTYP *name*;

10.3 Types

SECTION	READABILITY

An *sc-type* IS:

5.4 　　　　　　$[stor\text{-}cl]\ [qualifier]\ type$

A *type* IS:

2.2	integer	char	signed char	unsigned char
		short	signed short	unsigned short
		int	signed int	unsigned $[int]$
		long	signed long	unsigned long

2.3	floating-point	float
		double
		long double

3.21　*defined_type*　typedef *type* *defined_type*;

8.1　structure　struct *structyp*

8.1　structure
(typedef'*ed*)　　*STRUCTYP*

A *stor-cl* IS:

3.21　　　　　typedef

5.3　　　　　auto

5.7　　　　　static

5.12　　　　extern

5.13　　　　register

A *qualifier* IS:

5.4　　　　　const

　　　　　　volatile *(beyond the scope of this book)*

10.4 Statements

SECTION   READABILITY

    A *stmt* IS:

4.1	*expression* *statement*	*expr;*
4.1	null *statement*	;
4.1	return *statement*	return; return *expr;*

4.1	*block*
	(compound
	statement)
		{
		*stmt**
		}

4.2	if *statement*	if *(expr)* *stmt*

4.3	if
	statement
		if *(expr)*
		   stmt
		else
		   stmt

4.4	if
	statement
		if *(expr)*
		   stmt
		else if *(expr)*
		   stmt
		else if *(expr)*
		   stmt
		else
		   stmt

| 4.5 | switch *statement* | ```
switch (expr)
    {
case constant:
    stmt*
    break;
case constant:
case constant:
    stmt*
    break;
default:
    stmt*
    break;
    }
``` |

4.6   while *statement*

```
while (expr)
    stmt
```

4.7   for *statement*

```
for (expr; expr; expr)
    stmt
```

4.7   for *statement* (N + 1/2)

```
FOREVER
    {
    stmt*
    if (expr)
        break;
    stmt*
    }
```

4.8   do-while *statement*

```
do
    {
    stmt*
    } while (expr);
```

4.10   break *statement*

```
break;
```

4.10   continue *statement*

```
continue;
```

4.11   goto *statement*

```
goto label;   /* reason */
```
```

10.5 Expressions

SECTION		READABILITY
	AN *expr* IS:	
3.	unary *expr*	*unary-op* (NO SPACE) *expr*
3.9	postfix *expr*	*expr* (NO SPACE) *inc-dec-op*
3.	dyadic *expr*	*expr dyadic-op expr*
3.13	conditional	*expr* ? *expr* : *expr*
3.8	*function* call	*name*([*expr*[, *expr*]*])
3.14	subscript	*name*[*expr*]
5.11	two subs	*name*[*expr*][*expr*]
7.1	indirect	**name*
8.2	dot (*member*)	*name.member*
8.6	arrow (*member*)	*name->member*

Operator Type	Precedence Level	Operators	Associativity
Primary	15	( ) [] -> .	Left->Right
Unary	14	! ~ ++ -- + - (cast) * & sizeof	Right->Left
Arith-metic	13	* / %	Left->Right
	12	+ -	Left->Right
Shift	11	>> <<	Left->Right
Rel-ational	10	< <= > >=	Left->Right
	9	== !=	Left->Right
Bitwise	8	&	Left->Right
	7	^	Left->Right
	6	|	Left->Right
Logical	5	&&	Left->Right
	4	||	Left->Right
Cond.	3	?:	
Asst.	2	= += -= *= /= %= |= ^= &= >>= <<=	Right->Left
Comma	1	,	Left->Right

10.6 Selected C Library (Provided by local.h)

BOOK SECTION	STANDARD HEADER	SYNOPSIS	
5.18	<assert.h>	void	assert(int expr)
3.19	<stdlib.h>	double	atof(const char s[])
3.19	<stdlib.h>	int	atoi(const char s[])
3.19	<stdlib.h>	long	atol(const char s[])
3.17	<math.h>	double	ceil(double x)
3.17	<math.h>	double	cos(double x)
3.22	<stdlib.h>	void	exit(int n)
3.17	<math.h>	double	exp(double x)
3.22	<stdio.h>	char	*fgets(char s[], size_t size, FILE *fp)
3.17	<math.h>	double	floor(double x)
3.22	<stdio.h>	int	fprintf(FILE *fp, const char fmt[], ...)
3.4	<stdio.h>	int	getchar(void) /* : metachar */
3.14	"local.h"	int	getln(char s[], n) [not Standard C]
3.5	<ctype.h>	int	isalnum(int c) /* : bool */
3.5	<ctype.h>	int	isalpha(int c) /* : bool */
3.5	<ctype.h>	int	iscntrl(int c) /* : bool */
3.5	<ctype.h>	int	isdigit(int c) /* : bool */
3.5	<ctype.h>	int	isgraph(int c) /* : bool */
3.5	<ctype.h>	int	islower(int c) /* : bool */
3.5	<ctype.h>	int	isprint(int c) /* : bool */
3.5	<ctype.h>	int	ispunct(int c) /* : bool */
3.5	<ctype.h>	int	isspace(int c) /* : bool */
3.5	<ctype.h>	int	isupper(int c) /* : bool */
3.5	<ctype.h>	int	isxdigit(int c) /* : bool */
3.17	<math.h>	double	log(double x)
3.17	<math.h>	double	log10(double x)
3.17	<math.h>	double	pow(double x, double y)
2.8	<stdio.h>	int	printf(const char fmt[], ...)
3.4	<stdio.h>	int	putchar(int c)
5.8	<stdlib.h>	int	rand(void)
3.12	<stdio.h>	int	scanf(const char fmt[], ...)
3.17	<math.h>	double	sin(double x)
3.19	<stdio.h>	int	sprintf(char s[], const char fmt[], ...)
3.17	<math.h>	double	sqrt(double x)
5.8	<stdlib.h>	void	srand(int n)
3.19	<stdio.h>	int	sscanf(const char s[], const char fmt[], ...)
3.14	<string.h>	char	*strcat(char s1[], const char s2[])
6.3	<string.h>	char	*strchr(char s1[], int c)
3.14	<string.h>	int	strcmp(const char s1[], const char s2[])
3.14	<string.h>	char	*strcpy(char s1[], const char s2[])
3.14	<string.h>	size_t	strlen(const char s[])
5.4	<string.h>	int	strncmp(const char s1[], const char s2[], size_t size)
5.4	<string.h>	char	*strncpy(char s1[], const char s2[], size_t size)
6.3	<string.h>	char	*strrchr(const char s[], int c)
3.13	<ctype.h>	int	tolower(int c)
3.13	<ctype.h>	int	toupper(int c)

10.7 Formats for Printf

format-string:
    item●

item:
    non-%   ordinary character to print
    %%   print single %
    specification format for one data *item*

specification:
    % [*flags*] [*width*] [*.precision*] [*size*] *conversion-char*

flags:
    -                print left-adjusted
    +   print either a minus-sign or a plus-sign
    space   print either a minus-sign or a space
    #   use "alternate form" (see each *conversion-char*)
    0   print leading zeros

size:
    h   short (for integer formats)
    l   long (for integer formats)
    L   long double (for floating-point formats)

conversion-char:
    c   character
    d   decimal integer
    u   unsigned integer
    o   octal integer
                     (with # flag, forces a leading zero)
    x   hexadecimal integer (with lower-case abcdef)
                     (with # flag, forces a leading 0x)
    X   hexadecimal integer (with upper-case ABCDEF)
                     (with # flag, forces a leading 0X)
    f   fixed-point
                     (with # flag, forces a decimal-point)
    e   E-format (with lower-case e)
                     (with # flag, forces a decimal-point)
    E   E-format (with upper-case E)
                     (with # flag, forces a decimal-point)
    s   string

width:
    digit digit● Pad field to this *width* (with spaces or zeros)

precision:
    digit digit● d o u x X Min number of (zero-padded) *digit*s to print
                    e E f   Number of *digit*s after decimal point
                    s   Max number of characters to print

10.8 Formats for Scanf

format-string:
    *item**

item:
    non-%   ordinary character to match
    %%   match single %
    specification format for one data *item*

specification:
    % [*flags*] [*width*] [*size*]   *conversion-char*

flags:
    *   Match input, but suppress assignment

width:
    *digit digit** Maximum number of input characters to take

size:
    h   short (for integer formats)
    l   long (for integer formats)
    l   double (for floating-point formats)
    L   long double (for floating-point formats)

conversion-char:
    c   character
    d   decimal integer
    u   unsigned integer
    o   octal integer
    x   hexadecimal integer
    e f   floating-point value
    s   string

10.9 Common C Bugs

General

Uninitalized variables □ Off-by-one errors □ Treating an array as though it were 1-origin (instead of 0-origin) □ Unclosed comments □ Forgetting semicolons □ Misplaced braces □

Types, Operators, and Expressions

Using `char` for the returned value from `getchar` □ "Backslash" typed as "slash"; e.g., `'/n'` instead of `'\n'` □ Arithmetic overflow □ Using relational operators on strings; e.g. `s == "end"` instead of `strcmp(s, "end")` □ Using = instead of == □ "Grey expressions", which depend upon the order of side effects; e.g., `a[n] = n++;` □ Off-by-one errors in loops with increment □ Precedence of bitwise operators. (Always parenthesize them.) □ Right-shifting negative numbers (not equivalent to division) □ Assuming the order of evaluation of expressions □ Forgetting null-terminator on strings □

Control flow

Misplaced `else` □ Missing `break` in `switch` □ Loop with first or last case abnormal in some way □ Loop mistakenly never entered □ Indexing an array with `for (i = 0; i <= NELEMENTS; ++i)` which goes one step too far □ Putting semicolon on the control line of `for`, `while`, `if`, etc □

Functions and program structure

Wrong type of arguments (relying on memory instead of manual) □ Wrong order of arguments □ Omitting `static` on function's abiding storage □ Assuming that `static` storage is re-initialized at each re-entry □

Pointers and arrays

Passing pointer instead of value — or value instead of pointer □ Confusing `char` with `char *` □ Using pointers for strings without allocating storage for the string □ Dangling pointer references — references to storage no longer used □ Confusing single quotes (`'\n'`) with double quotes (`"\n"`) □

10.10 Table of ASCII Characters

Table of ASCII characters: ASCII, decimal, octal, hexadecimal

nul	0	0000	0x00	sp	32	0040	0x20	@	64	0100	0x40	'	96	0140	0x60	
soh	1	0001	0x01	!	33	0041	0x21	A	65	0101	0x41	a	97	0141	0x61	
stx	2	0002	0x02	"	34	0042	0x22	B	66	0102	0x42	b	98	0142	0x62	
etx	3	0003	0x03	#	35	0043	0x23	C	67	0103	0x43	c	99	0143	0x63	
eot	4	0004	0x04	$	36	0044	0x24	D	68	0104	0x44	d	100	0144	0x64	
enq	5	0005	0x05	%	37	0045	0x25	E	69	0105	0x45	e	101	0145	0x65	
ack	6	0006	0x06	&	38	0046	0x26	F	70	0106	0x46	f	102	0146	0x66	
bel	7	0007	0x07	'	39	0047	0x27	G	71	0107	0x47	g	103	0147	0x67	
bs	8	0010	0x08	(	40	0050	0x28	H	72	0110	0x48	h	104	0150	0x68	
ht	9	0011	0x09	)	41	0051	0x29	I	73	0111	0x49	i	105	0151	0x69	
lf	10	0012	0x0a	*	42	0052	0x2a	J	74	0112	0x4a	j	106	0152	0x6a	
vt	11	0013	0x0b	+	43	0053	0x2b	K	75	0113	0x4b	k	107	0153	0x6b	
ff	12	0014	0x0c	,	44	0054	0x2c	L	76	0114	0x4c	l	108	0154	0x6c	
cr	13	0015	0x0d	-	45	0055	0x2d	M	77	0115	0x4d	m	109	0155	0x6d	
so	14	0016	0x0e	.	46	0056	0x2e	N	78	0116	0x4e	n	110	0156	0x6e	
si	15	0017	0x0f	/	47	0057	0x2f	O	79	0117	0x4f	o	111	0157	0x6f	
dle	16	0020	0x10	0	48	0060	0x30	P	80	0120	0x50	p	112	0160	0x70	
dc1	17	0021	0x11	1	49	0061	0x31	Q	81	0121	0x51	q	113	0161	0x71	
dc2	18	0022	0x12	2	50	0062	0x32	R	82	0122	0x52	r	114	0162	0x72	
dc3	19	0023	0x13	3	51	0063	0x33	S	83	0123	0x53	s	115	0163	0x73	
dc4	20	0024	0x14	4	52	0064	0x34	T	84	0124	0x54	t	116	0164	0x74	
nak	21	0025	0x15	5	53	0065	0x35	U	85	0125	0x55	u	117	0165	0x75	
syn	22	0026	0x16	6	54	0066	0x36	V	86	0126	0x56	v	118	0166	0x76	
etb	23	0027	0x17	7	55	0067	0x37	W	87	0127	0x57	w	119	0167	0x77	
can	24	0030	0x18	8	56	0070	0x38	X	88	0130	0x58	x	120	0170	0x78	
em	25	0031	0x19	9	57	0071	0x39	Y	89	0131	0x59	y	121	0171	0x79	
sub	26	0032	0x1a	:	58	0072	0x3a	Z	90	0132	0x5a	z	122	0172	0x7a	
esc	27	0033	0x1b	;	59	0073	0x3b	[	91	0133	0x5b	{	123	0173	0x7b	
fs	28	0034	0x1c	<	60	0074	0x3c	\	92	0134	0x5c	|	124	0174	0x7c	
gs	29	0035	0x1d	=	61	0075	0x3d	]	93	0135	0x5d	}	125	0175	0x7d	
rs	30	0036	0x1e	>	62	0076	0x3e	^	94	0136	0x5e	~	126	0176	0x7e	
us	31	0037	0x1f	?	63	0077	0x3f	_	95	0137	0x5f	del	127	0177	0x7f	

10.11 Idioms of C Programming

Certain constructions of C are familiar patterns to experienced programmers but puzzle the novice. Herewith, a few of the common ones. Each brief discussion references a section number of *Learning to Program in C*.

c i j n p s *(as variable names)*
> Conventional variable names: c is a *character*, i and j are *integer indexes*, n is a *number of something*, p is a *pointer*, and s is a *string*. (2.6)

for (n = 10; n >= 0; --n) *(or)* for (c = 0; c <= 127; ++c)
> In an ordinary for loop that counts from a high limit to a low limit, or vice versa, the limit values appear in the control line. (3.2, 3.3)

d != 0 && n/d < 10
> The "short-circuit" logical operator && prevents the second expression from being evaluated if the first expression tests *false*. (3.3)

for (i = 0; s[i] != '\0'; ++i)
> Run the loop until a terminating value is hit. (3.14)

for (i = 0, j = MAX; i < j; ++i, --j)
> Two indexes, i and j, are given equal status in the loop. (3.15)

if (c) *(or)* if (iswhite) *(or)* if (p)
> The comparison to zero of a character, Boolean, or pointer is implied by the "test" of an if, for, while. However, comparisons of *numeric* data against zero should always be written in full. (4.2, 7.5)

while ((c = getchar()) != EOF)
> The "initialization" of the loop is the same as the "step" to the next case. (4.6)

for (;;)
> A "forever" loop, perhaps terminated by a break in the body. We suggest the definition of FOREVER. (4.7)

for (i = 0; i < NCARDS; ++i)
> A loop over the elements of an array, with a "test" that compares the subscript with the number of array elements, using <, not <=. (5.9)

short ndisks[3] = {0};
> The initialization = {0} when applied to an array or structure fills the entire aggregate with zeroes (a special case). (5.11)

for (p = s; *p; ++p)
> A loop over the characters in the string s using a pointer p. (7.5)

APPENDIX B: ANSWERS TO QUESTIONS

2.1 Bits and Numbers

Question [2-1] What is the decimal value of the following binary numbers?

00001111	01010101	10000001
15	85	129

Question [2-2] What is the 8-bit sum? What does each number equal in decimal? Do each problem both in unsigned and twos complement signed interpretation.

binary	unsigned decimal	signed decimal (twos complement)
00101011 =	43	43
+ 10000011 =	131	-125

10101110	174	-82
11110000 =	240	-16
+ 00001111 =	15	15

11111111	255	-1
10000000 =	128	-128
+ 00001010 =	10	10

10001010	138	-118

Now compute these 8-bit sums, using ones complement interpretation:

binary	signed decimal (ones complement)
00101011 =	43
+ 10000011 =	-124

10101110	-81
11110000 =	-15
+ 00001111 =	15

11111111	0
11111101 =	-2
+ 11111110 =	-1

11111100	-3

2.4 Constants

Question [2-3] What is the type of each constant:

123	int	1.2	double
'x'	int	1.5E4	double
5L	long	'2'	int

What does this string constant look like in memory:

"000"

```
| 48 | 48 | 48 |  0  |
| '0'| '0'| '0'|'\0' |
```

2.5 Octal and Hexadecimal Numbers

Question [2-4] Write down the octal equivalent for each binary number:

10110010   11111111

0262   0377

1101100100110110   1111111111111111

0154466   0177777

Question [2-5] Write down the binary equivalent (8 or 16 bits) for each octal number:

    014   0177

    00001100   01111111

      0200   014662   052525

    10000000   0001100110110010   0101010101010101

Question [2-6] Write down the hexadecimal equivalent for each binary number:

    10110010   11111111

       0xB2   0xFF

    1101100100110110   1111111111111111

          0xD936   0xFFFF

Question [2-7] Convert from the hexadecimal to the corresponding binary?

       0xFE   0x40

    11111110   01000000

       0x7FFF   0x9A6E

    0111111111111111   1001101001101110

2.6 Atoms of a C Program

Question [2-8] Write the category of atom next to each atom of `hello3.c`.

separator #	*keyword* include *header-name* <stdio.h>
name	main
separator	(
separator	)
separator	{
name	printf
separator	(
constant	"hello, world\n"
separator	)
separator	;
separator	}

2.8 Output and Printf

Question [2-9] What does the output of `asst2.c` look like (in our Typical Environment with ASCII codes and 16-bit `int`'s)?

```
c: dec=65 oct=101 hex=41 char=A
i: dec=65 oct=101 hex=41 unsigned=65
c: dec=88 oct=130 hex=58 char=X
i: dec=-4 oct=177774 hex=FFFC unsigned=65532
```

Question [2-10] If each format in `asst2.c` is changed to a 6-position width, what does its output look like?

```
c: dec=    65 oct=   101 hex=    41 char=     A
i: dec=    65 oct=   101 hex=    41 unsigned=    65
c: dec=    88 oct=   130 hex=    58 char=     X
i: dec=    -4 oct=177774 hex=  FFFC unsigned= 65532
```

2.10 Define and Include

Contents of "local.h" header:

```
/* local.h - local standard header file */
/* (A subset of full Plum Hall  local.h ) */
#ifndef LOCAL_H
#define LOCAL_H
#include <assert.h>
#include <ctype.h>
#include <errno.h>
#include <float.h>
#include <limits.h>
#include <math.h>
#include <stddef.h>
#include <stdlib.h>
#include <stdio.h>
#include <string.h>
#include <time.h>
#define FOREVER        for (;;)    /* endless loop */
#define NO             0           /* : bool */
#define YES            1           /* : bool */
#define getln(s, n)    ((fgets(s, n,stdin)==NULL) ? EOF : strlen(s))
#define ABS(x)         (((x) < 0) ? -(x) : (x))
#define MAX(x, y)      (((x) < (y)) ? (y) : (x))
#define MIN(x, y)      (((x) < (y)) ? (x) : (y))

typedef signed char    schar;
typedef unsigned char  uchar;
typedef unsigned short ushort;
typedef unsigned int   uint;
typedef unsigned long  ulong;
typedef int            bool;      /* : bool */
typedef short          metachar;  /* : metachar */

#endif  /* LOCAL_H */
```

3.1 Arithmetic Operators

Question [3-1] Draw expression trees for the following expressions:

     a + b % c   -a / b   a * -b

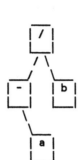 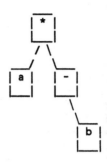

Question [3-2] How many subexpressions are there in this expression?
11
List them.

     (a + b) * (c + d) + e

     1.   a
     2.   b
     3.   c
     4.   d
     5.   e
     6.   a + b
     7.   (a + b)
     8.   c + d
     9.   (c + d)
     10. (a + b) * (c + d)
     11. (a + b) * (c + d) + e

Question [3-3] What does `arith.c` print?

```
3 2 -8 2
3.00000 2.50000 -8.00000
```

Question [3-4] If `a` equals 8, `b` equals 2, and `c` equals 4, what is the resulting value of each expression:

a + b % c	-a / b	a * -b
10	-4	-16

3.3 Logical Operators

Output file codes1.out (output from codes1.c in an ASCII environment):

0 0x00 0000		32 0x20 0040 ' '	
1 0x01 0001		33 0x21 0041 '!'	
2 0x02 0002		34 0x22 0042 '"'	
3 0x03 0003		35 0x23 0043 '#'	
4 0x04 0004		36 0x24 0044 '$'	
5 0x05 0005		37 0x25 0045 '%'	
6 0x06 0006		38 0x26 0046 '&'	
7 0x07 0007		39 0x27 0047 '''	
8 0x08 0010		40 0x28 0050 '('	
9 0x09 0011		41 0x29 0051 ')'	
10 0x0A 0012		42 0x2A 0052 '*'	
11 0x0B 0013		43 0x2B 0053 '+'	
12 0x0C 0014		44 0x2C 0054 ','	
13 0x0D 0015		45 0x2D 0055 '-'	
14 0x0E 0016		46 0x2E 0056 '.'	
15 0x0F 0017		47 0x2F 0057 '/'	
16 0x10 0020		48 0x30 0060 '0' digit	
17 0x11 0021		49 0x31 0061 '1' digit	
18 0x12 0022		50 0x32 0062 '2' digit	
19 0x13 0023		51 0x33 0063 '3' digit	
20 0x14 0024		52 0x34 0064 '4' digit	
21 0x15 0025		53 0x35 0065 '5' digit	
22 0x16 0026		54 0x36 0066 '6' digit	
23 0x17 0027		55 0x37 0067 '7' digit	
24 0x18 0030		56 0x38 0070 '8' digit	
25 0x19 0031		57 0x39 0071 '9' digit	
26 0x1A 0032		58 0x3A 0072 ':'	
27 0x1B 0033		59 0x3B 0073 ';'	
28 0x1C 0034		60 0x3C 0074 '<'	
29 0x1D 0035		61 0x3D 0075 '='	
30 0x1E 0036		62 0x3E 0076 '>'	
31 0x1F 0037		63 0x3F 0077 '?'	

Output file codes1.out (continued):

64 0x40 0100 '@'		96 0x60 0140 '`'	
65 0x41 0101 'A' uppercase		97 0x61 0141 'a' lowercase	
66 0x42 0102 'B' uppercase		98 0x62 0142 'b' lowercase	
67 0x43 0103 'C' uppercase		99 0x63 0143 'c' lowercase	
68 0x44 0104 'D' uppercase		100 0x64 0144 'd' lowercase	
69 0x45 0105 'E' uppercase		101 0x65 0145 'e' lowercase	
70 0x46 0106 'F' uppercase		102 0x66 0146 'f' lowercase	
71 0x47 0107 'G' uppercase		103 0x67 0147 'g' lowercase	
72 0x48 0110 'H' ,uppercase		104 0x68 0150 'h' lowercase	
73 0x49 0111 'I' uppercase		105 0x69 0151 'i' lowercase	
74 0x4A 0112 'J' uppercase		106 0x6A 0152 'j' lowercase	
75 0x4B 0113 'K' uppercase		107 0x6B 0153 'k' lowercase	
76 0x4C 0114 'L' uppercase		108 0x6C 0154 'l' lowercase	
77 0x4D 0115 'M' uppercase		109 0x6D 0155 'm' lowercase	
78 0x4E 0116 'N' uppercase		110 0x6E 0156 'n' lowercase	
79 0x4F 0117 'O' uppercase		111 0x6F 0157 'o' lowercase	
80 0x50 0120 'P' uppercase		112 0x70 0160 'p' lowercase	
81 0x51 0121 'Q' uppercase		113 0x71 0161 'q' lowercase	
82 0x52 0122 'R' uppercase		114 0x72 0162 'r' lowercase	
83 0x53 0123 'S' uppercase		115 0x73 0163 's' lowercase	
84 0x54 0124 'T' uppercase		116 0x74 0164 't' lowercase	
85 0x55 0125 'U' uppercase		117 0x75 0165 'u' lowercase	
86 0x56 0126 'V' uppercase		118 0x76 0166 'v' lowercase	
87 0x57 0127 'W' uppercase		119 0x77 0167 'w' lowercase	
88 0x58 0130 'X' uppercase		120 0x78 0170 'x' lowercase	
89 0x59 0131 'Y' uppercase		121 0x79 0171 'y' lowercase	
90 0x5A 0132 'Z' uppercase		122 0x7A 0172 'z' lowercase	
91 0x5B 0133 '['		123 0x7B 0173 '{'	
92 0x5C 0134 '\'		124 0x7C 0174 '	'	
93 0x5D 0135 ']'		125 0x7D 0175 '}'	
94 0x5E 0136 '^'		126 0x7E 0176 '~'	
95 0x5F 0137 '_'		127 0x7F 0177	

Question [3-5] When the variable c reaches the value 0x20 (ASCII blank, or ' ') how many of the relational expressions in codes1.c evaluate to a *true* (1) result? *2*

```
' ' <= c
c <= '~'
```

(Remember that if the left-hand operand of && evaluates to *false*, the right-hand operand is not even evaluated.)

How many evaluate to *true* for the value 126 (tilde, '~')? *5*

```
' ' <= c
c <= '~'
'0' <= c
'A' <= c
'a' <= c
```

Write the value of each expression (0 or 1):

```
1 < 4 && 4 < 7          1
1 < 4 && 8 < 4          0
!(2 <= 5)               0
!(1 < 3) || (2 < 4)     1
!(4 <= 6 && 3 <= 7)     0
```

3.4 Character Input/Output

Question [3-6] If you typed one line of input to this program, consisting of the characters 1aA! followed by a newline, what would its output be?

```
49 0x31 0061 '1' digit
97 0x61 0141 'a' lowercase
65 0x41 0101 'A' uppercase
33 0x21 0041 '!'
10 0x0A 0012
```

The fifth line of output comes from the newline ('\n') at the end of your typed input line.

3.5 Character-type Tests

Output file codes4.out (output from codes4.c in an ASCII environment):

0	0x00	0000	C		32	0x20	0040	' '	S				
1	0x01	0001	C		33	0x21	0041	'!'	G	P			
2	0x02	0002	C		34	0x22	0042	'"'	G	P			
3	0x03	0003	C		35	0x23	0043	'#'	G	P			
4	0x04	0004	C		36	0x24	0044	'$'	G	P			
5	0x05	0005	C		37	0x25	0045	'%'	G	P			
6	0x06	0006	C		38	0x26	0046	'&'	G	P			
7	0x07	0007	C		39	0x27	0047	'''	G	P			
8	0x08	0010	C		40	0x28	0050	'('	G	P			
9	0x09	0011	S C		41	0x29	0051	')'	G	P			
10	0x0A	0012	S C		42	0x2A	0052	'*'	G	P			
11	0x0B	0013	S C		43	0x2B	0053	'+'	G	P			
12	0x0C	0014	S C		44	0x2C	0054	','	G	P			
13	0x0D	0015	S C		45	0x2D	0055	'-'	G	P			
14	0x0E	0016	C		46	0x2E	0056	'.'	G	P			
15	0x0F	0017	C		47	0x2F	0057	'/'	G	P			
16	0x10	0020	C		48	0x30	0060	'0'	G	D	X	AN	
17	0x11	0021	C		49	0x31	0061	'1'	G	D	X	AN	
18	0x12	0022	C		50	0x32	0062	'2'	G	D	X	AN	
19	0x13	0023	C		51	0x33	0063	'3'	G	D	X	AN	
20	0x14	0024	C		52	0x34	0064	'4'	G	D	X	AN	
21	0x15	0025	C		53	0x35	0065	'5'	G	D	X	AN	
22	0x16	0026	C		54	0x36	0066	'6'	G	D	X	AN	
23	0x17	0027	C		55	0x37	0067	'7'	G	D	X	AN	
24	0x18	0030	C		56	0x38	0070	'8'	G	D	X	AN	
25	0x19	0031	C		57	0x39	0071	'9'	G	D	X	AN	
26	0x1A	0032	C		58	0x3A	0072	':'	G	P			
27	0x1B	0033	C		59	0x3B	0073	';'	G	P			
28	0x1C	0034	C		60	0x3C	0074	'<'	G	P			
29	0x1D	0035	C		61	0x3D	0075	'='	G	P			
30	0x1E	0036	C		62	0x3E	0076	'>'	G	P			
31	0x1F	0037	C		63	0x3F	0077	'?'	G	P			

Output file codes4.out (continued):

```
64 0x40 0100 '@' G P                              96 0x60 0140 '`' G P
65 0x41 0101 'A' G X UC L AN tolower(c) = 'a'     97 0x61 0141 'a' G X LC L AN toupper(c)='A'
66 0x42 0102 'B' G X UC L AN tolower(c) = 'b'     98 0x62 0142 'b' G X LC L AN toupper(c)='B'
67 0x43 0103 'C' G X UC L AN tolower(c) = 'c'     99 0x63 0143 'c' G X LC L AN toupper(c)='C'
68 0x44 0104 'D' G X UC L AN tolower(c) = 'd'    100 0x64 0144 'd' G X LC L AN toupper(c)='D'
69 0x45 0105 'E' G X UC L AN tolower(c) = 'e'    101 0x65 0145 'e' G X LC L AN toupper(c)='E'
70 0x46 0106 'F' G X UC L AN tolower(c) = 'f'    102 0x66 0146 'f' G X LC L AN toupper(c)='F'
71 0x47 0107 'G' G UC L AN tolower(c) = 'g'      103 0x67 0147 'g' G LC L AN toupper(c)='G'
72 0x48 0110 'H' G UC L AN tolower(c) = 'h'      104 0x68 0150 'h' G LC L AN toupper(c)='H'
73 0x49 0111 'I' G UC L AN tolower(c) = 'i'      105 0x69 0151 'i' G LC L AN toupper(c)='I'
74 0x4A 0112 'J' G UC L AN tolower(c) = 'j'      106 0x6A 0152 'j' G LC L AN toupper(c)='J'
75 0x4C 0113 'K' G UC L AN tolower(c) = 'k'      107 0x6B 0153 'k' G LC L AN toupper(c)='K'
76 0x4C 0114 'L' G UC L AN tolower(c) = 'l'      108 0x6C 0154 'l' G LC L AN toupper(c)='L'
77 0x4D 0115 'M' G UC L AN tolower(c) = 'm'      109 0x6D 0155 'm' G LC L AN toupper(c)='M'
78 0x4E 0116 'N' G UC L AN tolower(c) = 'n'      110 0x6E 0156 'n' G LC L AN toupper(c)='N'
79 0x4F 0117 'O' G UC L AN tolower(c) = 'o'      111 0x6F 0157 'o' G LC L AN toupper(c)='O'
80 0x50 0120 'P' G UC L AN tolower(c) = 'p'      112 0x70 0160 'p' G LC L AN toupper(c)='P'
81 0x51 0121 'Q' G UC L AN tolower(c) = 'q'      113 0x71 0161 'q' G LC L AN toupper(c)='Q'
82 0x52 0122 'R' G UC L AN tolower(c) = 'r'      114 0x72 0162 'r' G LC L AN toupper(c)='R'
83 0x53 0123 'S' G UC L AN tolower(c) = 's'      115 0x73 0163 's' G LC L AN toupper(c)='S'
84 0x54 0124 'T' G UC L AN tolower(c) = 't'      116 0x74 0164 't' G LC L AN toupper(c)='T'
85 0x55 0125 'U' G UC L AN tolower(c) = 'u'      117 0x75 0165 'u' G LC L AN toupper(c)='U'
86 0x56 0126 'V' G UC L AN tolower(c) = 'v'      118 0x76 0166 'v' G LC L AN toupper(c)='V'
87 0x57 0127 'W' G UC L AN tolower(c) = 'w'      119 0x77 0167 'w' G LC L AN toupper(c)='W'
88 0x58 0130 'X' G UC L AN tolower(c) = 'x'      120 0x78 0170 'x' G LC L AN toupper(c)='X'
89 0x59 0131 'Y' G UC L AN tolower(c) = 'y'      121 0x79 0171 'y' G LC L AN toupper(c)='Y'
90 0x5A 0132 'Z' G UC L AN tolower(c) = 'z'      122 0x7A 0172 'z' G LC L AN toupper(c)='Z'
91 0x5B 0133 '[' G P                             123 0x7B 0173 '{' G P
92 0x5C 0134 '\' G P                             124 0x7C 0174 '|' G P
93 0x5D 0135 ']' G P                             125 0x7D 0175 '}' G P
94 0x5E 0136 '^' G P                             126 0x7E 0176 '~' G P
95 0x5F 0137 '_' G P                             127 0x7F 0177 C
```

Output file codes4.out (continued):

128 0x80 0200	160 0xA0 0240	192 0xC0 0300	224 0xE0 0340
129 0x81 0201	161 0xA1 0241	193 0xC1 0301	225 0xE1 0341
130 0x82 0202	162 0xA2 0242	194 0xC2 0302	226 0xE2 0342
131 0x83 0203	163 0xA3 0243	195 0xC3 0303	227 0xE3 0343
132 0x84 0204	164 0xA4 0244	196 0xC4 0304	228 0xE4 0344
133 0x85 0205	165 0xA5 0245	197 0xC5 0305	229 0xE5 0345
134 0x86 0206	166 0xA6 0246	198 0xC6 0306	230 0xE6 0346
135 0x87 0207	167 0xA7 0247	199 0xC7 0307	231 0xE7 0347
136 0x88 0210	168 0xA8 0250	200 0xC8 0310	232 0xE8 0350
137 0x89 0211	169 0xA9 0251	201 0xC9 0311	233 0xE9 0351
138 0x8A 0212	170 0xAA 0252	202 0xCA 0312	234 0xEA 0352
139 0x8B 0213	171 0xAB 0253	203 0xCB 0313	235 0xEB 0353
140 0x8C 0214	172 0xAC 0254	204 0xCC 0314	236 0xEC 0354
141 0x8D 0215	173 0xAD 0255	205 0xCD 0315	237 0xED 0355
142 0x8E 0216	174 0xAE 0256	206 0xCE 0316	238 0xEE 0356
143 0x8F 0217	175 0xAF 0257	207 0xCF 0317	239 0xEF 0357
144 0x90 0220	176 0xB0 0260	208 0xD0 0320	240 0xF0 0360
145 0x91 0221	177 0xB1 0261	209 0xD1 0321	241 0xF1 0361
146 0x92 0222	178 0xB2 0262	210 0xD2 0322	242 0xF2 0362
147 0x93 0223	179 0xB3 0263	211 0xD3 0323	243 0xF3 0363
148 0x94 0224	180 0xB4 0264	212 0xD4 0324	244 0xF4 0364
149 0x95 0225	181 0xB5 0265	213 0xD5 0325	245 0xF5 0365
150 0x96 0226	182 0xB6 0266	214 0xD6 0326	246 0xF6 0366
151 0x97 0227	183 0xB7 0267	215 0xD7 0327	247 0xF7 0367
152 0x98 0230	184 0xB8 0270	216 0xD8 0330	248 0xF8 0370
153 0x99 0231	185 0xB9 0271	217 0xD9 0331	249 0xF9 0371
154 0x9A 0232	186 0xBA 0272	218 0xDA 0332	250 0xFA 0372
155 0x9B 0233	187 0xBB 0273	219 0xDB 0333	251 0xFB 0373
156 0x9C 0234	188 0xBC 0274	220 0xDC 0334	252 0xFC 0374
157 0x9D 0235	189 0xBD 0275	221 0xDD 0335	253 0xFD 0375
158 0x9E 0236	190 0xBE 0276	222 0xDE 0336	254 0xFE 0376
159 0x9F 0237	191 0xBF 0277	223 0xDF 0337	255 0xFF 0377

3.6 Bitwise Logical Operators

Question [3-7] Convert each number to 16-bit binary, and then negate it:

0x40 =	0000000001000000	01 =	0000000000000001
~0x40 =	1111111110111111	~01 =	1111111111111110

Question [3-8] Write the binary result of these operations:

```
  0000000001111111        0000000011000000        1111111111111100
& 0111010110011010      | 1000000000000100        1000000001111111

  0000000000011010        100000011000100         0111111110000011
```

Question [3-9] Write the ones complement and twos complement of these numbers:

```
9U = 0000000000001001    0xFF00U = 1111111100000000

     1111111111110110            0000000011111111
     (ones complement)           (ones complement)

     1111111111110111            0000000100000000
     (twos complement)           (twos complement)
```

3.7 Shift Operators

Question [3-10] What output will getbn produce for input 100001?

```
33 0x0021 0000041
```

For input 1111111111111111?

```
65535 0xffff 0177777
```

3.8 Functions

Question [3-11] If the input to getbn2 consists of these three lines

```
101
1111
00000
```

what does the output look like:

```
 5 0x0005 0000005
15 0x000f 0000017
```

(Remember that a return of 0 from getbin is taken as end-of-file, so the line 00000 generates no output.)

Question [3-12] Referring to the printf manual page, how can the output be printed *left-adjusted* in its field width?

By prefixing a minus-sign to its field width, as in %-5d.

Question [3-13] What output will bdrill produce from this input?

```
10101
11001
```

```
    a = 0000000000010101
    b = 0000000000011001
a + b = 0000000000101110
a & b = 0000000000010001
a | b = 0000000000011101
a ^ b = 0000000000001100
```

3.12 Address-of Operator and Scanf

Question [3-14] Write a program, pr2a.c, to read two hexadecimal numbers into long variables, and print the two variables and their sum.

```
pr2a.c:
    /* pr2a - print the sum of two long inputs
     */
    #include "local.h"
    main()
        {
        long a, b;

        scanf("%lx %lx", &a, &b);
        printf("    a = %8lx\n", a);
        printf("    b = %8lx\n", b);
        printf("a + b = %8lx\n", a + b);
        }
```

Make another such program, pr2b.c, with double variables, using the proper formats.

```
pr2b.c:
    /* pr2b - print the sum of two double inputs
     */
    #include "local.h"
    main()
        {
        double a, b;

        scanf("%lf %lf", &a, &b);
        printf("    a = %12.6e\n", a);
        printf("    b = %12.6e\n", b);
        printf("a + b = %12.6e\n", a + b);
        }
```

3.13 Conditional Operator

Question [3-15] Modify your pr2b.c program to create maxmin.c which prints the max and min of the two input numbers.

```
maxmin.c:
    /* maxmin - print the max and min of two double inputs
     */
    #include "local.h"
    main()
        {
        double a, b;

        if (scanf("%lf %lf", &a, &b) == 2)
            {
            printf("  a = %12.6e\n", a);
            printf("  b = %12.6e\n", b);
            printf("max = %12.6e\n", a < b ? b : a);
            printf("min = %12.6e\n", a < b ? a : b);
            }
        }
```

3.14 Arrays and Subscripting

Question [3-16] What does string.c print?

every good boy does fine

3.16 Order of Evaluation

Question [3-17] Mark Y or N whether each of these statements contains a *grey expression*:

```
Y     n = n++;

Y     printf("%d %d\n", ++n, ++n);

N     n = ++m;

N     n = y *= 2;

N     a[i++] += 3;

Y     a[i++] = a[i++] + 3;
```

3.18 Precedence and Associativity

Question [3-18] Parenthesize to show the binding:

```
(a  ==  b)  &&  (c  !=  d)

y  =  (3.14  *  (-  d))
```

3.21 Defined-types, Constants, and Properties

Question [3-19] What does bits.c print?

```
b1=0x1030,  b2=0x1070
b1=0306,  b2=0061
b1=0xF801,  b2=0xB800
```

Will it give the same results on any C machine? *Yes.*

4.2 If

Question [4-1] Which of these are valid if statements according to the syntax descriptions? Which agree with the readability format?

	VALID SYNTAX?	READABILITY FORMAT?
`if (x < 0)` `    y = x;`	Y	Y
`if (n) ;`	Y	N
`if(c == EOF)` `    done = YES;`	Y	N

4.3 If-else

Question [4-2] What does this if statement print, for each value of n:

```
if (n < 5)
    {
    if (n % 2 == 1)
        printf("A\n");
    else
        printf("B\n");
    }
else
    {
    if (n % 2 == 1)
        printf("C\n");
    else
        printf("D\n");
    }

n = 1      A
n = 2      B
n = 3      A
n = 4      B
n = 5      C
n = 6      D
n = 7      C
```

4.4 Else-If

Question [4-3] If the guesser had four tries, how big a range could it handle? *31* Five tries? *63*

5.1 Syntax and Readability of Functions

Question [5-1] What is the type of each expression:

The type of log(x)   *is* double

The type of log   *is* double (double)

The type of exp   *is* double (double)

The type of exp(log(y) * y)   *is* double

5.4 Array Arguments

Question [5-2] Assume the following machine state just before calling

strncpy1(save, line, 4)

VARIABLE ADDRESS   STORAGE

line   800 | 97 | 98 | 99 | 0 |
                     | 'a' | 'b' | 'c' | '\0' |

save   1800 | 119 | 120 | 121 | 118 |
                     | 'x' | 'y' | 'z' | 'w' |

What does the parameter storage look like when strncpy1 is entered?

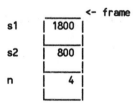

Question [5-3] At what address is s1[0] located? *1800*

Question [5-4] At what address is s2[3] located? *803*

Question [5-5] What does the storage of save look like when strncpy1 returns?

save	1800		97	98	99	0
			'a'	'b'	'c'	'\0'

5.6 Initializing Automatic Scalars

Question [5-6] What does inits print?

1 2 x

Question [5-7] What does recpt1 print?

```
First = 1
Second = 1
```

5.7 Storage Class and Internal Static

Question [5-8] What is the output of recpt2?

```
First = 1
Second = 2
```

5.9 External Static Storage

Question [5-9] Suppose a program were to call

```
nfrom(1, 10)
```

and rand1() were to return 1003. What would nfrom return? *4*

Question [5-10] Suppose a program were to call

```
nfrom(1, 6)
```

and rand1() were to return 3605. What would nfrom return? *6*

5.10 Initializing Arrays

Question [5-11] What are the initial values?

```
static char st[5] = "std";
```

115	116	100	0	0
's'	't'	'd'	'\0'	'\0'

```
static char s[2] = "ab";
```

97	98
'a'	'b'

```
static short a[5] = {1, 2, 3};
```

1	2	3	0	0

```
static short b[] = {1, 3, 5, 7,};
```

1	3	5	7

5.14 Scope Rules

Question [5-12] What does the program x print?

37

5.15 Summary of Initialization

Question [5-13] In this incorrect sample program, which lines have invalid initializers?

```
        /* noinit - some invalid initializers
         */
        #include "local.h"
        short a = 0;
BAD     short b = a + 1;
        short c[5] = {4, 3, 2, 1};
        main()
            {
            short d = a + 2;
            short e[3] = {1, 2, 3};
BAD     static short f = d + 1;
BAD     static short g[2] = {4, 5, 6};

            printf("initializers\n");
            }
```

6.3 Design

Question [6-1] Write the program outline of this revised syntax.

```
for each hand
    if (deck is low on cards)
        shuffle cards
    deal the cards
    if (dealer shows Ace)
        offer insurance
    while (player can hit and asks for hit)
        hit player
    while (dealer can hit)
        hit dealer
    score the outcome
```

Question [6-2] Using this syntactic approach, it is fairly easy to modify the design to accommodate multiple players. Do so.

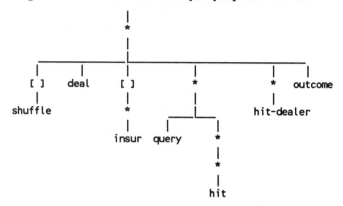

> *for each hand*
>   *if (deck is low on cards)*
>   *shuffle cards*
>   *deal the cards*
>   *if (dealer shows Ace)*
>   *for each player*
>   *offer insurance*
>   *for each player*
>   *query -- split pair, double down?*
>   *for each hand of player*
>   *while (player can hit and asks for hit)*
>   *hit player*
>   *while (dealer can hit)*
>   *hit dealer*
>   *score the outcome*

Question [6-3] Write a more detailed outline for the main program, bj.c. Note any new functions that you discover in the process, and note all data that the top-level program needs to administer. Hand-simulate some simple cases for each function to determine if it has the information it needs. Do not include any miscellaneous printf calls that may be needed, but consider whether new functions are needed for printing results.

bj/bj.c (partial):

```
main()
    {
    CASH action;      /* how much money has crossed the table */
    CASH bet;         /* amount of player's current bet per hand */
    CASH result;      /* net result of this hand, plus or minus */
    CASH standing;    /* how much has player won or lost */
    bool canhit;      /* can player's hand take hit? */
    bool isdbl;       /* did player take DBLDN? */
    bool isinsur;     /* did player take insurance? */
    short hand;       /* current hand number : {1:2} */
    short reply;      /* player's reply : {NONE, DBLDN, SPLIT} */
    short tophand;    /* how many hands is player playing : {1:2} */

    Print welcoming messages
    action = standing = 0;
    opndek();
    while ((bet = getbet()) != 0)
        {
        tophand = 1;
        isinsur = isdbl = NO;
        if (deklow())
            shuffl();
        deal();
        if (val(DEALER, 0) == 11)
            isinsur = takes insurance;
        reply = query();
        if (reply == SPLIT)
            tophand = split();
        else if (reply == DBLDN)
            give one hit and double the bet
        for (hand = 1; hand <= tophand; ++hand)
            {
            determine canhit
            while (canhit && takes hit)
                canhit = hit(hand);
            if (score(hand) > 21)
                printf("Bust\n");
            }
        if (!allbst())
            while (score(DEALER) < 17)
                hit(DEALER);
        result = outcom(bet, tophand, isinsur, isdbl);
        score and announce standing
        }
    }
```

6.5 Implementation: The Latter Phases

Question [6-4] Apply these three methods to designing test cases for the outcom function in bj/outcom.c.

bet	toph	ins	dbl	bj[0]	bj[1]	sc[0]	sc[1]	sc[2]
2000	1	1	1	1	0	21	20	0
4	1	1	1	0	0	21	21	0
1000	1	1	0	1	0	21	20	0
2	1	1	0	0	0	20	22	0
2	1	0	0	1	1	21	21	0
4	1	0	1	0	1	20	21	0
2	1	0	0	0	0	20	21	0
2	1	0	0	0	0	22	21	0
2	1	0	0	0	0	21	20	0
2	2	0	0	0	0	20	20	21

Question [6-5] Predict what values outcom should give for each of your test cases. Compile outcom.c with the symbol TRYMAIN defined, to obtain the test driver for outcom. Run the driver, using your file of test cases as input. Compare the output with your predictions.

bet	toph	ins	dbl	bj[0]	bj[1]	sc[0]	sc[1]	sc[2]
2000	1	1	1	1	0	21	20	0

Insurance wins

Dealer BJ beats all but BJ
outcom() = -500

bet	toph	ins	dbl	bj[0]	bj[1]	sc[0]	sc[1]	sc[2]
4	1	1	1	0	0	21	21	0

Insurance loses

Push
outcom() = -1

bet	toph	ins	dbl	bj[0]	bj[1]	sc[0]	sc[1]	sc[2]
1000	1	1	0	1	0	21	20	0

Insurance wins

Dealer BJ beats all but BJ
outcom() = -500

bet	toph	ins	dbl	bj[0]	bj[1]	sc[0]	sc[1]	sc[2]
2	1	1	0	0	0	20	22	0

Insurance loses

outcom() = -3

bet	toph	ins	dbl	bj[0]	bj[1]	sc[0]	sc[1]	sc[2]
2	1	0	0	1	1	21	21	0

Both BJ: push
outcom() = 0

bet	toph	ins	dbl	bj[0]	bj[1]	sc[0]	sc[1]	sc[2]
4	1	0	1	0	1	20	21	0

Your BJ wins 3 for 2
outcom() = 6

bet	toph	ins	dbl	bj[0]	bj[1]	sc[0]	sc[1]	sc[2]
2	1	0	0	0	0	20	21	0

Win
outcom() = 2

bet	toph	ins	dbl	bj[0]	bj[1]	sc[0]	sc[1]	sc[2]
2	1	0	0	0	0	22	21	0

Win
outcom() = 2

bet	toph	ins	dbl	bj[0]	bj[1]	sc[0]	sc[1]	sc[2]
2	1	0	0	0	0	21	20	0

Lose
outcom() = -2

bet	toph	ins	dbl	bj[0]	bj[1]	sc[0]	sc[1]	sc[2]
2	2	0	0	0	0	20	20	21

On hand 1, Push
On hand 2, Win
outcom() = 2

bet	toph	ins	dbl	bj[0]	bj[1]	sc[0]	sc[1]	sc[2]

7.1 Basics of Pointers

Question [7-1] Which of the following are *invalid?*

GOOD	p = &i;	GOOD	p = &a[i];
BAD	p = &(i + 1);	BAD	p = &regvar;
BAD	p = &++i;	GOOD	p = &a[regvar];

7.2 Declaring and Using Pointers

Question [7-2] Assuming the following initial configuration of memory, and assuming two-byte addresses, after this series of statements is executed, what is the resulting configuration of memory?

	1100	9		9
pi	1300	1100		1350
t	1350	14		2
		20		21
pj	1380	1100		1352
pl	1400	1410		1410
	1410	7		7
	1430	0.0		9.0
pd	1440	1430		1430

7.3 Pointers as Function Parameters

Question [7-3] At the time that swap is entered, what is the value of *pi? *5* What is the value of *pj? *10*

Question [7-4] At the time the swap returns, what is the value of *pi? *10* What is the value of *pj? *5*

7.4 Pointers and Arrays

Question [7-5]
In the following example, what value will be given to i? *10*

```
pq = &q[1];
i = *pq;
```

In this next example, what value will be given to i? *5*

```
pq = &q[0];
i = *pq;
```

7.7 Arrays of Pointers

Question [7-6] Write the *type* and *value* of each expression:

	type	value
cities[1][1]	char	'H'
&cities[1][1]	char *	1104
*cities[1]	char	'P'

7.8 Command Line Arguments

Question [7-7] If we execute echo1 with the command

    echo1 abc xyz 123

how many pointers are passed in the array that argv points to? *5 (Including the command name and the null pointer.)* What is the value of argc? *4*

8.1 Basics of Structures

Question [8-1] What is the size of ti on a machine with 2-byte addresses? With 4-byte addresses?

	2-byte machine	4-byte machine
sizeof(ti)	14	16

But note that a few unusual environments actually allocate some minimum number of bytes (e.g., 16) for *any* structure whatever.

8.3 Initialization

Question [8-2] Write a short program `vacat.c` containing this declaration for `vacation`. In the program, assign the value 1983 to the members `start` and `finish`. Print the resulting values of all members, using `printf`.

```
vacat.c:
    /* vacat - structure practice
     */
    #include "local.h"
    #include "task.h"
    main(void)
        {
        TASK vacation = {"leave for Hawaii", 1984, 0, 0};

        vacation.start = vacation.finish = (long)1983;
        printf("vacation.desc = %s\n", vacation.desc);
        printf("vacation.plan = %ld\n", vacation.plan);
        printf("vacation.start = %ld\n", vacation.start);
        printf("vacation.finish = %ld\n", vacation.finish);
        }
```

Output:

```
vacation.desc = leave for Hawaii
vacation.plan = 1984
vacation.start = 1983
vacation.finish = 1983
```

BIBLIOGRAPHY

Gelperin, David, and Bill Hetzel. [1988].
"The Growth of Software Testing." *Communications of the ACM*, Vol 31, No 6, Pp 687-695, June 1988.

Kernighan, Brian W., and Dennis M. Ritchie [1978].
The C Programming Language. New Jersey, Prentice-Hall.

Kernighan, Brian W., and Dennis M. Ritchie [1988].
The C Programming Language (Second Edition). New Jersey, Prentice-Hall.

Kernighan, Brian W., and P. J. Plauger [1978].
The Elements of Programming Style (Second Edition). New York, McGraw-Hill.

Kernighan, Brian W., and P. J. Plauger [1981].
Software Tools in Pascal. Reading, MA, Addison-Wesley.

Myers, Glenford [1979].
The Art of Software Testing. New York, John Wiley & Sons.

Parnas, David L. [1972].
"On the Criteria to be used in decomposing systems into modules." *Communications of the ACM*, December, 1972.

Plauger, P. J., and Jim Brodie [1989].
Standard C. Redmond, WA, Microsoft Press.

Plum, Thomas [1985].
Reliable Data Structures in C. Cardiff, NJ, Plum Hall.

Plum, Thomas, and Jim Brodie [1985].
Efficient C. Cardiff, NJ, Plum Hall.

Plum, Thomas [1989].
C Programming Standards and Guidelines (Second Edition). Cardiff, NJ, Plum Hall.

Press, William, Brian P. Flannery, Saul A. Teukolsky, and William T. Vetterling [1988].
Numerical Recipes in C. New York, Cambridge University Press.

Ritchie, D. M., S. C. Johnson, M. E. Lesk, and B. W. Kernighan [1978].
"The C Programming Language." In *The Bell System Technical Journal*, Vol. 57, No. 6, July-August 1978.

Walston, C. E., and C. P. Felix [1977].
"A Method of Programming Measurement and Estimation." *IBM Systems Journal*, Vol. 16, No. 1, Pp. 54-73, IBM G321-5045.

Yourdon, Edward, and Larry Constantine [1978].
Structured Design. Englewood Cliffs, NJ, Prentice-Hall.

Adams, Doug [1987].
Dirk Gently's Holistic Detective Agency. New York, Simon & Schuster.

INDEX

PLUM HALL PRODUCTS

Please give Plum Hall a call or an e-mail for information on the following products and services:

License for Machine-Readable C++ Programming Guidelines

Your entire organization, or one specific site, can license the reproduction of this *C++ Programming Guidelines* book. You can use it as the starting point for your own in-house programming standard, modifying, adding, and deleting as your group desires. You can then distribute it internally in printed form or on-line.

Suite++™: The Plum Hall Validation Suite for C++

Source code of test cases comparing compiler behavior to the (draft) ANSI/ISO C++ standard. Includes positive tests (for required behavior) and negative tests (for production of diagnostic messages).

The Plum Hall Validation Suite for C

The authoritative test suite for ANSI/ISO C, with positive and negative tests for all requirements of the ANSI/ISO C Standard. Used for accredited certification by the European Compiler Testing Service (British Standards Institution, AFNOR, IMQ), and by JQA (Japan).

C Programming Guidelines Machine-Readable

The Plum Hall textbook *C Programming Guidelines* is licensed by over 100 companies world-wide as the basis for their internal C programming standard.

P. J. Plauger's "Standard C Library"

P. J. Plauger's best-selling textbook *The Standard C Library* (published by Prentice-Hall) contains full source code for a library conforming to the ANSI/ISO C Standard. Plum Hall serves as the licensing agency for organizations who wish to distribute this library as part of their C or C++ implementations.

PLUM HALL INC
PO Box 44610
Kamuela HI 96743
+1-808-882-1255
info@plumhall.com